Doing Evil to Achieve Good

Doing Evil to Achieve Good

Moral Choice in Conflict Situations

Edited by

Richard A. McCormick, S.J.
Rose Kennedy Professor of Christian Ethics
Kennedy Institute of Ethics
Georgetown University

and

Paul Ramsey
Harrington Spear Paine Professor of Religion
Princeton University

Loyola University Press
Chicago, Illinois

© 1978

LOYOLA UNIVERSITY PRESS

Printed in the United States of America

LIBRARY OF CONGRESS

CATALOGING IN PUBLICATION DATA

Main entry under title:

   Doing evil to achieve good.

   1. Christian ethics—Address, essays, lectures.
I. McCormick, Richard A., 1922-   II. Ramsey,
Paul.

BJ1251.D64   241   78-11316

ISBN 0-8294-0285-3

Cover by Deborah Brown Callahan

Contents

To
Eunice and Sargent Shriver
Who
Have Done so Much for God's Needy Ones

Contributors

BARUCH A. BRODY, Chairperson of the Department of Philosophy at Rice University, taught philosophy at M.I.T. for six years before accepting appointment at Rice. Widely known as a lecturer in philosophical circles, and the author of numerous articles, his attention to fundamental issues is evidenced by two volumes he has written: *Abortion and the Sanctity of Life* (M.I.T. Press, 1975) and *Identity and Essence* (forthcoming). He edited *Reid's Philosophical Works* and several anthologies, among which are *Moral Rules and Particular Circumstances* (Prentice-Hall, 1970), *Readings in the Philosophy of Science* (Prentice-Hall, 1970) and *Philosophy of Religion* (Prentice-Hall, 1974).

WILLIAM K. FRANKENA, Roy Wood Sellars Professor of Philosophy at the University of Michigan, taught philosophy there from 1937 until his retirement in 1978. He is a past president of the Western Division of the American Philosophical Association, and is perhaps the most distinguished philosopher in the United States who has shown a marked interest in ethical theory, philosophy of law, philosophy of education, and in the status and contours possible for a distinctive Christian or religious ethics. He has lectured in many of the leading universities in the United States and abroad. Notable among his publications are the widely used volume *Ethics* (Prentice-Hall, 2nd ed., 1973), and *Three Questions about Morality,* his Carus Lectures published by Open Court in 1977. Many of his landmark essays have been collected in *Perspectives on Morality* (William E. Goodpaster, ed., University of Notre Dame Press, 1977).

RICHARD A. McCORMICK, S.J. is Rose F. Kennedy Professor of Christian Ethics at the Kennedy Institute of Ethics, Georgetown University. He is past president of the Catholic Theological Society of America and was awarded its Cardinal Spellman Award as Outstanding Theologian of the Year in 1969. Father McCormick writes frequently for many medical and moral-theological journals. Since 1965 he has authored the highly respected "Notes on Moral Theology" for *Theological Studies*. His forthcoming books include *The Church as a Moral*

1

Teacher (Paulist Press) and *Persons, Patients and Problems* (Louisiana State University Press).

PAUL RAMSEY, Harrington Spear Paine Professor of Religion, has taught Christian ethics at Princeton since 1944. He is a past president of the American Theological Society and of the American Society of Christian Ethics. His publications include *Basic Christian Ethics* (Scribner's, 1950), *War and the Christian Conscience* (Duke, 1961) and *Deeds and Rules in Christian Ethics* (Scribner's, 1967). For the past ten years he has turned his attention to medical ethical issues, beginning with the Lyman Beecher Lectures at Yale Medical and Divinity Schools, published as *The Patient as Person* (Yale University Press, 1970), and continuing with the Bampton Lectures in America at Columbia University, published under the title *Ethics at the Edges of Life: Medical and Legal Intersections* (Yale University Press, 1978).

BRUNO SCHÜLLER, S.J. is professor of moral theology at the University of Münster (Westfälische Wilhelms-Universität) and a former professor at the University of Bochum and the Jesuit scholasticate in Frankfurt (St. Georgen). Perhaps the most influential moral theologian on the continent, Father Schüller lectures widely throughout the world. His many publications include: *Die Herrschaft Christi und das weltliche Recht* (Gregorian University, 1963), *Gesetz und Freiheit* (Patmos, 1966), *Die Begründung sittlicher Urteile* (Patmos, 1973), and *Christlich Glauben und Handeln* (edited with Klaus Demmer, 1977).

Introduction

In the past ten or fifteen years there have been any number of developments that have had a profound influence on the discipline of Christian ethics. There have been social problems of the first magnitude, waxing and waning, but nevertheless never far from our consciousness. One thinks of the tragedy of Vietnam, the widespread abuse of human rights in some areas of the Third World and elsewhere, the problem of hunger and food distribution, racial disturbances in the United States, the liberalization of abortion in so many places in the Western World, the struggle with equitable health care delivery, the many-faceted assault on the environment in the industrialized world, the women's movement. And so on.

Christian ethics exists as a discipline to extend into these areas the abiding insights of the Judaeo-Christian tradition in a disciplined and persuasive way. These insights must be applied in a variety of settings to a variety of complex instances. Furthermore, they must be communicated through the educational process at all stages. Application and communication of value judgments leads quite naturally to the high usefulness and even necessity of moral norms encapsulating these insights, limiting them, modifying them. Some of these normative statements are more general (formal), and even tautologous. Others are more concrete (material) and attempt to apply more general value judgments to concrete pieces of human conduct.

The wording of a significant number of concrete normative statements has been influenced by the rules of practice known widely as the principle of the double effect. This is especially the case in the Catholic world. In our ecumenical age, ethicists from other religious traditions are beginning to take this principle into account, and some philosophers have addressed themselves to the moral dilemmas it is said to resolve. Moreover, in important areas of our common life elements of the principle of double effect are employed without the name. In efforts to develop limits on warfare and treaties to control its violence, there is special concern to protect noncombatants from direct attack. In criminal law, an appraisal of *mens rea* (the guilty mind) in terms of intention to kill determines first degree murder—apart from motives of mercy or the action's conspicuous consequences (when the victim would die soon anyway).

In resolving hard cases in the church-state area, the Supreme Court frequently asks what was the "primary purpose and immediate effect" of a piece of legislation or of musical performances in the public schools. Thus, the concrete norms under discussion in this volume have an importance not limited to the religious tradition—in which, no doubt, the principle of double effect was nicely honed and given centrality.

In the religious tradition, certain actions, if they had to be described as direct, were *never* to be done: direct killing, direct abortion, direct sterilization, and so on. Furthermore, these formulations have been used by the official teaching office of the Catholic Church on many occasions and thus became part of what is widely referred to as "official Catholic teaching."

On October 11, 1962 the Second Vatican Council officially opened. It was officially closed on December 8, 1965. Between those dates, the Council elaborated and issued sixteen documents that required no less than 103,014 words, exclusive of footnotes. Such an explosion was bound to have an enormous influence on moral theology both within and without the Catholic community. It did. In the theological community, one of the most significant offshoots of the Council was a more intense, and even in a sense new, ecumenism of methodology. Catholic and non-Catholic scholars worked together cooperatively as never before. It is perhaps no coincidence that the editors of this volume trace their colleagueship and friendship to this very period.

This intensifying ecumenism of procedure brought together two interesting currents that might otherwise have passed in the night. First there was a growing practical rigor in non-Catholic circles—a kind of new casuistry in dealing with the many personal and social moral problems of the contemporary world. On the Catholic side, however, there was a move away from what had been an all too often one-sided preoccupation with such casuistry. This move involved a reexamination of some of the traditional and hallowed analyses that structured such casuistry. Indeed, the Council encouraged and even enjoined this. After noting that other theological disciplines should be renewed by livelier contact with the mystery of Christ and the history of salvation, the Council stated bluntly: "Special attention needs to be given to the development of moral theology." (*Decree on Priestly Formation*)

During the past six or seven years moral theology has experienced this special attention so unremittingly, some would say, that the Christianity has been crushed right out of it. When reform is in human hands, the results will inevitably bear the imprint of human handling. Be that as it may, it was this special attention that led to restudy of the meaning of direct and indirect intention in various parts of the Catholic world. This broad restudy provided the proximate stimulus for the Pere Marquette Lecture of 1973 at Marquette University, published under title of *Ambiguity in Moral Choice* and republished as the first chapter of this volume.

Because the matter treated in *Ambiguity in Moral Choice* is of great theoretical as well as practical importance, and because the matter is difficult and the discussion far from complete, we thought it could prove fruitful to subject the original monograph and/or the problems raised therein to extensive commentary.

The issue addressed in this volume is both simple and complex. It is simple because it concerns a single and narrowly focused issue in ethics and moral theology: the moral relevance and decisiveness of the distinction between what is directly intended and what is *only* indirectly intended or actively permitted. For instance, a long tradition has maintained that if an abortional intervention must be said to be directly intended, it is never permissible. For it involves the direct taking of human life. If, however, the death of the fetus is the foreseen but unavoidable byproduct of surgery aimed at removal of a pathological organ (for example, a cancerous uterus), the abortion was said to be only indirectly intended, and justifiable if a truly proportionate reason were present. This same approach was applied in many other areas such as the conduct of warfare, complicity with the evildoing of others, sterilizing interventions, and so on.

The issue becomes much more complex when one questions the decisive moral relevance of the direct/indirect distinction and yet maintains that it is still morally right at times to perform actions inseparably joined with causing harm or death. For this means that one apparently is forced to adopt a teleological understanding of moral norms, that is, one that also weighs consequences in deciding whether and when certain moral rules are exceptionless. Thus the entire discussion opens on the issue of methodology where moral norms are concerned, and especially the philosophical debates on utilitarianism.

We believe we have a fairly good representative sample from the theological (Ramsey, Schüller) and philosophical (Brody, Frankena) communities as commentators. The authors approach the issue from different points of view and from different traditions and therefore manifest different concerns and reveal different emphases. It is clear that two authors (Schüller, McCormick) come from the same Catholic

theological tradition but are modifying the classical language and
method of that tradition, a modification that is shared by many other
well-known theological ethicists (Joseph Fuchs, Franz Böckle, Bernard
Häring, Peter Knauer, Franz Scholz, Charles Curran, Louis Janssens).
It is also clear that other well-known philosophers and theologians
believe this modification is unjustified (Paul Ramsey, Germain Grisez)
or not without some serious residual problems (William Frankena,
Baruch Brody). To what extent this modification is justified and is
problematic is the subject of this volume. It is our hope that the lively
exchanges presented here will lead to a better knowledge (or at least a
more organized confusion) of moral decision making among human
beings, and therefore of the *humanum*, and therefore of the Perfect
Human whose love nourishes our efforts and whose understanding
supplies for our lack of it.

Richard A. McCormick, S.J.

Paul Ramsey

CHAPTER ONE

Ambiguity in Moral Choice

by

Richard A. McCormick, S.J.

The distinction between what is directly voluntary and indirectly voluntary has been a staple of Catholic moral thought for centuries.[1] It has been used to face many practical conflict-situations where an evil can be avoided or a more or less necessary good achieved only when another evil is reluctantly caused. In such situations the evil caused as one goes about doing good has been viewed as justified or tolerable under a fourfold condition. (1) The action is good or indifferent in itself; it is not morally evil. (2) The intention of the agent is upright, that is, the evil effect is sincerely not intended. (3) The evil effect must be equally immediate causally with the good effect, for otherwise it would be a means to the good effect and would be intended. (4) There must be a proportionately grave reason for allowing the evil to occur. If these conditions are fulfilled, the resultant evil was referred to as an "unintended byproduct" of the action, only indirectly voluntary and justified by the presence of a proportionately grave reason.[2]

The practical importance of this distinction can be gathered from the areas where it has been applied in decision making: killing (self-defense, warfare, abortion, euthanasia, suicide), risk to life (dangerous missions, rescue operations, experimentation), sterilization, contraception, cooperation in another's evil action, scandal. Its appeal is attested to by the long line of prominent theologians who have used it in facing problems of the first magnitude such as the conduct of war. The most articulate contemporary exponent of the just-war theory (Paul Ramsey) appeals to it frequently in his writings, as did John C. Ford, S.J. in his excellent work on obliteration bombing.[3] Many other theologians fall

7

back on the distinction, sometimes unwittingly, sometimes when it suits a rather obvious purpose. So settled, indeed, had the usage become in theological circles that the direct/indirect distinction has achieved a decisive prominence in some of the most influential and authoritative documents of the Church's magisterium.

For instance, in discussing the problem of abortion, Pius XI asked: "What could ever be a sufficient reason for excusing in any way the direct murder of the innocent (*directam innocentis necem*)?"[4] Pius XII repeatedly condemned the "deliberate and *direct* disposing of an innocent human life"[5] and insisted that "neither the life of the mother nor that of the child can be subjected to an act of *direct* suppression."[6] Similarly Pius XII employed the distinction in dealing with sterilizing drugs. He noted that

> if the wife takes this medication not with a view to preventing conception, but solely on the advice of a physician, as a necessary remedy by reason of a malady of the uterus or of the organism, she is causing an *indirect* sterilization, which remains permissible according to the general principle concerning actions having a double effect. But one causes a *direct* sterilization, and therefore an illicit one, whenever one stops ovulation in order to preserve the uterus and the organism from the consequences of a pregnancy which they are not able to stand.[7]

Where the conduct of war is concerned, recent documents of the magisterium have insisted on what theologians refer to as noncombatant immunity or the principle of discrimination. Thus Pius XII, after stating that an aggrieved nation may licitly turn to warfare as a last defensive resort, immediately rejected a use of nuclear weapons which "entirely escapes from the control of man" and represents "the pure and simple annihilation of all human life within the radius of action."[8] The Second Vatican Council condemned as a crime against God and humankind "any act of war aimed indiscriminately at the destruction of entire cities. . . ."[9] The principle of discrimination proposed in such statements has commonly been explained and applied through the distinction direct/indirect.[10]

In 1968 Pope Paul VI made explicit use of the distinction between direct and indirect in *Humanae Vitae*. He stated:

> We must once again declare that the *direct* interruption of the generative process already begun, and above all, *directly* willed and procured abortion, even if for therapeutic reasons, are to be absolutely excluded as licit means of regulating birth.

He immediately added:

> Equally to be excluded, as the teaching authority of the Church has
> frequently declared, is *direct* sterilization, whether perpetual or temporary,
> whether of the man or of the woman.[11]

More recently the "Ethical and Religious Directives for Catholic
Hospitals," approved overwhelmingly by the American bishops in
November 1971, refers repeatedly to the distinction between direct/
indirect. Directive 10 reads: "The directly intended termination of any
patient's life, even at his own request, is always morally wrong." Similarly, prohibited abortion is described as "the *directly* intended termination of pregnancy before viability." Furthermore, the revised
Directives define what direct must be taken to mean: "Every procedure
whose sole immediate effect is the termination of pregnancy before
viability is an abortion."[12]

It is safe to say, therefore, that the rule of double effect has had an
honored and very important place in the formulation of Catholic moral
theology and teaching. However, in the past four or five years, there
have been rumblings of dissatisfaction, uncertainty, disagreement—or
all three.[13] These sentiments have surfaced in several studies which
reapproach the distinction between direct and indirect, to test its traditional understanding, to challenge its decisiveness, or even to deny its
moral relevance. Clearly we have here an issue of the greatest theoretical and practical importance, one that deserves most careful reflection.
The purpose of this essay is to review critically several recent studies on
direct/indirect voluntariety and to offer some personal reflections in an
attempt to identify the present state of the moral question.

It should be said at the outset that these reflections should be regarded
as no more than gropings and explorations undertaken with the confidence that others more competent will carry them further and bring
greater clarity to the question. A distinction with a history as imposing
and long-lived as that between the direct and indirect voluntary should
not be abandoned unless its inadequacy is rather clearly and systematically established. I say this because in these our times there are far too
many ready and eager to turn a theological question into a new discov-
ery, and to promulgate this *urbi et orbi* in terms which the professional
theologian can only regret, and most often disown completely.

The recent discussion was, I believe, largely put in motion by the
writings of Peter Knauer, S.J.[14] Knauer, it will be recalled, began with
the insistence that moral evil consists in the permission or causing of a

physical evil without commensurate reason. In explaining this, Knauer relied heavily on St. Thomas's analysis of self-defense. The defense of one's life against an assailant is not exactly an effect, but rather an aspect of the act. Therefore, the *finis operis* or meaning of an action is not derived simply from its external effect but is really that aspect of the act which is willed. For example, almsgiving is not simply a physical act; it gets its sense and becomes a moral act through the intention of the donor.

Knauer argues that it is with this in mind that we must understand the terms *direct* and *indirect*. In the past we have tied these terms too closely to physical causality.[15] Actually, "the permission or causing of a physical evil is direct or indirect as there is or is not present a commensurate reason," for when such a reason is present, it

> occupies the same area as what is directly willed and alone determines the entire moral content of the act. If the reason of an action is commensurate, it alone determines the *finis operis,* so that the act is morally good.[16]

What, then, is a commensurate reason? This is crucial to Knauer's presentation. It is not just any reason, meaningful or important as it may be. Rather a reason is commensurate if the value realizable here and now by measures involving physical evil in a premoral sense is not in the long run undermined and contradicted by these measures but supported and maximized. Thus "a refusal to bear children is only commensurately grounded if it is ultimately in the interests of the otherwise possible child."[17] Or again,

> to prove that a particular act is contraceptive in the moral sense it must be shown that the act in the last analysis does not serve the end of preservation and deepening of marital love, but in the long run subverts it.[18]

To the objection that this amounts to proposing that a good end justifies an evil means, Knauer would reply that a means can be judged to be evil only if it is caused without commensurate reason. One cannot, in other words, isolate certain physical evils and say of them that they are, in all circumstances, moral evils. The distinction between physical and moral evil is not, of course, new. For instance, in discussing the principle that a good end does not justify an evil means, the late and renowned Gerald Kelly, S.J., wrote:

> This principle, so simple in itself, can be very complicated in its explanation. It does not mean that no evil may be done in order to obtain good. It

refers primarily to *moral* evil; and in this respect it is absolute, because *moral* evil may never be done to obtain any kind of good.

The principle is not absolute as regards *physical* evil, because there are some physical evils that we have a right to cause in order to obtain a good effect. An example of this latter that is very common in medicine is mutilation. Mutilation is certainly a physical evil; yet as we shall see, there are some circumstances in which man has a right to mutilate himself or to authorize such mutilation.[19]

This explanation of Kelly is absolutely correct. What is not clear is what is to count (and why) for *moral* evil. Kelly clearly regarded contraceptive interventions and directly sterilizing interventions, for example, as falling in this category. Knauer has questioned—and I believe rightly—just that type of conclusion and insisted that what is morally evil can only be determined after we have examined the reason for the procedure. What is to be said of Knauer's understanding of direct and indirect intent? My earlier reaction was critical. Since that time, however, I have come to accept the substance of Knauer's presentation, though not without serious qualifications about his use of the terms *direct* and *indirect* as will become clear in the course of this study.

German Grisez says of Knauer that he "is carrying through a revolution in principle while pretending only a clarification of traditional ideas."[20] As Grisez sees it, Knauer's basic failing is that he overlooks a very important mode of obligation. He

ignores the obligation that we not turn directly against the good. This omission opens the way for his redefinition of "directly intended" in a way that bears no relation to any previous use of the expression. To support his position, Knauer also finds it necessary to claim that moral intent is completely distinct from psychological intent."[21]

I shall discuss later the notion of "turning directly against the good" as proposed by Grisez. However, his criticism of Knauer's neglect of psychological intent is, I believe, justified. The notions of direct and indirect intention have become so utterly identified with the existence of a commensurate reason in Knauer's thought that direct and indirect really do not function. This is not to deny the decisive nature of commensurate reason or to challenge the substance of Knauer's approach. It is only to note that Knauer seems to give no meaning to psychological intent. One can only wonder why Knauer retained the terminology at all. Secondly, Knauer does not satisfactorily indicate the limitations of intention in determining the meaning of concrete human actions and therefore he is unable to deal convincingly with cases like that of Mrs. Bergmeier who committed adultery to free herself from prison and rejoin her family.[22]

The next theologian to turn a critical eye to the direct/indirect distinction was William Van der Marck.[23] His critique is intelligible only within the larger framework of his thought. Van der Marck's treatment is anchored in the notion of intersubjectivity. He notes:

> The fact that human action is intersubjective means that it necessarily has consequences favorable or detrimental to the mutual relationship of the persons concerned. To state this more directly, intersubjectivity is a form of either communication or the disruption of communication; it is a form of either community or the destruction of community. When we now speak of act and consequences, of act and effect, of means and end, we are, in the first place, not speaking of something that happens *now* and has results, consequences, or effects, or that achieve an end *later*; rather, we are speaking of a particular corporeal action that, precisely as a human act, has immediate implications with respect to the relationship between subjects.[24]

Now the essential meaning of *good* and *evil* is simply a qualification of the implications, effects, consequences. In other words, it is only a qualification of the human content of the act. Good and evil, he insists, refer to the success or failure of intersubjectivity,

> and for this reason there cannot be any question of good and evil unless there is first a question of intersubjectivity; furthemore, we may speak of good and evil only to the extent that we speak of intersubjectivity.

Van der Marck feels that the disease of traditional moral theology is that it began to maneuver among categories of good and evil before it touched intersubjectivity. Thus traditional theology would characterize something as a means and a bad one prior to consideration of intersubjectivity. For example, it would say that to have children is good, but artificial insemination is a bad means to it.

Van der Marck does not deny the usefulness of the categories object-circumstances, means-end. But he argues that the

> reality itself, however, is much more important than categories and the tools they provide, and when we do gain insight into the reality itself, these categories and other ways of approach will themselves become more intelligible.[25]

Thus Van der Marck sets out to criticize the categories in light of the reality.

What is the reality of a human being? A human being is both corporeal and intersubjective. "Corporality qualifies man under all aspects in which he coincides with and forms part of the nonhuman world." Intersubjectivity, on the other hand, points him out in his human uniqueness. Now if this is true of a human being, it is true of his action also. Therefore, the most fundamental thing to be said about human action is the distinction between corporeity and intersubjectivity. Human action is a reality which is wholly corporeal, yet we see its uniqueness only when we view it as intersubjective.

A few examples offered by Van der Marck will throw light on his analysis. The physical, bodily reality of killing can be, as an intersubjective reality, murder, waging war, administering the death penalty, self-defense, suppressing an insurrection and so on. Taking something from another can be intersubjectively stealing, borrowing, satisfying dire need, repossessing one's property. Removing a nonviable fetus from the womb can be intersubjectively abortion (murder), removal of the effects of rape, saving the life of the mother and so on. Van der Marck feels that too often the reality of action is identified with one single form of intersubjectivity to the total exclusion of others. Why? Because the qualification good and bad is derived from the corporeal act as such, the physical act, in spite of the explicitly made distinction between *esse physicum* and *esse morale*. The criticism he levels against traditional manuals of moral theology is this:

> That the same material, bodily act may possibly have a *different* intersubjective significance is something that, in principle, lies outside its field of vision.[26]

Van der Marck then applies the corporeity-intersubjectivity distinction to the means-end and act-intention categories. Thus, means is related to end in the same way as corporeity is related to intersubjectivity. That is, just as intersubjectivity is the ultimate determinant of *human* action, so the end is the ultimate determinant of *human* action.

> For example, termination of pregnancy could be called "means," and intersubjectivity would be indicated by "end," whether it be murder, removal of the effects of rape, or saving the life of the mother.

Similarly with act (object) and intention.

> Act refers to the whole action as a physiological reality, while intention
> refers to the same action, but precisely as human and intersubjective.

In summary, intersubjectivity demands special consideration before
we can speak about good and evil, for "what is material in human action
is able to be intersubjective in the most diverse and varied of ways."[27]

Against this background, Van der Marck approaches the principle of
double effect. The double effect principle is very helpful, according to
Van der Marck, in overcoming the tendency to ascribe a meaning to an
action independent of intersubjectivity. For the double effect principle,
in distinguishing between action and effects, thereby distinguishes between corporeity and intersubjectivity. However, the problem with the
principle according to Van der Marck, is that

> a twofold intersubjectivity is ascribed to the act (two effects) and then one
> aspect is immediately canceled out ("indirectly willed" for "sufficient
> reason)."[28]

According to him, both effects or aspects constitute the intersubjectivity of the act, its human meaning. They are there and are determinative of the meaning (and morality) of the act whether I will them or not.
To hold that one is only indirectly willed (unintended) he sees as "canceling it out."[29] And he seems to find that objectionable. What Van der
Marck approves in the double effect idea is not, then, its validity as an
adequate account of the human meaning (and morality) of our actions,
but rather the fact that it moves a step away from assigning meaning
independently of intersubjectivity. For effects are the intersubjective
aspects of acts and to take them seriously is to take intersubjectivity
seriously.

Ultimately, then, Van der Marck would abandon the distinction between direct and indirect. It is not an adequate tool to get at the meaning
of our actions, and for two reasons, if I understand him correctly. First,
it "cancels out" as indirect one aspect of intersubjectivity—the evil
effect. Secondly, the morality of our actions requires a larger setting
than that present in the assessment of immediate effects—that of
community-building or destruction of community. Every action, as an
intersubjective reality, is either a form of community or destruction of it.
That *determines* its objective moral quality.

To call something *good* or *evil* is therefore, in the first instance, a highly pragmatic statement that can be made only after the event, after one has been able to establish the "results" actually produced by the action."[30]

Van der Marck's argument is basically this: we must first describe our conduct and its meaning in categories which respect our social nature before speaking of this conduct as good or evil. The conduct so described is then judged to be good or evil depending on whether it is community-building or not. This judgment is not adequately elaborated out of the categories of direct and indirect intent. His analysis, while a helpful corrective at key points, reveals, I believe, the symptoms and problems of a reaction. I see three serious problems in his approach.

The first difficulty raised by Van der Marck's analysis is the problem of the application of the categories corporeity-intersubjectivity to the categories of means-end and act-intention, and the implications of this application. As for the application itself, the author says: means and end are formally, not materially distinct. They are related to each other just as corporeity and intersubjectivity. Therefore, it is the end which contributes human meaning to action. This is true, it seems, with regard to those effects which are rather the immediate implications of one's activity than genuine, later-on effects. Van der Marck is aware of this distinction. For in writing of means-end, act-effect, he says:

> When we now speak of act and consequences, of act and effect, of means and end, we are, in the first place, not speaking of something that happens *now* and has results, consequences; rather, we are speaking of a particular corporeal action that, precisely as a human act, has immediate implications with respect to the relationship between "subjects."[31]

Therefore he does distinguish "later-on effects" from "immediate implications." It is these latter which are only formally distinct from the action and which give human significance to my action.

But how does one make this distinction in practice? Perhaps saving the life of the mother is not a later-on effect, but an *immediate implication* of the action giving it its basic human description and meaning. But Van der Marck has given us no satisfactory criterion for distinguishing the two. Grisez, as I shall indicate later, uses the criterion of indivisibility. But as I understand him, Van der Marck gives none. In other words, perhaps a case can be made for saying that terminating pregnancy to save the mother is actually not a use of a means to achieve an end, a means-to-end act. Rather the saving of the mother is an immediate implication of the act, its intersubjectivity. Van der Marck should have attempted to show why in this instance we are not dealing with a true means at all, but with the immediate intersubjective implications of an act which define its basic human meaning. If one fails to do this, then eventually any intended effect can be grouped under title of end and be said to specify the act in its human meaning. In summary, there is a cutoff point between the physiological description of the action and the consequentialist (or intentional) description. It is this cutoff point that is not clear in Van der Marck. And it is this cutoff point, I think, that is precisely the practical problem.

Secondly, there is the matter of canceling out the evil effect. *Canceling out* is terribly loose theological language and it is not clear what Van der Marck intends by it. But it seems to convey the idea of not counting, ignoring. I do not believe that the evidence justifies the statement that the rule of double effect was denying that one aspect (the evil) of the action had intersubjective significance. To say that it was canceled out by indirectness implies this. The rule was rather insisting on just the contrary, and for this reason demanding a truly proportionate reason. If the evil effect had been canceled out by use of the double effect, no proportionate reason would have been demanded. One can argue that Van der Marck's fear of a merely physiological analysis of the meaning of an act has brought him to a contrary extreme—where physiological realities are totally dominated by intent, and therefore, where he is the one who cancels out the evil. For instance, to redescribe emptying the womb of a nonviable fetus as "destroying or removing the effects of rape" could be a rather hasty way of depersonalizing the fetus. The intention is, indeed, removing the effects of rape. But the most immediate, obvious, irrevocable implication of this removing is the destruction of nascent life. The language of intention dare not disguise this fact and suffocate the full implications of our conduct. To be consistent intersubjectivity must include all the subjects and the fetus cannot be that easily verbalized out of significance. We may characterize the action as "removing the effects of rape," but the question remains: is this morally appropriate when these effects are a person, or nascent human life?

The third problem is the criterion of community-building. There is, of course, a sense in which one cannot quibble with such a criterion. That is, if an action is, in its *full* intersubjective reality, eventually destructive of community, then clearly it is immoral and any criterion which approves it is inadequate. But at this point one asks: has experience and reflection given us no practical presumptive judgments about what is community-building? I think it has. Van der Marck suggests the contrary when he says that good and evil are pragmatic statements "that can be made only after the event." Clearly we have more to learn, but by that same token we have learned something already. We know, for instance, that killing of others is, except in the most extreme and tragic circumstances, destructive of the *humanum* in every way, and is therefore destructive of community. And there are other things that we know before the event. Otherwise experience and reflection generate nothing by way of valid (I do not say exceptionless) generalization. In summary, if in the past we have identified good and evil too narrowly with the physical structure of the action, Van der Marck has backed off so far from this shortcoming that intention seems to swallow up the physical reality of the action. A balance is missing.

Another interesting discussion of the principle of double effect is that of Cornelius J. Van der Poel, C.S.Sp.[32] His thought-structure is very close to that of Van der Marck. Van der Poel believes that the standard interpretation of the double effect has two weaknesses. First, it fragments the human action. For instance, in the tragic case where termination of pregnancy is the only way to save the mother's life, traditional casuistry has spoken of the "direct killing" of the child in order to save the mother. Van der Poel rejects this as the proper reading of what is going on. He notes:

> The termination of the pregnancy is seen as a negative value, the saving of the mother as positive. One effect viewed as a completely independent human act in itself seems to be weighed against the other effect, also viewed as a completely independent human act in itself. . . . Thus we get the impression that the unity of the human act of saving the mother (which includes the most regrettable but inseparably connected element of the death of the child) is divided into two independent realities.[33]

Obviously, the thought of Van der Marck hovers over this rendering.

Secondly, the traditional understanding overemphasizes the importance of the *physical* effect in judging the *moral* value of the human action. Thus, in determining what is directly intended, moralists narrowed their focus too much to the physical structure of the act. If the *finis operis* of the act was killing, then that action was direct killing. The weakness of this approach was manifested, Van der Poel believes, in the moral discussion of organ transplants. Transplantation of organs demands the direct physical excising of an organ from the donor. However, this physical structure of the action must be put into its total context.

> The physical excision of the organ is a part of the total human action of transplantation. The example shows that the physical structure of the act is merely a premoral consideration, and not itself determinant of morality.[34]

Thus physical occurrences which represent intermediate stages of a human action get *moral* determination from the totality of the human action. What gives this totality or unity? "The total intention or reason of the action." It is precisely this intention or purpose which unites the intermediate stages and makes the action *human*. For example, "the human action of surgical intervention . . . is in its totality directed toward the saving of the mother's life."[35]

At this stage of his analysis Van der Poel makes two important points. First, not any material effect can be used to obtain a good result. There must be a proportionate reason which makes the occurrence of physical evil acceptable within the whole act. Thus of an abortion to avoid shame or inconvenience, Van der Poel says that these purposes enter "into the act of terminating the pregnancy" and are the goals that "determine the human meaning of it." But they are (I presume he would say, though he nowhere says it) disproportionate, not sufficient to render the evil caused acceptable.

Secondly, the intermediate stages within a total action are certainly voluntary but they are "willed only in relation to the purpose." The agent wills and wants "the means of the intermediate stages only insofar as the final goal *is contained in these means*." Van der Poel gives the example of a person who loves nature and beauty and wants to view the countryside from the highest mountain peak in the area. The climb is long, fatiguing, and perhaps dangerous. But the inseparable fatigue and danger do not constitute a separate object of the will. "There is only one object, the vision, which communicates its meaning to all the intermediate stages of the one *human* act." If we consider the fatiguing and dangerous climb as an independent entity we rob it of its specific *human* determination and ascribe a human value to an abstract physical entity.

This same analysis should be applied, he argues, to those actions which have a double effect. Thus,

> the amputation of a leg may be an absolute requirement for the life and health of a person. In such a case the act of the will directs itself not to two

different actions of amputation and cure, but the one act of curing includes the amputation unavoidably and defines the *human* meaning of the amputation itself.[36]

In all such instances, we should not speak of an effect which is in *itself evil* but which can be permitted. For that ascribes a human meaning to the material effect independent of the total human action. Thus, once we concentrate our attention on the total human action and the proportion between the evil caused (means) and the purpose (end) within this single action, we need not speak of direct and indirect willing. Rather the evil is voluntary *in se sed non propter se*.

Van der Poel, therefore, rejects the classical methodology that would face conflict situations by appeal to the notions of direct and indirect. But the question remains: how do we know whether the end or good of the action is proportionate to the evil caused within it? Here Van der Poel states that the "ultimate moral criterion is the community-building or destroying aspect of the action." Thus

> the means for a particular action may never be so grave that the total result of the whole action would be damaging for the community.[37]

Van der Poel's analysis raises several problems. For instance, when are occurrences (of evil) to be viewed as only intermediate stages of a single action? May *every* premoral evil that occurs in any way in conjunction with my activity be reduced to an "intermediate stage"? For example, is the killing of innocent children to get at the enemy's morale simply an "intermediate stage" of the action describable as *national self-defense?* What is the criterion here? Somewhat similarly, because it seems legitimate to intend some premoral evils *in se sed non propter se,* does it follow that all evils which occur in conjunction with one's activity can be said to be intended *in se sed non propter se?* For instance, does one intend and choose the death of the fetus in a cancerous uterus situation in the same way one intends and chooses the fatigue and danger involved in a mountain climb? This can be doubted, as I will attempt to show later. How one intends premoral evil would seem to depend on how that evil relates to the action—whether as effect, aspect, or integral and inseparable means.

It is, however, the matter of proportionate reason to which I wish to attend here. Van der Poel seems quite ambiguous on what this term should mean. When he says that not any good will justify any evil, he seems to suggest that proportionate reason is found in a balancing of the identifiable values immediately at stake. For instance, one may not abort a pregnancy simply to avoid shame. Yet at another point, he backs off from such a calculus and insists that

> there needs to be a proportionate reason which makes the occurrence of the physical evil acceptable *in view of the total human existence.*

Or again:

> This total human action should be projected against the background of the whole of human existence in this world, to see whether it is contributing to it or destructive in its results.

The evil in the action "may never be so grave that the total result of the whole action would be damaging for the community."[38] Briefly, the proportionate reason is determined by whether the action is community-building or not.

Van der Poel is, I believe, both right and wrong. First the good news. Obviously—as was pointed out above where Van der Marck is concerned—if an action is reasonably foreseen or eventually known to be ultimately community-damaging, it is, regardless of its immediate meaning and rewards, immoral. The criterion is clearly correct in this rearview-mirror sense. But now for the bad news. To propose as the only criterion of the morality of an act a measure so utterly ultimate is to suggest (at least) that more proximate criteria are useless or invalid. That is, in my judgment, to bypass a good deal of accumulated experience and wisdom. Furthermore, pastorally it is a general invitation to creeping exceptionism and to all kinds of self-serving and utilitarian decisions under the guise of community building.

The problem, then, is not the validity of the ultimate criterion of community-building. It is rather the existence of more proximate norms. For instance, Van der Poel says:

> When the life of the mother is certainly threatened by the fetus, the moralist (following the community-building criterion) can conclude to the taking of the life of the fetus in these circumstances.[39]

Just how *that* criterion leads to *this* conclusion remains almost totally mysterious. This is not to deny the conclusion, not at all. It is only to say that unless one specifies a bit what counts for community-building and how we know this, then that criterion can be squeezed to yield almost any conclusion—for instance, the immorality of all abortions, or the morality of abortion on demand.

A criterion is like a weapon. If not carefully and precisely constructed, it can impale its user. This has happened, I believe, to Van der Poel. Speaking of self-defense, he says:

> We do not weigh the independent value of the human life of the unlawful attacker against the independent value of the life of the person who legitimately defends himself against the attack. We place the total action in the social setting of human existence and we call the whole action morally good provided that this was the only way to defend himself.[40]

Here Van der Poel is left dangling helplessly on his own *petitio principii*. For the precise point of his own criterion is not whether "this was the only way to defend himself," but whether self-defense in such desperate circumstances is community-building or not. I believe self-defense is a legitimate Christian response. And I know of no studies that tell us that this response is more community-building than its opposite. Once again, I believe that behind this difficulty in Van der Poel is an overreaction. His legitimate dissatisfaction with a narrow physicalism has led him to presume too readily that once he has shown that an action ought to be viewed and described as mother saving, self-defense, or transplantation, it is community-building. It may be, but that is precisely the issue.

Against Van der Poel, I think we must also and first wrestle realistically with proportion in much narrower terms. That is, if the more immediate good achieved by the total act itself is not at least proportionate to the evils within it or accompanying it, then we must conclude that the action will be *de facto* community-damaging. This type of calculus could turn out to be shortsighted and wrong. But it should not be overlooked. For instance, if the purpose of a truly dangerous mountain climb is simply a view of natural beauty, one might easily conclude (in lack of other criteria) that such a climb represents an unjustified risk and is immoral. If, however, the same climb and same danger is undertaken to rescue another, a different assessment of proportion would be in place. Van der Poel himself suggests, perhaps unwittingly, that we need not always go foraging in the community-building forest but that the morality of an action which causes premoral evil can be found in a less sweeping and more modest criterion. In dealing with abortion of a pregnancy to avoid shame or burden or an unwanted child—an abortion I presume he considers immoral—he says:

> The ultimate goal (in this case avoidance of shame or burden) enters into the act of terminating the pregnancy. It is this goal, therefore, that determines the human meaning of it.[41]

Granted, the intention does shade the meaning. But the question remains: is an action with this meaning morally acceptable? If he considers the act immoral (as he seems to), it can only be because there is no proportion between "avoiding shame or burden" and destroying fetal life. The perception of this disproportion is not secured by reference to community-building or destroying. Indeed, it seems clear that anyone who does such disproportionate things does *thereby* something that is likely to be community-destroying.

Philippa Foot approaches the double effect from a different perspective.[42] After admitting the legitimacy of the distinction between "direct intention" and "oblique (or indirect) intention," she claims that the distinction plays only a very subsidiary role in determining what is right in difficult situations. Much more important is the distinction between avoiding injury and bringing aid, a negative duty and a positive duty. The former weighs on us more strictly than the latter.

Foot uses several examples to illustrate her thesis. First there is the case of a runaway tram which the driver can steer only on either of two tracks. Five men are working on one track, only one on the other. Anyone working on either track is bound to be killed if the tram comes through. The second example, is that of a group of rioters demanding that a culprit be found for a certain crime and threatening to kill five hostages if he is not. The real culprit being unknown, the judge sees himself as able to prevent the death of five by framing one innocent person and having him executed. Foot says that we would unhesitatingly steer the tram down the track where it killed but one rather than five. But we would balk at framing one innocent man to save five. "Why can we not argue from the case of the steering driver to that of the judge?"

To that question Foot admits that the double effect provides an answer. The death of the innocent man framed by the judge would have to be intended. Whereas if he refrained, the deaths of the hostages would be unintended by him. But she believes that such situations should be solved in another way: by distinguishing positive and negative duties. In both cases we have a conflict of duties, but the steering driver faces a conflict of *negative* duties. His duty is to avoid injuring five men and his duty is also to avoid injuring one. "It seems clear he should do the least injury he can." The judge, however, is weighing the duty of not inflicting injury (negative) against the duty of bringing aid (positive). If our only choice is between conflicting negative duties or conflicting positive duties, we reasonably opt for the least harm or most good. But when the conflict is between negative (inflicting injury) and positive (bringing aid) we do not inflict injury to bring aid.

This is a thoughtful and intriguing study. I would agree with Foot that the double effect probably plays a lesser role in at least some conflict decisions than we have thought. Furthermore, her distinction between positive and negative duties is certainly valid and meaningful, although it is not new. It has been known for centuries. But tidy as it is, it still leaves unanswered questions. First of all, in applying the distinction to the case of abortion to save the mother (where nothing can be done to save mother and child, but where the mother can be saved), Foot states that "it is reasonable that the action that will save someone should be done." I would agree, but it is not clear how the distinction between bringing aid and avoiding injury functions here. Presumably Foot would say that abortion in this instance is "bringing aid." However, it is precisely the contention of traditional moralists that taking the child in this instance is "causing injury," even though the child is to perish. Foot nowhere shows why the operation should not be called "causing injury." Similarly, it is difficult to see how Foot would argue the moral legitimacy of self-defense and warfare if her overarching categories are "bringing aid" and "avoiding injury."

Secondly, and more importantly, Foot states that her

> conclusion is that the distinction between direct and oblique intention plays only a quite subsidiary role in determining what we say in these cases, while the distinction between avoiding injury and bringing aid is very important indeed.

What is this "subsidiary role"? This is not clear. Indeed, it would seem that it is ultimately no role at all. For at one point she states: "If you are permitted to bring about the death of the child, what does it matter how it is done?" If Foot had clarified the moral role of intention in human conflict situations, perhaps she would have clarified *why* and therefore *where* it is or is not permissible to inflict injury to bring aid. Not having done so, she retreats to the statement that "to refrain from inflicting injury ourselves is a stricter duty than to prevent other people from inflicting injury." Is it? That is precisely the point.

One of the most ranging and profound recent discussions of the double effect is that of Germain Grisez.[43] Grisez's analysis is developed with relentless consistency and subtlety. His treatment of the distinction between direct and indirect intention interlocks logically with his overall moral theory. This moral theory is developed somewhat as follows. The basic human goods (life, knowledge pursued for its own sake, interior integrity, justice, friendship, and so on) present themselves as goods-to-be-realized. They appeal to us for their realization. Thus these goods are the nonhypothetical principles of practical reason. "As expressions of what is-to-be, the practical principles present basic human needs as fundamental goods, as ideals."[44] But the appeal of these goods is not the direct determinant of moral obligation. They clarify the possibilities of choice but do not determine why some choices are morally good and others evil.

What determines this? The attitude with which we choose. What, then, is a right attitude? A realistic one.

> To choose a particular good with an appreciation of its genuine but limited possibility and its objectively human character is to choose it with an attitude of realism.[45]

The right attitude does not seek to belittle the good that is not chosen, but only seeks to realize what is chosen. This open, realistic attitude shapes itself into specific moral obligations. For instance, we must take all the goods into account in our deliberations; we must avoid ways of acting which inhibit the realization of any one of the goods to the extent possible; we must contribute our effort to their realization in others. A final and most important mode of obligation is this: we must never act "in a way destructive of a realization of any of the basic goods." For to act *directly* against a good is to subordinate it to whatever leads to that choice. And one may not morally do that, because the basic goods are equally basic.

But clearly not every inhibition of a good that occurs as a result of my action is directly destructive of this good. Some inhibitions are unsought and unavoidable side effects of an effort to pursue another value. Thus one *directly* goes against a basic good when its inhibition is directly intended.

When is the destruction of a basic good directly intended? Here Grisez modifies the textbook understanding of the double effect. He believes that the modern formulation is too restrictive. It insists too much on the behavioral aspect, the physical causality, in determining the meaning of the act. In the textbook tradition, if evil is the sole immediate effect of the physical act, then it is directly produced and hence directly intended. For example, one may not "shell out" an ectopic fetus that represents a mortal threat to the mother, though he may excise a pathological tube which contains a fetus. Similarly one may not abort the fetus to save the mother.

Grisez rejects this understanding. Rather he insists that

> from the point of view of human moral activity, the initiation of the indivisible process through one's own causality renders all that is involved in that process equally immediate. . . . For on the hypothesis that no other human act intervenes or could intervene, the moral agent who posits a natural cause *simultaneously* (morally speaking) posits its foreseen effects.[46]

For instance, the saving of the mother is an aspect of the abortifacient act equally immediate, morally speaking, to the death of the child. Thus he writes:

> The justification is simply that the very same act, indivisible as to its behavioral process, has both the good effect of protecting human life and the bad effect of destroying it . . . the entire process is indivisible by human choice and hence all aspects of it are equally present to the agent at the moment he makes his choice.[47]

Central in Grisez's analysis is the indivisibility of the action or behavioral process. It is this indivisibility which allows one to conclude to the equal immediacy of the good and bad effects —and therefore to direct intent of the good and indirect intent of the evil. If, however, the process is divisible and the good effect occurs as a result of a subsequent act, we are dealing with means to end, or with effects not equally immediate. Thus one may not commit adultery to save one's children from a prison camp "because the saving effect would not be present in the adulterous act, but in a subsequent human act—that of the person who releases them." Similarly, organ transplants that will involve deprivation of life or health to the donor are immoral because the two aspects (excision, implant) are factually separable.

Grisez applies this analysis to many instances involving killing. He contends that it is *never* permissible *directly* to take human life. For him, capital punishment cannot be justified. The argument from deterrence, even if factually defensible, is "ethically invalid, because the good is achieved in other human acts, not in the execution itself." Similarly, Grisez argues that killing in warfare is indirect (and must be to remain morally tolerable) much as it is in self-defense.

Thus far Grisez. His ranging analysis of the direct/indirect distinction is by far the most subtle, consistent, and plausible defense of that distinction that I have seen in recent literature. What is to be said of it? First of all, Grisez's notion of an indivisible process seems certainly correct. If the evil effect or aspect occurs within an indivisible process, then "the moral agent who posits a natural cause *simultaneously* (morally speaking) posits its foreseen effects." In other words, the evil effect is not a means, morally speaking, to the good effect. Hence, it is not, or need not be, the object of an intending will. So far so good. What is not clear is why one must be said to turn against a basic good when the evil occurs as a means, and is the object of an intending will. This is the very problem posed by Schüller, as we shall see. The problem I am raising centers around the notion of proportionate reason. A closer examination of proportionate reason might have forced Grisez to admit that it need not be ultimately decisive whether the will is intending or permitting, but whether the reason in either case is proportionate. Grisez's reluctance to examine proportionate reason more thoroughly allows him to concentrate his full attention on the posture of the will with reference to the evil in a narrow sense and to frame the problem of unavoidable evil in these terms. If he had discussed what constitutes a proportionate reason more adequately, perhaps we would see a different understanding of what it means to go directly against a basic good.

Behind Grisez's failure to examine more thoroughly the notion of proportionate reason is his deep repugnance to anything resembling a utilitarian calculus. In discussing the four conditions for use of the double effect, Grisez says of the last (proportionately grave reason):

> The last condition can easily become a field for a covert, although limited, utilitarianism. However, that is not necessary. Though human good is not calculable and though diverse modes of human good are incommensurable, the basic human goods do require protection when possible. Human life may not be destroyed frivolously or gratuitously . . . where safer methods of achieving desirable objectives are readily available.[48]

After this brief statement, Grisez fairly runs from the notion of proportion and returns to it only to indicate here and there what reasons are *not* proportionate. However, the heart of the matter has been passed over a bit too quickly here. If one insists—as we should—that there must be a proportionate reason, we ask: what is a proportionate reason for taking another human life? Or in Grisez's terms above: what does *when possible* mean concretely in the phrase "the basic human goods do require protection when possible"? When is destruction of human life not "frivolous or gratuitous" and why? We know that lesser goods such as convenience, avoidance of shame, and health are not to be preferred to life. But what goods are to be preferred, or at least are of equal status? Grisez does not clarify this because on his own terms he cannot. The basic goods are simply incommensurable, and to start weighing and balancing them is to succumb to utilitarianism.

Perhaps. But I agree with Stanley Hauerwas that ultimately Grisez cannot "avoid the kind of consequentialist reasoning that our human sensibilities seem to demand in such (conflict) cases."[49] For if a good, like life, is simply incommensurable with other goods, what do we mean by a proportionate reason where death is, in Grisez's terms, indirect? Proportionate to what? If some goods are to be preferred to life itself, then we have compared life with these goods. And if this is proper, then life can be weighed against other values too, even very basic values. Granted, there are real dangers and genuine difficulties in a merely utilitarian calculus. But I believe that some such calculus can be avoided only at the cost of artificiality and contrivance. Our problem is rather to do all we can to guarantee that our calculus will be truly adequate and fully Christian.

Let me put the matter very concretely. In cases (admittedly rare) where abortion is necessary to save the mother's life, Grisez writes:

> The justification is simply that the very same act, indivisible as to its behavioral process, has both the good effect of protecting human life and the bad effect of destroying it . . . the entire process is indivisible by human choice and hence all aspects of it are equally present to the agent at the moment he makes his choice.[50]

This is not, in my judgment, the *justification* at all. It is only one way of explaining how the evil that I do is not direct, according to one understanding of what that term means. In other words, this is the justification only on the assumption that an intending will necessarily involves one in turning against a basic good, that is, if directly intended killing is evil *in se*. What is the true justification for allowing abortion here? It cannot be that one may prefer the life of the mother to that of the fetus. For that preference is simply not clear. Furthermore, such a preference gets one into the functional and utilitarian valuations of life that Grisez so rightly abhors. What is the justification—or proportionate reason? Is it not that we are faced here with two alternatives (either abort, or do not abort)? Both alternatives are destructive but one is more destructive than the other. We could allow both mother and child (who will perish under any circumstances) to die; or we could at least salvage one life. Is it not because, *all things considered,* abortion is the lesser evil in this tragic instance? Is it not precisely for this reason, then, that abortion in this instance is proportionate? Is it not for this reason that we may say that the action is truly lifesaving? And is it not for this reason that abortion in these circumstances does not involve one in turning against a basic good?

The matter can be urged in another way. Suppose we are faced with a situation (suggested by Philippa Foot) with the following alternatives: an operation which saves the mother but kills the child, versus one that kills the mother but saves the child. In either choice Grisez's use of double effect would seem to apply. That is, there is a single indivisible process one of whose aspects is good, one evil. And the act is lifesaving. But unless one uses functional criteria (the "greater value" in some sense of the mother's or child's life) is there a proportionate reason for choosing mother over child, or child over mother? If Grisez would say that in this instance we may save the mother, I ask: why? Why *prefer* the mother to the child when I have a choice? On the other hand, if Grisez says that I may do neither since to do either would involve one in a preference of one life over another, then it seems that what has functioned as proportionate reason in instances where he allows abortion to save the mother is this: it is better to save one life than to lose two. Or more generally, a proportionate reason exists because that choice represents the lesser evil.

Frankly, I do not know what Grisez would say to an either/or case of this kind. But I suspect he would hesitate long and hard. But he would not and does not hesitate in the simple instance where abortion (of a fetus who will perish under any circumstances) is necessary to save the mother's life. Does this not indicate that in this latter instance the crucial and decisive consideration is that it is better on all counts in such circumstances to save one life where my only alternative is to lose two? Does it not indicate that the procedure is legitimate precisely for this reason? And does it not then follow that "acting directly against a basic good" need not be interpreted within the deontological understanding of direct and indirect that Grisez provides?

Ultimately, then, Grisez has provided only an ingenious criterion to loosen the notion of direct killing to accommodate the instances where common sense seems to allow it. This is a further relaxation of a deontological norm. But it still presupposes that direct killing is evil *in se* and necessarily involves a morally reprehensible attitude. As I shall indicate later, it can be argued that our moral posture must be measured by a broader intentionality that relates it to a plurality of values. In brief, it is the presence or absence of a proportionate reason which determines whether my action—be it direct or indirect psychologically or causally—involves me in turning against a basic good in a way which is morally reprehensible.[51] Or as Hauerwas puts it:

> Grisez does not seem to provide the necessary theoretical account of why so many of our moral arguments take the form of choices between "lesser evils."[52]

The most precise and searching challenge to the distinction between direct and indirect voluntariety is that of Bruno Schüller.[53] Schüller notes four areas where the distinction has been used by traditional theology: scandal, cooperation, killing, and contraception. But according to Schüller it was used for different reasons where scandal and cooperation are involved. These reasons must be isolated.

The sin of another, Schüller notes, is a moral evil and as such is an absolute disvalue. It would seem to follow that an action (scandal) which has such a disvalue as a foreseen effect must be absolutely avoided. But this would lead to impossible consequences. No lawmaker, for example, could attach a punishment to a violation of law because he would know in advance that this would be the occasion of sinful bribery for a certain undetermined number of people. More fundamentally, it is hard to reconcile an absolute duty to avoid foreseen evil with the will of the creator who created a being capable of sin. The way out has always been sought in distinguishing will, intention, and purpose from permission and toleration—or direct from indirect. The absolute disvalue of sin demands only that one not will and intend it under any circumstances. However, for a proportionate reason it may be permitted.

The reason the distinction is necessary is that we are dealing here with *moral* evil. The absoluteness of the disvalue forces some such distinction. However, when we are dealing with nonmoral evils (error, pain, sickness, death) the reason for the distinction between directness and indirectness disappears precisely because these disvalues, fundamental as they are, are *relative* disvalues. These we must, of course, also avoid—but conditionally. The condition under which we must avoid a relative disvalue is that it does not concur with a greater relative disvalue or an absolute one. For example, sickness must be avoided but not at any price, not, for example, at the price of plunging one's family into destitution. Schüller argues that when we justifiably cause a relative disvalue in our conduct, we should not call it *indirect*. Thus when health officers quarantine one with typhoid fever, should we say that they intend only the prevention of its spread and "merely permit" the isolation of the sick individual? Hardly. The isolation is a necessary means to an end. And where means are concerned we speak of an intending will, a direct choice.

We should not abandon this usage. Indeed it brings out the difference between the attitude to moral evil and that to nonmoral evil. For a proportionate reason we may *permit* a moral evil, but we may directly will and directly cause a nonmoral evil if there is a proportionate reason for doing so.

This has been a tenet of Catholic moral theology for centuries. For instance, one may reveal the hidden defects of another and thereby hurt his reputation "to ward off a relatively important harm from oneself or the neighbor." Similarly with a promise. But this breaking of a promise is experienced by the one to whom the promise was made as an evil. In such cases we do not demand that the negative effect be unintended.

Schüller next turns to killing and contraception. Why did traditional theology feel it necessary to use "direct" and "indirect" when dealing with these subjects? It was because it viewed them as evil *in se*. This can be sustained, however, only if the death of a person is an absolute evil in the sense of a moral evil. Once it is granted that the killing of an innocent person is the destruction of a fundamental but nonmoral value, there is no need for the distinction direct/indirect. Rather the assessment is made teleologically, that is, from presence or absence of proportionate reason.

Schüller concludes, therefore, that death and contraception must be judged according to teleological, not deontological norms (these latter being norms independent of proportionate reason). He further concludes that since this is so, it is superfluous to distinguish between indirect and direct action. All of them must be judged according to proportionate reason.

My first reaction to Schüller's analysis was that it is absolutely correct.[54] After further reflection, I think that there is still some unfinished business in it. Here I should like to raise a question which is not clearly resolved in his study.

Schüller concludes that the distinction between direct and indirect is necessary and functional only where the *sin* of another (scandal) is concerned. In other instances the distinction is merely descriptive. This suggests the following problem. If one says there is a crucial difference between an intending and a permitting will where *moral* evil is concerned—as one must—then that must mean that the will relates differently to what it intends and what it permits. Otherwise the distinction is meaningless and arbitrary. But if the will relates differently to what it intends and merely permits in this one instance, then it must do so wherever that distinction is legitimately made. That is, there is a different relation to the will when it intends and merely permits even where *nonmoral* evil is concerned. The only question then is the following: is this different relationship of moral significance where *nonmoral* evil is concerned? As I read him, Schüller says it is not, because in all instances the action (whether one intends or merely permits the nonmoral evil) is to be judged teleologically (that is, by proportionate reason). However, it can be doubted that, because both indirect and direct causing of nonmoral evil are to be judged teleologically, the same teleological judgment applies to both.

Here something more must be said. Because *direct* (descriptively) killing must also be judged teleologically, it does not seem to follow that the same proportionate reason which would justify what is indirect (descriptively) would always justify what is direct. In other words, there may be a proportionate reason for doing something in one way which is not proportionate to doing it another way.

Let us take the death of noncombatants in warfare as an example. Traditonal theology has concluded that it can be permissible (proportionate) at times to attack the enemy's war machine even though some noncombatants (innocents) will be tragically and regretfully killed in the process. The difficulty of applying this distinction in practice (that is, determining the noncombatants) does not affect its theoretical legitimacy. It has also concluded that it is not morally permissible to make these noncombatants the target of one's attack, to kill them as a means to bringing the enemy to his knees and weakening his will to fight. This latter conclusion is, I believe, a teleological judgment (one based on proportionate reason defined by forseeable or suspected consequences in the broadest sense), not a deontological one. Equivalently it means that direct attacks on noncombatant civilians in wartime, however effective and important they may seem, will in the long run release more violence and be more destructive to human life than the lives we might save by directly attacking noncombatants. But this teleological assessment is concretely different from the teleological assessment made where the deaths are incidental. The difference is not in the number of deaths here and now. They could be numerically the same—for instance, one hundred civilians killed incidentally, one hundred directly killed. The deaths are equally regrettable and tragic simply as deaths and *in this sense* how they occur does not affect their status as nonmoral evils. But how they occur has a good deal to say about the present meaning of the action, the effect on the agent and others, and hence about the protection and security of life in the long run. These considerations are certainly a part of one's teleological calculus. There are those who argue that it makes little difference to a person whether he is killed by a direct or indirect action, hence that a "love ethic" abandons this distinction. I would urge, contrarily, that it is precisely a "love ethic" which demands the distinction; for a love ethic is concerned not simply with this or that effect, but also with the *overall* implications and repercussions of human conduct. And these implications and repercussions are affected very much at times by whether a certain evil is visited by an intending or merely permitting will.

In summary, Schüller's effort has been to show that the norms governing killing and contraception must be built and interpreted teleologically, not deontologically. In this I believe he is correct. But his study leaves the impression that therefore the distinction between direct and indirect is totally superfluous in these areas, and others too. I am not persuaded of this. The nonmoral evil is, to be sure, quantitatively the same whether it is chosen or merely permitted. But the act is not necessarily thereby the same. The relation of the evil to the will, how it happens, not only can tell us what kind of act we are performing, but can have enormously different immediate and long-term implications, and therefore generate a quite different calculus of proportion. I am suggesting, therefore, that the terms direct/indirect are not superfluous, or at least not at all times, but only that a different teleological calculus may apply in each instance.

This problem can be restated in terms of Schüller's analysis of cooperation in another's evildoing. Schüller argues that the distinction between direct and indirect is not necessary here. For whether one performs or refuses the cooperation has no influence on the *moral* violation of the other, but only on the effects of this moral violation. Schüller takes the example of a bank cashier during a robbery. The cashier may and should hand over the money not because this leaves the robber less morally guilty, but because the loss of money is a lesser nonmoral evil than loss of life. The moral guilt of the robber is in his determination to kill during the robbery if necessary. The cashier, Schüller notes, cannot lessen this. But he can lessen the nonmoral disvalues that the robber is prepared to commit. In this instance the cashier can *intend* to cause the harm to the bank to save his own life. There is, says Schüller, no need to appeal to indirectness here. The problem is analyzed teleologically.

I agree with this analysis, but I believe that something more must be said. Schüller says the cashier should hand over the money because the loss of money is a lesser nonmoral evil than loss of life. That is certainly true. But must we not add also that preserving one's life in this way will not in the long run threaten more lives and undermine the very value I am protecting in this instance?

Let us return to the case of the rioting mob and the judge. In Schüller's analysis we would have to say that the *moral* guilt of the mob is already there in its determination to kill five men unjustly if the judge does not frame one innocent man and execute him. Therefore this moral evil cannot be lessened. But the judge can lessen the nonmoral disvalues the mob is prepared to commit by executing one innocent man. Certainly the death of one innocent man is a lesser evil than the death of five innocent men. Schüller (if his analysis stops where it does) would be forced to conclude that the judge should execute the one innocent man. Yet I think we are appalled at this conclusion. Is it not precisely because we sense that taking the life of this innocent man in these circumstances would represent a capitulation to and encouragement of a type of injustice which in the long run would render many more lives vulnerable? Yet our judgment would be different if the death of the one innocent man were incidental. In summary, proportion must be measured also in terms of long-term effects. And in terms of such effects, whether one directly intends (or not) certain nonmoral evils he now does may make quite a difference.

In other words, the teleological character of all our norms does not eliminate the relevance of the distinction between direct/indirect where nonmoral values and disvalues are involved. Rather precisely because these norms are teleological is the direct/indirect distinction relevant. For the relation of the evil-as-it-happens to the will may say a great deal about the meaning of my action, its repercussions and implications, and therefore what will happen to the good in question over the long haul. If one asks why, I believe the answer is to be found in the fact that an intending will represents a closer relation of the agent to the disvalue and therefore indicates a greater willingness that the disvalue occur.

These are some of the recent attempts to deal with conflict situations in a sinful and imperfect world. All of these studies make valid and necessary points and I have found all of them illuminating. If a single thread or theme is common to all of them, it is, as Charles Curran has repeatedly pointed out, dissatisfaction with the narrowly behavioral or physical understanding of human activity that underlies the standard interpretation of direct and indirect. I agree with this dissatisfaction. On the other hand, in making their points they all seem in one way or another incomplete, and even misleading when dealing with the distinction between direct and indirect intention.

For instance Knauer rightly rejects the use of *moral evil* to describe actions independently of the reasons for which they are done, hence independently of their context and intention. However, in interpreting the direct/indirect distinction in an exclusively moral way (that is, with no relation to psychological intentionality), he underestimates the real differences in the meaning of our conduct that could be generated by psychological intentionality. Grisez provides a satisfying account of the origin of moral obligation with his analysis of basic human goods. But his interpretation of what it means "to turn directly against these goods" seems too contrived and incapable of accounting for the complexity of reality, especially of the conflict situations we have been considering. This is traceable to his reluctance to examine more realistically the notion of proportionate reason, a reluctance rooted in his nervous fear of any utilitarian calculus.

Van der Marck and Van der Poel rightly insist that the meaning of our actions must take account of intersubjectivity (Van der Marck) and intentionality (Van der Poel). However, both authors seem too readily to accept the idea that once an action is described in terms of its dominant intentionality (for example, "removing the effects of rape") it has been justified, or that the only calculus which is of any help in weighing the moral quality of the decision is community-building or destroying.

Schüller is certainly correct in his insistence on the difference between moral and nonmoral evil and therefore on the profound difference between actions occasioning the *sin* of another and actions visiting nonmoral disvalues on the neighbor. Similarly, I believe he is correct in insisting that the meaning of moral norms concerning nonmoral evils must be interpreted within the confines of a teleological calculus (as long as a greater evil would not result). However, his preoccupation with this point leads him to suggest that direct and indirect intention are altogether morally irrelevant where nonmoral evil is associated with our activity. This fails to take seriously enough the real contribution of intentionality to the significance of human actions. In doing so it could leave him somewhat vulnerable to the weaknesses of a merely numerical calculus of proportionality.

In conclusion I should like to attempt a synthesis that takes advantage of the above positions but seems identifiable with no one of them. Such a critical synthesis will remain incomplete, and even vulnerable, I am sure. Not only does the problem we are dealing with involve one's whole moral theory (an area where there is considerably less clarity and certainty than is desirable), but it also brings this theory to bear on practical day-to-day problems. One is asked to be both theoretically consistent and practically sensitive to the complexity and intransigence of reality—in other words, to plug all the loopholes in a prudent and persuasive way. This is particularly difficult in times where theologians have different views on how the loopholes ought to be plugged, if they should be plugged at all! The following reflections must, therefore, remain a thought-experiment and will represent above all a useful invitation to other theologians to correct the shortcomings, inconsistencies, and even errors they may contain. My own very tentative conclusions would be summarized in the following statements:

1. There is a difference between an intending and permitting will, and therefore in the human action involving the one or the other.

2. In a conflict situation, the relation of the evil to the value sought is partially determinative of the posture of the will (whether intending or permitting).

3. The basic structure, however, in conflict situations is avoidable/ unavoidable evil, the principle of the lesser evil.

4. Both the intending and the permitting will (where evil is involved) are to be judged teleologically (that is, by presence or absence of proportionate reason).

5. Proportionate reason means three things: (a) a value at stake at least equal to that sacrificed; (b) no other way of salvaging it here and now; (c) its protection here and now will not undermine it in the long run.

6. The notion of proportionate reason is analogous.

An explanation of each of these will provide the context for my own modified understanding of the moral relevance of the direct/indirect distinction.

1. *There is a difference between an intending and permitting will.* If the distinction between an intending and permitting will is utterly essential and profoundly meaningful where the moral evil (sin) of another is concerned, as Schüller rightly maintains, that can mean but one thing:

there is a real difference between an intending and permitting will. Otherwise we are dealing with mere words, as was pointed out above. Now if there is a real difference between an intending and permitting will, then this difference must show where nonmoral evil is concerned. That in turn means that the human action involving an intending will (of evil) is or at least can be a different human action from that involving a permitting will. To say anything else is to say that intentionality does not affect the meaning of human activity, a tenet that becomes inconsistent if one reverses it where *sin* is concerned. This difference between an intending and permitting will generates two important conclusions, one negative, one positive. First of all, it is not simply and exclusively the existence or nonexistence of an evil effect that determines the meaning of the action that occasioned it. *How* this evil relates to the human will is also relevant. A love ethic is, indeed, concerned with effects; but it must also be concerned with how they occur. Why? Because secondly, actions which are different because of differing intentionality have a different immediate meaning and may lead to different social and long-term effects.

To admit that there is a difference between an intending and permitting will within an action is not to deny that the overall significance of the action is affected by intention of the end, a point clearly made by Van der Marck and Van der Poel. Nor is it to deny a certain unity of the action rooted in this intentionality. It is simply to say that within such ultimate purposefulness the will can assume at least two different postures vis-à-vis the evil that is associated with one's choice. That this difference can be morally significant is suggested by the instance of the intention or permission of the *sin* of another. How should this difference be explained? The matter remains somewhat mysterious, as Schüller notes. But we can say this much at least: the intending will (hence the person) is more closely associated with the existence of evil than the merely permitting will. Furthermore I believe we must say that an intending will is more willing that the evil be than is a permitting will. That this can have morally significant repercussions I shall attempt to indicate later.

2. *In a conflict situation, the relation of the evil caused to the value sought is partially determinative of the posture of the will (whether intending or permitting).*[55] It seems that nonmoral evil can be immediately associated with human activity in at least two distinguishable ways: as an aspect of the act with no causal relation to the good effect; as means with a necessary causal relationship to the good envisaged. That

which stands in a relationship of means to end is necessarily the object of an intending will, even if not *propter se*. That which is merely effect or aspect need not be. When is the evil in a causal relationship to the good, a means to it, and therefore necessarily the object of an intending will? I would be willing to accept Grisez's criterion: if the evil occurs within an indivisible process, then in the moral sense it is equally immediate with the good effect, and hence not a means. If, however, the process is divisible so that the good effect occurs as the result of a subsequent act, we are clearly dealing with a means, and an intending will. There are difficulties in this criterion because it moves a step away from our psychological experience of permission. Concretely, it is much clearer that we are dealing with a means when there is divisibility than it is that we are not when the process is indivisible. For some evils that are part of an indivisible process do seem to be means. Be that as it may, Grisez's criterion can be accepted provisionally.

An example will bring out the difference between the intending and permitting will. If a woman has cancer of the ovaries, a bilateral oophorectomy is performed. The result: sterility. If a family has seven children, the wife is weak, the husband is out of a job, the woman may have a tubal ligation on the occasion of the last delivery. The result: sterility. The immediate effect (nonmoral evil) is the same in both cases—sterility. Obviously these actions are different human actions in terms of their overall intentionality—the good sought. One is a lifesaving intervention, the other a family-saving or family-stabilizing act, so to speak. But even within this larger difference, the bearing of the will toward the sterility is, I believe, distinguishable in the two instances. For the moment no moral relevance will be assigned to this difference. But it seems that there is a difference and the difference originates in the relation of the nonmoral evil to the good sought. In the one instance, the nonmoral evil is chosen as a means; in the other it is not. Van der Marck and Van der Poel have been reluctant to admit the category of means in this regard. But one need not unduly fragment the wholeness or unity of the overall action to allow the validity of this distinction within it.

Because the forms of associated evil are distinguishable within our actions, the psychological experience of "intention" is somewhat different in each case. General reluctance that the evil must be brought about (whether "intended" or "permitted") is presumably common to both instances. Still when the evil is an effect or aspect with no necessary causal relationship to the good being pursued, one does indeed have a different psychological awareness of the evil involved than he does when there is a necessary causal relationship between the evil and good achieved. I have suggested that this psychological difference is traceable to the fact that an intending will is more closely associated with the evil, more willing that the evil exist. The crucial question is whether (and why) this single form of psychological awareness—that associated with evil as aspect—is normative for a proper human intentionality. The traditional answer has been yes, at least in the instances involving human life and our sexual faculties. That is, the evil involved must be unintended *in that one psychological sense*. I believe that there are good reasons to doubt this conclusion and to assert that the meaning of human intentionality toward nonmoral evil is to be determined by reference to a larger canvas.

3. *The basic analytic structure in conflict situations is the lesser evil, or morally avoidable/unavoidable evil.* The rule of double effect is a vehicle for dealing with conflict situations. When we see the situations it was trying to meet, we can discern its essential elements. It was facing conflict situations where only two courses are available: to act or not to act, to speak or remain silent, to resist or not to resist. The concomitant of either course of action was harm of some sort. Now in situations of this kind, the rule of Christian reason, if we are governed by the *ordo bonorum,* is to choose the lesser evil. This general statement is, it would seem, beyond debate; for the only alternative is that in conflict situations we should choose the greater evil, which is patently absurd. This means that all concrete rules and distinctions are subsidiary to this and hence valid to the extent that they actually convey to us what is factually the lesser evil. This is true of the distinction between direct and indirect voluntariety. It is a vehicle, not a principle—and a vehicle as useful as its accuracy in mediating and concretizing the more general principle. Now, if in a conflict situation one does what is, in balanced Christian judgment (and in this sense "objectively"), the lesser evil, his intentionality must be said to be integral. It is in this larger sense that I would attempt to read Thomas's statement that moral acts *"recipiunt speciem secundum id quod intenditur."*[56] Thus the basic category for conflict situations is the lesser evil, or avoidable/unavoidable evil, or proportionate reason.

Because the evil caused was so often genuinely incidental and associated with a permitting will (psychologically), the distinction between direct and indirect came to be identified with proper intentionality. That is, from being a subordinate vehicle in service of the determination of the lesser evil, it became a principle of this determination. Awareness of its broad rootage gave way to a concentration on the actions, their causality and the psychological posture of the will in explaining the idea of twofold effect. Actually, where nonmoral evil is concerned, direct voluntariety says but one thing: the evil has a causal relation to the good and is willed as a means. This becomes morally decisive only when the posture of the will affects the determination of what is, all things considered, the lesser or greater evil.

I am arguing, therefore, that the essential ingredients that led to the formulation of the rule of double effect are two: (1) the legitimacy, desirability, or above all necessity of a certain good (self-defense, saving the mother, resisting national aggression, rescuing another, and so on); (2) the inseparability of this good from harm or evil in the circumstances. But evil-as-effect (or aspect) of the action is only one form of this inseparability of evil from a desirable good. Another form is evil-as-means.

Concretely, it can be argued that where a higher good is at stake and the only *means* to protect it is to choose to do a nonmoral evil, then the will remains properly disposed to the values constitutive of human good. (Griesez's basic goods, Schüller's *ordo bonorum),* that the person's attitude or intentionality is good because he is making the best of a destructive and tragic situation. This is to say that the intentionality is good even when the person, reluctantly and regretfully to be sure, intends the nonmoral evil if a truly proportionate reason for such a choice is present.

To face conflict situations exclusively in terms of a psychological understanding of the terms *direct* and *indirect* could be to give a narrow and restrictive reading to the overall intent of St. Thomas. Be that as it may, we know that later theologians moved away from this analysis of self-defense and stated that some conflict situations could legitimately involve one in intending (reluctantly) nonmoral evil as a means. For instance, M. Zalba, S.J., in his treatment of capital punishment, defends the *direct* killing of criminals by appeal to the common good: "Without it (capital punishment) the public common good cannot survive, if one considers the malice and daring of criminals. . . . ."[57] The factual validity of this argument can be denied; but what is important here is the theoretical structure of the argument. Zalba, with many other theologians, is arguing that there are greater goods than an individual human life and when they are threatened and there is no other way to circumvent this threat, then it is reasonable to choose to do the evil to achieve the good, or avoid the evil.

Similarly Zalba (with many others) holds that in situations of self-defense against unjust aggression one may legitimately intend the wounding or death of the assailant as "a legitimate and upright means instituted by God for the prosecution of one's right. . . ."[58] The appeal to the double effect, he says, appears *"obscurior"* precisely because "the preservation of one's own life is achieved *through* the wounding of another life rather than as a concomitant of this wounding." Once again, the structure of the argument is similar: one may intend nonmoral evil as a means if it is the only way of protecting a good judged to be at least proportionate.

There are other instances where we see a similar teleological model operative. One may legitimately intend the deception of another through falsehood to preserve a professional secret. To say that the deception is indirect and unintended (psychologically) as Zalba does, is unnecessary—and, in his case, inconsistent if he argues as he does where self-defense and capital punishment are concerned. Why did he not argue that deliberate, intended deception of another is a legitimate means to a proportionately grave good otherwise unobtainable? In the recent past theologians argued (correctly in my view) that women could directly sterilize themselves against the very real possibility of pregnancy by rape.[59] Once again, what is this but an avowal that I may reasonably choose to do nonmoral evil (as a means) if it is justified by a truly proportionate reason?

These reflections suggest that the moral integrity of one's intentionality cannot be restrictively defined in terms of the psychological indirectness associated with evil-as-an-effect(or aspect)of an indivisible process even where the basic goods are concerned. Psychologically unintended evil effects are but an example of legitimate intentionality. But if the unintended effect is but one example of integral intentionality, and if intended means can be another, then it seems clear that integral intentionality traces not to psychological indirectness as such when evil occurs, but exclusively to the proportionate reason for acting. If there is a truly proportionate reason for acting, the agent remains properly open and disposed toward the *ordo bonorum* whether the evil occurs as an indivisible effect or as a means within the action. However, since evil-as-means and evil-as-effect are different realties, they may demand different proportionate reasons. What is sufficient for *allowing* an evil may not in all cases be sufficient for *choosing* it as a means.

4. *Both the intending and permitting will are to be judged teleologically (that is, by presence or absence of proportionate reason).* Even though there is a real difference between an intending and permitting will, and hence a real difference between actions involving the one or other, the moral relevance of this distinction must be approached delicately. In the past it was too readily concluded that if an evil occurred in conjunction with an intending will it was thereby immoral. This was especially true where the values of life and sexuality were concerned. The present reaction against this is a statement to the effect that it is simply the existence of the evil, not its relation to the intending or permitting will, which has moral significance. Both positions are, I believe, one-sided, and, if urged, extreme. The mediating position suggested here is that there is a difference between an intending and permitting will where concomitant premoral evil is concerned, but that both must be judged teleologically.

Concretely, the supposition behind the assertion that certain evils are morally tolerable only if they are indirect with regard to human intentionality is either one of the following two: there are no higher values; or if there are, they are never in conflict with lesser values. For if there are higher values and if they will be lost or threatened unless one sacrifices the lesser values, and if this choice will not subvert the relevant values in the long run, then what is wrong with choosing, reluctantly to be sure, to do the nonmoral evil that the greater good may be achieved? Is there a reasonable, defensible alternative to this? If there is, I do not see it. This leads to the conclusion that in those instances where nonmoral evil has been viewed as justified because it is indirect, the psychological indirectness was not radically decisive at all. What was and is decisive is the proportionate reason for acting. Similarly, in those instances that have been traditionally viewed as immoral because the intentionality was direct, the psychological directness itself is not decisive. The immorality must be argued from lack of proportionate reason. An example of each instance will clarify the point of the argument.

In discussing indirect sterilization, Edwin Healy, S.J. presents the following case:

> The patient has had many vaginal deliveries and as a result lacerations, infections, and erosions have occurred in the *cervix uteri*. Moreover, there has been subinvolution of the uterus and the organ itself has become heavy, boggy, enlarged and weakened, and is now causing the patient great physical debility, pain and distress. May the physician excise the uterus for the

present relief of the patient?[60]

The operation will, of course, result in sterilization—an evil effect, a disvalue when viewed abstractly. Healy approves the operation as a justified *indirect* sterilization, for "the condition described above would be sufficiently grave to justify this operation if less radical treatment would not prove effective." Is this not simply at root a calculus which asserts that the pain, debility, and distress caused by the uterus are greater disvalues than the loss of fertility entailed in its removal, and that sacrificing fertility in this instance will not subvert its value in the long run? *Indirect* here means one thing: the sterility is not chosen as a means. The term should not imply that one may never choose infertility as a means.

The principle of discrimination in the conduct of war (noncombatant immunity) may serve as the second instance. This principle has traditionally been presented as a moral absolute, and the direct killing of innocent persons viewed as intrinsically evil, evil *in se*. That is, such killing is morally evil regardless of the circumstances and independently of the consequences. Here I should like to suggest that it is precisely because of foreseen consequences that such a principle is a practical absolute. In this perspective its meaning would be: even though certain short-term advantages might be gained by taking innocent life in warfare, ultimately and in the long run, the harm would far outweigh the good. Taking innocent human life as a means, for example, to demoralizing the enemy, totalizes warfare. The action is radically different in human terms from the incidental death of innocents as one attempts to repel the enemy's war machine, even though the evil effects are numerically the same. It is radically different because of the intentionality involved, and to deny this is to deny to intentionality any realistic place in determining the meaning of human choice. Taking innocent human life as a means removes restraints and unleashes destructive powers which both now and in the long run will brutalize sensitivities and take many more lives than we would now save by such action. We cannot prove this type of assertion with a syllogistic click, but it is a good human bet given our knowledge of ourselves and our history—at least good enough to generate a practically exceptionless imperative, the type of moral rule Donald Evans refers to as "virtually exceptionless."[61]

What is responsible for this difference? This is the crucial question, of course, and one that cannot be answered (or at least has not been) with full satisfaction. Above it was suggested that the intending will (hence the person) is more closely associated with the evil than is a permitting will. This bespeaks (in some admittedly obscure way) a greater willingness that it occur. Now such a willingness is morally acceptable only to the extent that such an intention represents a choice of what is the lesser evil.

This analysis is not without its weaknesses. Suppose, for instance, two situations where one and the same good could be realized. In the first situation it can be realized only by intending the evil; in the second it can be realized by permitting the evil. If someone is ready to bring the good into existence only by permitting the evil, it has been suggested that he is less willing that the evil exist. Yet it must be said that he is also less willing that the good exist. Furthermore, the person who is prepared to realize the good even by intending the evil is more willing that the evil exist, but only because he is more willing that the good exist. Ultimately, therefore, to say that the intending will is more closely associated with evil than a merely permitting will is somewhat circular and considerably less than satisfying.

Joseph L. Allen views the principle of noncombatant immunity from direct attack as one generated teleologically, by a consideration of consequences. Of this principle he states:

> Such limits represent the fact that in the overwhelming number of cases, the strategist will be far more destructive by transgressing the rule than by following it.[62]

Therefore the rule of noncombatant immunity is a virtually exceptionless moral principle not independently of a calculation of consequences, but precisely because of an adequate calculation. Thus Allen writes:

> Calculation over whether to obliterate a city is too narrow if it asks only whether this action would "shorten the war" or assist in the attaining of military objectives. The strategist must also consider several other possible effects of the proposed action, if he is actually concerned for the total result: the destruction of people who have little direct relation to the war effort; the destruction of the social fabric of the city and its surrounding area; the invitation the raid gives, both to the opponent and to one's own side, to conduct more and more attacks of this sort, perhaps out of revenge and often out of all proportion to some "better peace"; and the increased callousness to creaturely beings that tends to accompany such acts. . . . The effect of an act on the whole range of creaturely beings must be considered, not merely its effect on a narrowly conceived military goal.[63]

What Allen is saying is that killing innocent people *as a means* in warfare is wrong because there is no proportionate reason for doing this, if our calculation of proportionality is adequate. This leads him to conclude that the end does not justify the means, but that the *ends* do. That is, before an adequate moral assessment of an act can be made, its effect on all the ends or values must be weighed. In the case of indiscriminate warfare, our experience and reflection tell us that all the ends or values will not be best served by such actions. Or, as Charles Curran puts it, "all of the moral values must be considered and a final decision made after all the moral values have been compared."[64] It is this weighing of all the moral values that has made of noncombatant immunity a virtually exceptionless moral rule. Proportionality is always the criterion where our actions cause damage. Our major problem is to make sure that we do not conceive it narrowly. The strength of our moral norms touching concrete conduct is an elaboration of what we judge, within our culture, with our history and experience, to be proportionate or disproportionate.

If there are norms that are teleologically established and yet are "virtually exceptionless"—as I believe there are—the remaining theological task is to clarify those metaethical assertions in view of which these norms are held as exceptionless. Above I referred to the fact that "we sense that taking the life of this innocent man in these circumstances would . . . in the long run render many more lives vulnerable." Of the direct destruction of noncombatants in warfare I have said that it would "in the long run . . . take many more lives than we would now save by such action." These are nondemonstrable calculations, prudential judgments based on both the certainties of history and the uncertainties of the future. Our sense of what we ought to do and ought not to do is informed by our past experience and a certain agnosticism with regard to our future behavior and its long-term effects. This leads to the suggestion—and it is only that—that where we view norms as "virtually exceptionless," we do so or ought to do so because of the prudential validity of what we refer to technically as *lex lata in praesumptione periculi communis* (a law established on the presumption of common and universal danger).

The notion of a presumption of universal danger is one most frequently associated with positive law. Its sense is that even if the action in question does not threaten the individual personally, there remains the further presumption that to allow individuals to make that decision for themselves will pose a threat for the common good. For instance, in time of drought, all outside fires are sometimes forbidden. This prohibition of outside fires is founded on the presumption that the threat to the common welfare cannot be sufficiently averted if private citizens are allowed to decide for themselves what precautions are adequate.

It seems to me that the exceptionless character of the norm prohibiting direct killing of noncombatants in warfare might be argued in a way analogous to this. The risk in alternative policies is simply too great. There are enormous goods at stake, and both our past experience of human failure, inconstancy, and frailty, and our uncertainty with regard to long-term effects lead us to believe that we *ought* to hold some norms as virtually exceptionless, that this is the conclusion of prudence in the face of dangers too momentous to make risk tolerable.

5. *Proportionate reason means three things:* (a) a value at least equal to that sacrificed is at stake; (b) there is no less harmful way of protecting the value here and now; (c) the manner of its protection here and now will not undermine it in the long run. If one examines carefully all instances where the occurrence of evil is judged acceptable in human action, a single decisive element is at the heart of the analysis: proportionate reason as here described. Under scrutiny this term must include the three elements mentioned. This understanding of proportionality is very close to that of Knauer. However, he maintains that when the reason is proportionate in the sense stated, the evil caused or permitted is indirect. I would prefer to say that the evil is direct or indirect depending on the basic posture of the will, but that it is justified in either case if a genuinely proportionate reason (in the sense stated) is present. The position suggested here is an attempt to incorporate into our moral reasoning all aspects of proportionality, immediate and long term, in contrast to a position that would appeal exclusively to the criterion of community-building, or rely too narrowly on psychological directness and indirectness as decisive without further ado.

The foregoing could be put negatively. An action is disproportionate in any of the following instances: if a lesser value is preferred to a more important one; if evil is unnecessarily caused in the protection of a greater good; if, in the circumstances, the manner of protecting the good will undermine it in the long run.

It is with reference to this third aspect of proportionality that the difference between an intending and permitting will (direct and indirect) reveals its potential moral relevance. Thus where nonmoral evil is involved, even if the good at stake is quantitatively proportionate to or greater than the loss, protecting it *in this way* could in the long run undermine this good. The principle of noncombatant immunity would seem to be an example of this.

The judgment of proportionality in conflict situations is not only a very decisive judgment; it is also a most difficult one. To see whether an action involving evil is proportionate in the circumstances we must judge whether this choice is the best possible service of all the values in the tragic and difficult conflict. What is the best possible promotion of all the values in the circumstances will depend on how one defines *in the circumstances*. A truly adequate account of the circumstances will read them to mean not just how much *quantitative* good can be salvaged from an individual conflict of values, but it will also weigh the social implications and reverberating aftereffects insofar as they can be foreseen. It will put the choice to the test of generalizability ("What if all persons in similar circumstances were to act in this way?"). It will consider the cultural climate, especially in terms of the biases and reactions it is likely to favor in a one-sided way. It will draw whatever wisdom it can from past experience and reflection, particularly as embodied in the rules peoples of the past have found a useful guide in difficult times. It will seek the guidance of others whose maturity, experience, reflection, and distance from the situation offer a counterbalance to the self-interested tendencies we all experience. It will allow the full force of one's own religious faith and its intentionalities to interpret the meaning and enlighten the options of the situation. This is what an adequate and responsible account of the circumstances must mean. So informed, an individual is doing the best he can and all that can be expected of him. But to say these things is to say that an individual will depend on communal discernment much more than our contemporary individualistic attitudes suggest.

6. *The notion of proportionate reason is analogous.* The comments made above should not lead us to believe that the concept of proportionate reason is reducible to a simple utilitarian calculus. Far from it. The notion is much more difficult than traditional casuistry would lead us to believe and, I believe, somewhat more fruitful and Christian than deontologists would allow us to imagine. Perhaps the problem can be introduced by a concrete instance. Moral theologians have judged as heroic charity the choice of a soldier to throw himself, at the cost of his own life, on a live explosive to save the life of a fellow soldier or soldiers. This means that they have asserted that, in technical terms, there is a proportionate reason for doing this. On the other hand, they have also asserted that an individual is not obliged to do this. In other words, there is a proportionate reason also for not making such a choice.

Somewhat similarly, if one has a proportionate reason for throwing himself on an explosive to save the life of his friend, then he also has a proportionate reason for allowing an assailant to kill him in preference to defending himself. Indeed, an unjust assailant is in a legitimate sense, precisely in his injustice, one's neighbor in greatest need. What then does proportionate reason mean if it can yield either conclusion?

The criterion of proportionality is that *ordo bonorum* viewed in Christian perspective, for it is the *ordon bonorum* which is determinative of the good one should attempt to do and the criterion of the objectively loving character of one's activity. In the light of this *ordo bonorum* there are three distinct possible and general senses of "proportionate reason."

First, there is the situation where the only alternative to causing or permitting evil is greater evil. This is the instance where both mother and fetus will certainly die without an abortion but where at least the mother can be saved with an abortion. It is also the case of the drowning swimmer where the hopeful rescuer cannot be of help because he cannot swim. The mother cannot save the child; under no condition can she do him any good. Similarly the bystander cannot save the drowning man. He can do him no good. It would be immoral to try. One who cannot save another but still tries is no longer governed by the *ordo bonorum*. For love (as involving, besides *benevolentia,* also *beneficentia*) is always controlled by the possible. There is no genuine *beneficentia* if no good can accrue to the individual through my sacrifice. An act of love (as *beneficentia*) is not measured by the mere desire or intention *(benevolentia)*. Therefore, in instances like this, abortion and not attempting to save the drowning swimmer are proportionately grounded decisions precisely because the harm cannot be avoided, whereas harm to the mother and prospective rescuer can and should be avoided. Into this first category of proportionality would fall also the standard case where falsehood is uttered as the necessary means to protect a patient's confidence and reputation.

Secondly, proportionate reason in a different sense is realized in situations where the alternatives are not so obvious. This is the instance where I lay down my life for another (or others). In this instance a good equal to what I sacrifice accrues to another and is the only way of securing that good for him. This is proportionate not because his life is preferable to mine—they are equally valuable as basic human goods— but because in case of conflict, it is a human and Christian good to seek to secure this good for my neighbor even at the cost of my life Indeed, other things being equal, such self-sacrifice is the ultimate act of human love. It is an assertion-in-action that "greater love than this no man has than that he lay down his life for his friends." To deny that such sacrifice could be proportionately grounded would be to deny that self-giving love after the model of Christ is a human good and represents the direction in which we should all be growing.

By saying that self-sacrifice to save the neighbor can truly be proportionate, traditional theology has implied that the goods being weighed, the alternatives, are not simply physical human life, my life versus that of another. Rather it has implied: (a) a world in which conflict occurs; (b) a world in which we are not mature in charity; (c) that the most maturing choices in such a world of conflict and sin are, other things being equal, those which prefer the good of others to self after the example of Christ. Preference of another to self is only thinkable as a good in a world both *objectively* and *subjectively* infected by sin and weakness: objectively in terms of conflict situations where death and deprivation are tragic possibilities that cannot be prevented except by corresponding or greater loss; subjectively in terms of the fact that being immature in grace and love, we tend to view such situations in terms of our own personal good exclusively and primarily—whereas our growth and perfection as human beings are defined in terms of our being, like the triune God himself, *ad alterum,* a being for others.

Thirdly, some actions or omissions were said to be proportionately grounded because the preference of a good for or in another at the cost of that good in or for myself should not, in view of human weakness and immaturity, be demanded. To say anything else would be to impose perfect love on imperfect creatures under pain of separation from divine friendship. This would be disproportionate because it would crush human beings and turn them from God. We know that the manuals of moral theology were often designed with confessional practice in mind. This means that casuistry was often concerned with what is sinful to do or omit rather than whether it was Christianly good to aspire to a particular value. Is it not to be expected that this perspective would also appear at the level of "proportionate reason"? Understandably, therefore, scholastic tradition has always maintained the axiom: *"Caritas non obligat cum gravi incommodo."* In other words, there is a proportionate reason for not aiding my neighbor in his distress or need. This axiom must be carefully understood if this third sense of proportionate reason is not to compromise genuine Christianity.

Could we approach it as follows? It is important, first of all, to admit that the allegation that Christ knew nothing of "excusing causes," "extraordinary measures," "excessive inconvenience," and so on, where fraternal love was involved, is assuredly correct. However, Christ was proclaiming an ideal after which we should strive and which we will realize perfectly only after this life and the purgations preparatory to eternal life. "Love one another as I have loved you" is a magnificent ideal. Our growth and maturity depend on our continued pursuit of it. But nobody has ever achieved it. This disparity between ideal and achievement suggests an explanation of the maxim under discussion which will show that it is not incompatible with, but even demanded by, the gospel message. That is, it suggests the imperfection of our charity in this life. What I have in mind is something like this. To propose a deep knowledge of physical science as desirable, as an ideal, is one thing. To demand of a ten-year-old that he master the subtleties of atomic physics under pain of deprivation of further instruction probably means that I will put an end to the individual's whole educational process. To propose bodily health as an ideal is proper and necessary. To demand that a tubercular patient recover his health all at once under pain of relapse into serious illness means that he is condemned to ill health. Similarly, to propose the Savior's love as an ideal is helpful and necessary. But to demand of human charity the perfection of virtue exemplified and preached by Jesus under pain of deprivation of charity itself (mortal sin) would be to condemn human beings to life in mortal sin. This can hardly be thought to be the message of One who knew human beings so thoroughly that he came to redeem them. Hence, when one asserts limits to charity, he is not emasculating the gospel message; he is rather asserting it, but insisting that it was proclaimed to imperfect beings who must grow to its fullness. One dare not forget this. For if charity can be minimalized out of existence, it can also be maximalized out of existence. When proclamation and immediate demand are confused, the proclamation can easily be lost in the impossibility of the demand.

The adage we are dealing with, therefore, simply recognizes human limits and the con equent imperfection of our charity. It is saying that we do not lose divine life for failing to have and express its fullness now. The ideal remains. It is there—to be sought, pursued, struggled after. But it is precisely because its achievement demands constant pursuit that it would be inconsistent with the charity of the gospel message to assert that its demands exceed the limitations of the human pursuer. This is the third sense of proportionate reason.

This study would very tentatively conclude, therefore, that the traditional distinction between direct and indirect is neither as exclusively decisive as we previously thought, nor as widely dispensable as some recent studies suggest. As descriptive of the posture of the will toward a particular evil (whether intending or permitting), it only aids us in understanding what we are doing. Whether the action so described represents integral intentionality more generally and overall depends on whether it is, or is not, *all things considered,* the lesser evil in the circumstances. This is an assessment that cannot be collapsed into a mere determination of direct and indirect voluntariety. Hence the traditional distinction, while morally relevant, cannot be the basis for deontologically exceptionless norms—which is not to say that there are no virtually exceptionless norms. Quite the contrary in my judgment.

This conclusion no doubt will appear rationally somewhat untidy. But it is, I believe, a reflection of the gap that exists between our moral sensitivities and judgments, and our ability to systematize them rationally. Moral awareness and judgments are fuller and deeper than rational arguments and rational categories. They are the result of evidence in the broadest sense—which includes a good deal more than mere rational analysis. While moral judgments must continually be submitted to rational scrutiny in an effort to correct and nuance them, in the last analysis, rooting as they do in the intransigence and complexity of reality, they remain deeper and more obscure than the systems and arguments we devise to make them explicit.[65]

ENDNOTES FOR CHAPTER ONE

1   See Joseph T. Mangan, S.J., "An Historical Analysis of the Principle of Double Effect," *Theological Studies* 10 (1949): 40-61; J. Ghoos, "L'Acte à double effet: Étude de Théologie Positive," *Ephemerides Theologicae Lovanienses* 27 (1951): 30-52.

2   See G. Kelly, S.J., *Medico-Moral Problems* (St. Louis: Catholic Hospital Association, 1958), pp. 13ff.; G. Grisez, *Abortion: The Myths, the Realities, and the Arguments* (Washington: Corpus Books, 1970), p. 329.

3   Paul Ramsey, *The Just War* (New York: Charles Scribner's Sons, 1968);

Paul Ramsey, *War and the Christian Conscience* (Durham: Duke University Press, 1961); John C. Ford, S.J., "The Morality of Obliteration Bombing," *Theological Studies* 5 (1944): 261-309.

4   *Acta Apostolicae Sedis (AAS)* 22 (1930): 563.

5   *AAS,* 43 (1951): 838-39.

6   Ibid., p. 857.

7   *AAS,* 50 (1958): 735-36.

8   *AAS,* 46 (1954): 589.

9   Walter Abbott, S.J., ed., *The Documents of Vatican II* (New York: America Press, 1966), p. 294.

10 See Ramsey, *War and the Christian Conscience,* pp. 34-59.

11 See Peter Harris, et al., *On Human Life* (London: Billing & Sons, 1968), p. 129. This book gives both the Latin text and an English translation.

12 *Ethical and Religious Directives for Catholic Health Facilities* (Washington: United States Catholic Conference, 1971), p. 4.

13 Earlier the distinction had been challenged by authors such as Joseph Fletcher, *Morals and Medicine* (Boston: Beacon Press, 1954); Glanville Williams, *The Security of Life and the Criminal Law* (New York: Alfred A. Knopf, 1951).

14 P. Knauer, S.J., "The Hermeneutic Function of the Principle of Double Effect," *Natural Law Forum* 12 (1967): 132-62. This is a revised version of his earlier article in *Nouvelle revue théologique,* "La détermination du bien et du mal moral par le principe du double effet" 87 (1965): 356-76.

15 Charles Curran, *A New Look at Christian Morality* (Notre Dame, IN: Fides, 1970), pp. 237ff.

16 Knauer, "Hermeneutic Function," p. 141.

17 P. Knauer, S.J., "Überlegungen zur moraltheologischen Prinzipienlehre der Enzyklika 'Humanae vitae'," *Theologie und Philosophie* 45 (1970): 73.

18 Knauer, "Hermeneutic Function," p. 161.

19 Kelly, *Medico-Moral Problems,* p. 4.

20 Grisez, *Abortion,* p. 331.

21 Ibid.

22 See ibid., and Noonan's footnote question to Knauer in "The Hermeneutic Function of the Principle of the Double Effect," p. 162.

23 William Van der Marck, *Toward a Christian Ethic: A Renewal of Moral Theology* (Westminster: Newman Press, 1967).

24 Ibid., p. 61.

25 Ibid., p. 54.

26 Ibid., p. 56. The sweeping character of Van der Marck's statement must be denied. Otherwise traditional theology would have proscribed all taking of another's property, all falsehood, all killing, etc. Obviously it did not.

27 Ibid., p. 59.

28 Ibid., p. 58.

29   This is a point of view expressed recently by Nicholas Crotty, C.P., in "Conscience and Conflict," *Theological Studies* 32 (1971): 208-32. See also my critique in "Notes on Moral Theology," *Theological Studies* 33 (1972): 68-119.

30   Van der Marck, *Christian Ethic,* p. 61.

31   Ibid.

32   Cornelius Van der Poel "The Principle of Double Effect," in *Absolutes in Moral Theology,* ed. Charles Curran (Washington: Corpus Books, 1968), pp. 186-210.

33   Ibid., p. 193.

34   Ibid., p. 194. See also Joseph Fuchs, "The Absoluteness of Moral Terms," *Gregorianum* 52 (1971): 415-58.

35   Where Van der Poel says "totality," Van der Marck speaks of "immediate implications" and Grisez (see below) of "indivisible aspects."

36   Van der Poel, "Principle of Double Effect," p. 201. See also Fuchs, "Absoluteness of Moral Terms."

37   Van der Poel, "Principle of Double Effect," p. 209.

38   Ibid., p. 198.

39   Ibid., p. 207.

40   Ibid., p. 210.

41   Ibid., p. 201.

42   Philippa Foot, "The Problem of Abortion and the Doctrine of the Double Effect," in *Moral Problems,* ed. James Rachels (New York: Harper and Row, 1971), pp. 29-41. The essay appeared originally in *Oxford Review* 5 (1967): 5-15.

43   Grisez, *Abortion,* pp. 307-46.

44   Ibid., p. 314.

45   Ibid., p. 315.

46   Ibid., p. 333.

47   Ibid., p. 340.

48   Ibid., p. 329.

49   Stanley Hauerwas, "Abortion and Normative Ethics," *Cross Currents* (Fall 1971), pp. 399-414. This is a very thoughtful critique of the work of Daniel Callahan and G. Grisez on abortion.

50   Grisez, *Abortion,* p. 340.

51   This does not imply that direct and indirect are indistinguishable realities and morally irrelevant. It merely means, as I shall argue later, that both forms of intention are subject to a theological judgment.

52   Hauerwas, "Abortion and Normative Ethics," p. 413.

53   Bruno Schüller, S.J., "Direkte Tötung—indirekte Tötung," *Theologie und Philosophie* 47 (1972): 341-57.

54   Richard A. McCormick, S.J., "Notes on Moral Theology," *Theological Studies* 33 (1972): 71.

55 I say "partially" because even a disvalue which has no necessary causal relation to the good can be, perversely indeed, desired.

56 Thomas Aquinas, *Summa Theologiae,* II-II, q. 64, a. 7.

57 M. Zalba, S.J., *Theologiae Moralis Summa* (Madrid: La Editorial Catolica, 1957), vol. II, p. 272.

58 Ibid., p. 278.

59 See Ambrogio Valsecchi, *Controversy* (Washington: Corpus Books, 1968), pp. 26-36. Valsecchi presents a thorough bibliography in this test case and digests the relevant articles fairly.

60 Edwin Healy, S.J., *Medical Ethics* (Chicago: Loyola University Press, 1956), p. 179.

61 Donald Evans, "Paul Ramsey on Exceptionless Moral Rules," *The American Journal of Jurisprudence* 16 (1971): 184-214.

62 Joseph L. Allen, "The Relation of Strategy and Morality," *Ethics* 72 (1963): 167-78.

63 Ibid., pp. 171-72.

64 Charles E. Curran, *Look at Christian Morality,* p. 239.

65 This monograph was composed at and supported by the Kennedy Center for Bioethics, Georgetown University, Washington, D.C.

CHAPTER TWO

The Problem of Exceptions in Medical Ethics

by

Baruch Brody

There are certain fundamental moral principles that are agreed upon by just about all writers on questions of medical ethics. Disputes in that area are not often then disputes about fundamental principles. What then are they about? They seem to be primarily about the application of these fundamental principles, and in particular about the permissibility of not applying them to certain cases, about the permissibility of making an exception in certain cases.

The disputes about euthanasia and abortion illustrate this point. Consider, for a moment, the dispute about euthanasia. It must always be remembered that every act of euthanasia is an act in which an individual takes the life of a second individual. Certainly, all of the disputants about euthanasia agree as to the validity of the moral principle forbidding one person to take the life of another. What they must therefore be disagreeing about is whether there are factors present in some cases (the benefits to the second individual, his consent, and so on) and that would make these cases valid exceptions to the general principle, that would make the principle inapplicable in these cases. The same thing, with one complication, holds for the dispute about abortion. The disputants about abortion also agree as to the validity of this moral principle. What they are disagreeing about is two things (and that is the complication), first, whether there is a person whose life is being taken, whether the principle is applicable at all (this is, of course, the dispute about the status of the fetus), and secondly, whether there are special factors connected with the interests and rights of the mother and/or the fetus that would, in any case, make abortions an exception to that otherwise valid principle.

Obviously, therefore, no progress can be made in solving these difficult questions of medical ethics without a satisfactory methodology for dealing with the question of the application of moral principles to particular cases and with the question of evaluating possible exceptions to these principles. Both Richard McCormick and Paul Ramsey have devoted themselves to articulating more fully their methodologies that have been implicit in many of their earlier writings. In this essay, I will argue against both of their approaches and suggest, as an alternative, an approach that I have implicitly employed in some of my work on abortion and euthanasia.[1] I will also suggest as a program for further research certain problems faced by this approach.

McCormick's Consequentialist Methodology

Let me begin by defining *a consequentialist* as someone who believes that the rightness and wrongness of an action is ultimately based upon the quality of the consequences produced by it. A consequentialist would, for example, say that one person's taking the life of another is wrong—when it is wrong—because doing so in those cases would lead to worse consequences than not doing so. If killing is generally wrong, says the consequentialist, this is only because it generally has undesirable consequences. Let me also define *a consequentialist methodology for exceptions* as the approach to making exceptions to valid moral rules whenever doing so will lead to more desirable consequences than following the rules.

It is clear that McCormick is not a consequentialist. He believes that certain types of actions are intrinsically right or wrong and that we can know this without having to consider their consequences. Thus, in his 1973 Hillenbrand Lecture, McCormick wrote:

> The first thing that must be said is that the issue is not precisely whether suicide and killing are generally wrong. This we grasp spontaneously and prethematically, a point well made by Germain Grisez and John Finnis. In this sense our basic moral commitments are not the result of discursive reflection. The issue is exception making, and the form of moral reasoning that both supports and limits in an intelligible way the exceptions we tolerate.[2]

Nevertheless, as I hope to show, McCormick is committed to a consequentialist methodology for exceptions and to all the difficulties of consequentialism. That McCormick is committed to that methodology emerges most clearly in his discussion of the principle of double effect:

> The basic analytic structure in conflict situations is the lesser evil, or morally avoidable/unavoidable evil. The rule of double effect is a vehicle for dealing with conflict situations. . . . It was facing conflict situations where only two courses are available: to act or not to act, to speak or remain silent, to resist or not to resist. The concomitant of either course of action was harm of some sort. Now in situations of this kind, the rule of Christian reason, if we are governed by the *ordo bonorum,* is to choose the lesser evil. . . . This means that all concrete rules and distinctions are subsidiary to this and hence valid to the extent that they actually convey to us what is factually the lesser evil.[3]

This passage must mean that in these conflict situations (the very situations in which morally serious individuals contemplate making exceptions to rules that they believe to be valid) we are to choose that action among the unfortunate alternatives that are open to us that has the best consequences. And this means that we are to make exceptions to our rules just in case doing so will lead to a more desirable consequence (a lesser evil) than would following the rule. In short, McCormick has a consequentialist methodology for exceptions.

All of this explains why McCormick is in agreement with some of the basic principles of Fletcher's situational ethics. Both advocate a consequentialist methodology for exceptions. The differences between them are only about the identification and the weighing of the relevant consequences:

> In summary, while rightly endorsing the principle of proportion as the measure of the deeds we do, Fletcher has failed to examine those aspects, values, and dimensions that would alone inform us whether certain forms of behavior are proportionate.[4]

What are the implications for action of such a consequentialist methodology for exceptions? It seems that they must be equivalent to the implications for action of full-fledged consequentialism. Consider, after all, a rule like killing is wrong, a rule whose intrinsic validity, says McCormick, can be seen by us spontaneously without an examination of the consequences of following it. When, however, does this rule apply? When should it be followed? According to McCormick, that rule should be broken whenever breaking it will lead to better results (such as a lesser evil) than would obtain if the rule were followed. But this is exactly the implication for action of full-fledged consequentialism, so

McCormick's consequentialist methodology for exceptions and full-fledged consequentialism have the same implications for human action, and any objections to the latter are also objections to the former.

What are the objections to full-fledged consequentialism? Ramsey and others have claimed that the fundamental objection is its failure to be concerned with the distribution of these consequences, is its failure to demonstrate rationally why greatest good or greatest happiness (or net greatest anything) required that the greatest number of participants share in that good, that all concerned be counted.

There are five points that should be noted about this claim. First, there is a great difference between the claim that all concerned be counted and the claim that the greatest number should share in that net greatest good. Second, the former claim, that all concerned be counted, follows trivially from the consequentialist idea of trying to produce the greatest net amount of good since, in measuring that good, everyone's good must be counted. Third, it is not clear that the latter claim, that the greatest number should share in the good, is always true. Would we not at least sometimes prefer that five people receive some great good rather than that thousands of people receive some very trivial good? Fourth, still Ramsey's fundamental point, that consequentialists have usually failed to consider the very relevant question of how the net good is distributed, is correct. And the failure of consequentialism to take this into account leads to some very unsatisfactory implications for human action. Fifth, nevertheless, this does not show that consequentialism has to be rejected, for there are a whole variety of ways in which distributional considerations can be built into a consequentialist position. Instead of trying to produce the most good (even if that merely means the least evil), one could try to maximize the median amount of good, some weighted function of the total good, and the standard deviation from the mean. Sidgwick had already suggested such a modification of consequentialism, and many such modifications have recently been explored by Professor Rescher.[5]

What then is the fundamental difficulty with both full-fledged consequentialism and McCormick's consequentialist methodology for exceptions? It seems to me that it lies in their failure to bring to bear on the question of exception-making considerations of human rights. After all, unless we are prepared to treat individuals as mere means, there are certain of their rights that cannot be violated even if doing so would lead to very desirable consequences (even widely spread desirable consequences).[6] It is a failure to keep this point in mind that has led consequentialism to many unacceptable implications for action.

All of this emerges very clearly if we examine McCormick's treatment of Zalba's defense of capital punishment. McCormick apparently does not agree with Zalba because he seems to be skeptical about some of Zalba's claims about deterrence and social survival. Nevertheless, he certainly commends the fundamental moral assumption underlying Zalba's argument, namely, that certain goods can outweigh the value of the individual human life and can justify its being taken. It is not surprising that McCormick accepts this assumption because it also underlies his own consequentialist methodology for exceptions. But this seems simply wrong. It is one thing to believe in capital punishment because one believes that the criminal, because of his actions, no longer has a full-fledged right to life. But it is very different to believe that the criminal has such a full-fledged right and yet that social benefits can outweigh that right. To believe that is to treat the life of all, criminal or noncriminal, as a means that can be used up or traded for some social benefit, and to do that is surely morally objectionable.

The same point really emerges in the case of abortion. Suppose that it were shown that a policy of abortion in certain cases would have socially desirable consequences, even if one took into account long-range consequences on the fabric of society and on people's moral sensitivity. Would it then be permissible to kill the fetus even if the fetus were a human being? Or would that not be an illegitimate use of the fetus as a means to acquiring some goal? The consequentialist methodology would have to permit such abortions, and would indeed have to permit doing the same thing to us as well. It is these implications that make consequentialism and Professor McCormick's consequentialist methodology unacceptable.

Ramsey on Direct and Indirect

We turn then to Paul Ramsey's views about moral conflicts and about the exceptions we have to make to our moral rules in order to deal with these conflicts. A good way to begin is to look at Ramsey's fundamental objection to McCormick's views (which he calls McCormick's use of proportional reason):

> Of course, if goods and evils are commensurable one commensurates them; if they are comparable one compares them, draws the proportionate conclusion, and chooses the lesser over the greater evil, or chooses the greater

good. But if any human goods or evils are incommensurate, then there is a genuine and irreducible ambiguity in moral choice. One cannot cut the Gordion knot by any calculus. . . .

As an example of what Ramsey has in mind, we might consider a conflict-of-lives case like an abortion to save the life of the mother or like the *Dudley* and *Holmes* lifeboat cases. If it is indeed true that the values of the lives in question cannot be compared, then Ramsey is surely right in saying that we cannot decide what to do by referring to the lesser evil of some set of consequences. What then are we to refer to? Ramsey says that:

> If then incommensurate rights to life come into conflict, one confronts decisional ambiguity whose grammar can be parsed only by never doing any more than indirectly intending to take a human life if unavoidably the deadly deed must be done.

As I understand Ramsey's position, then, it seems to come to the following claims about conflict cases: first, in many cases, where the values of the consequences can be compared, we should act to produce the greater good even if doing so involves an exception to our moral rules; second, there are cases, however, in which one must go against some basic moral rule and there is no way to choose the lesser evil because the values of the consequences of one's actions are incommensurable; third, in such cases, one should not act so as to intendingly violate such a rule. Instead, one should choose that course of action that involves at most an unintended, although certainly foreseen, violation of that rule.

There are many questions that can be raised about each of these claims and one might also wonder whether they are truly compatible with what Ramsey has said about such exceptions on other occasions. For now, however, I would like to focus in on two issues, the notion of incomparable values and the moral distinction between the directly intended (the intended) and the indirectly intended (the merely foreseen). These are, after all, at the heart of Ramsey's methodology for moral exceptions.

What is it for two values to be incomparable? It might mean one of two things: first, it is actually psychologically impossible for people to make comparative value judgments between the two values, to value one more than the other or to value them equally; second, while people can make such value judgments, they ought not to make them (presumably because there is no sound basis for making them). The former is, of course, a subjective notion of incomparable values while the latter is a far more objective notion. It seems to me, however, that Ramsey is in trouble whichever of these notions he has in mind.

Let us begin with the subjective notion of incomparable values. Could it ever be psychologically impossible for people to make comparative value judgments between two values? After all, the following seems to emerge from the analysis of valuation (of utility) in decision theory: if a person has open to him a course of action A that will, with probability P, cause the realization of value V_1 and a course of action B that will, with that same probability, cause the realization of value V_2, then, if there are no other consequences of these actions or if those other consequences are of equal value, that person values V_1 (V_2) more than V_2 (V_1) if he prefers to do A (B) rather than B (A) and he values V_1 and V_2 equally if he is equally willing to do either. So, if there are two values that are psychologically impossible to compare, all of us could neither prefer to do the appropriate action A or the appropriate action B nor be equally willing to do either. We would all presumably have to have some other attitude, say complete paralysis of will. This consequence seems to me to make it highly unlikely that there really are subjectively incomparable values. There are, no doubt, some values for which some (perhaps even many) people could not feel anything other than paralysis of will (at least for some time) if they had to make the appropriate choices of action. But I cannot think of any two values for which we would all, even after much reflection, feel complete paralysis of will if we had to make the appropriate choices of action. Even in conflict of lives cases, most people have some preferences among the courses of action open to them.[7]

I do not believe that Ramsey would be very troubled by this conclusion, for I suspect that he is really concerned with the objective notion of incomparable values. I suspect that what he is really saying is that there are values for which there are no sound bases for making comparative value judgments among them, even if people can and do make such judgments. After all, Ramsey is claiming that there is no *sound basis* for applying the principle of proportional reason in the cases of incomparable value judgments.

Let us suppose then that Ramsey means that two values are incomparable when there is no sound basis for making a comparative value judgment between them. I would like to show now that, even given this more plausible interpretation, he faces a very serious difficulty.

The classical principle of double effect went something like this: it is permissible to do an action A even though it can be foreseen that that necessarily involves the performance of an action B which is intrinsically wrong providing that (1) the performance of B is not intended either as an end or as a means to some end, and (2) the good to be obtained by performing A is sufficient to outweigh the evil produced by the performance of B. Clause (1) is, of course, the more famous of the two conditions, since it introduces that which is special to the principle of double effect, the moral significance of the distinction between the intended and the foreseen. But clause (2) is also vital. It would, after all, be absurd to do A if the evil that results from doing B is not of lesser weight than the gain that results from performing A. To put it schematically, it is that proportionate gain that gives us a reason to do A while it is the fact that the performance of B is unintended that makes it permissible to do A. So a comparison of the weight of the values in question is essential even if we do employ the distinction between the intended and the foreseen.

All of this means that Ramsey is in a difficult position. After all, his argument is that the distinction between the intended and the foreseen must be brought to bear in resolving decisional ambiguities just when the values in question are incommensurable. But if they really are incommensurable, then it is not clear that it can be brought to bear because, as we have just seen, a comparison of the weight of the values at stake seems needed as well.

We have so far focused our attention on Ramsey's crucial notion of incommensurable values. But we must also look at the way in which he wants to use the distinction between the intended and the foreseen. Ramsey wants to claim (1) that incommensurability of values means that we cannot use proportionate reason, and (2) that in conflict cases involving incommensurable values, we should use the distinction between the intended and the foreseen. Granting the meaningfulness of incommen surable values, we would certainly have to agree with (1). But what reason do we have for granting (2)? Why should we suppose that there is a moral distinction between an intended action and a merely foreseen action?

In thinking about this question, it is extremely important to distinguish between the moral evaluation of an action and the moral evaluation of an agent for performing that action. There are obviously factors relevant to the latter (the degree of competency of the agent, for example) which are not relevant to the former. The questions that we must distinguish therefore are: (a) should it make a difference, in our evaluating an agent for performing an action, whether the agent intended the performance of the action or merely foresaw the performance?; and (b) if it does, should that also make a difference in our evaluation of the action itself? It is important to keep in mind, moreover, that Ramsey needs an affirmative answer to the second question, for he is concerned with the evaluation of actions—with deciding how we should resolve decisional ambiguities and how we should determine what to do—and not with the evaluation of agents.

It is interesting to note, even in thinking about the first question, that the law rejects as an excuse the claim that the performance of the action in question, although foreseen, was unintended:

> We have seen that consequences which are foreseen as certain or highly probable need not be, but usually are, intended. A system of law, however, could provide that a man be held liable for such consequences, even though he did not intend them. In the first place, such a rule would obviate difficult inquiries into the mental element. But secondly, and more importantly, the rule could be justified on the ground that a man should not do acts which he sees will involve consequential harm to others, whether or not he intends to cause this harm.[8]

This legal attitude seems right. If I burn down my factory to collect the insurance, knowing but not intending that some of the workers will die, I am still responsible for my action. Now this does not prove that (a) should be responded to negatively, because (1) it does not show that there is *no* difference in my responsibility, *no* difference in the evaluation of me and (2) perhaps other cases are different. But it does at least seem to suggest that the answer to (a) should be negative. And if that were true, then surely the answer to (b) should be negative as well, for intentions are surely more relevant to the evaluation of agents than to the evaluation of actions.

In short, then, Ramsey is in trouble, both because of his notion of incommensurable values and because of his reliance on the significance of the distinction between the intended and the foreseen. But where does that leave us? In the next section, I hope to outline an alternative approach that will avoid all of these problems.

The Casuistry of Rights

Perhaps the best way to explain this third approach is to begin by looking, even briefly, at the claims that it makes about the moral problems concerning euthanasia and abortion.[9] Having done so, we will then be in a much better position to explain the theoretical bases of this approach.

Consider the issue of euthanasia. According to this approach, the fundamental issues surrounding euthanasia arise because any act of euthanasia deprives the person being killed of something to which he has a right, namely, his life. Now, in general, people can consent to their being deprived of something to which they have a right or they can request that they be so deprived. And, unless there are special circumstances raising further moral considerations, that consent and/or request is efficacious, so the person who acts on that consent and/or request has done no wrong. Returning then to the issue of euthanasia, if an individual consents to the taking of his life, or actively requests that his life be taken, then (unless there are special circumstances raising further issues) the taking of his life is permissible. Let me just add that in order for the consent and/or request to be efficacious, the individual must be competent and the consent must not be based upon fraud and/or duress. All of this means that the standard discussions about euthanasia have to be redone. It is not relevant for us to consider whether the individual gains or loses (for example, to consider the likelihood of an unusual recovery or the efficacy of the pain-killing drugs) because it is the individual's choice and not ours. Nor need we consider what means are to be employed (direct versus indirect) because the legitimacy of the means is determined by the nature of his consent. Our sole concern, at least in determining the permissibility of the act of euthanasia, is about whether there has been an efficacious consent.

But what if the individual does not now consent to and/or request euthanasia because he is unable to do so? Does our approach entail that euthanasia would not be permissible in such cases? How about administering pain-killing drugs in such cases even though that will shorten the life of the individual? Will we not have to appeal to proportionate reason or to direct versus indirect to solve these problems? I do not think so, for there are two additional points to be noted. First, individuals can, and often do, consent to and/or request the deprivation of that to which they have a right in advance and conditionally. Remembering this at least suggests the possibility of plans for arranging for euthanasia in advance. Secondly and more importantly, but more hesitantly, we should certainly consider the possibility of relying upon hypothetical consent, upon our judgment that the individual would consent if he could. It is, after all, that type of consent that we rely upon when we treat emergency patients whose consent to being treated cannot be obtained.

Let us look briefly at the claims this approach makes about the question of abortion to save the life of the mother. It makes four major claims (assuming for the sake of the argument that the fetus has the right to life of a human being).

a. The mother does not have the right to take the life of the fetus as a legitimate act of defense against a pursuer. It is true, of course, that the right to life of a pursuer is sufficiently weaker than a normal right to life that the life of a pursuer can be taken to save the life of the pursued. But the fetus is not a pursuer. While its continued existence poses a threat to the life of the mother, that is not enough to make it a pursuer (or else, you could kill anyone when necessary to save your own life, for that person would be a pursuer). Moreover, there is nothing else that the fetus does that would really make it a pursuer.

b. Abortions cannot be justified on the grounds of the hypothetical consent of the fetus, on the grounds that the fetus would consent if it could because it is better for it to be aborted than to be born as an unwanted child. Claims to this effect are irresponsibly speculative.

c. A course of action that results in the fetus's surviving because it has not been killed and the mother's not surviving because she has not been saved is preferable to one that results in the mother's surviving because she has been saved and the fetus's not surviving because it has been killed, not because one life is more important than another, but because the right to not be killed (and the corresponding obligation not to kill) is stronger than the right to be saved (and the corresponding obligation to save).

d. Still, if (as is commonly the case in the early stages of pregnancy) both mother and fetus will die if there is no abortion, and there is no way to save the fetus, one should kill the fetus to save the mother. The fetus is not being unjustly deprived of that life to which it has a right because it will inevitably die shortly anyway and the mother's right to be saved therefore takes precedence.

Naturally, much has to be said by way of explanation and defense of all these claims. What I want to do now, however, is explain the moral methodology of exception making involved in it.

It is clear that this approach to problems in medical ethics like abortion and euthanasia rests upon several fundamental assumptions.

First, human beings have certain rights. The rights that are particularly relevant in our cases are the right not to be killed and the right to be saved. The relevant moral rules either prohibit the performance of certain actions that would violate these rights or require the performance of certain actions needed to ensure the realization of these rights (we can, therefore, talk of these rules as protecting these rights).

Second, some of these rights are stronger than others, and this leads to some moral rules (the ones protecting the stronger rights) taking precedence over others (the ones protecting the weaker rights) when it is impossible to satisfy both.

Third, there are a number of ways in which rights go out of existence. These include those cases in which one voluntarily waives one's rights, in which one voluntarily consents to being deprived of that to which one has a right, and those cases in which one acts (as does the pursuer) in such a way as to at least weaken the strength, if not totally annihilate, one's rights.

Fourth, the facts mentioned above lead to certain important exceptions to moral rules, ones that are very important in the context of medical ethics. After all, if, on the basis of the strength of the rights they protect, one rule takes precedence over another, then that justifies an exception to the rule that is preceded. Again, if some rule protects some right, then, if that right goes out of existence in a given case, that case will be one in which one can legitimately act in violation of that rule.

Employing these assumptions, we approach problems in medical ethics like abortion and euthanasia by (1) identifying the relevant rights, (2) assessing their respective strengths in the relevant cases, (3) seeing if any have, in one way or another, gone out of existence, and (4) applying this information to determine what one ought to do in a given case. In short, this approach consists of a casuistry of rights.

It should be noted that in approaching these problems in this way, the sole moral considerations that we are taking into account are those concerning human rights. But there obviously are other types of moral considerations. One type is, of course, those considerations having to do with maximizing the good and distributing it in an equitable fashion. And there are other types as well. Now there are many moral problems where these have to be considered. These are problems where considerations of rights are of less importance. Our moral methodology would be inappropriate for dealing with such problems, and that is why we are only putting it forward as an approach to exception making for certain problems in medical ethics.

Previous writers in ethics have usually assumed that the whole of morality is woven of one fabric, and they have therefore usually proposed a monistic approach to morality. I cannot see any reason for supporting such an assumption, and I suspect that it is at the root of our failure to develop adequate ethical systems.

Some Further Questions

In order to apply the methodology we have outlined in the previous section, one would need a great deal of knowledge about rights. This includes knowledge about which rights people have, knowledge about how they can be lost, and knowledge of the relative strength of rights. What is the source of this knowledge?

In my opinion, the root of this knowledge is moral intuition. But even in a survey essay like this, something more than that is required, so let me say a little bit about these intuitions. To begin with, we must note the existence of two very different types of intuitions. The first is the intuition of the truth of certain general claims, for example, that each human being has a right not to be killed, or that although the right not to be killed is usually stronger than the right to be saved, the right of the pursued to be saved takes precedence over the right of the pursuer not to be killed. The second is the intuition about a particular case, about whether a right has been lost in that case or about which right takes precedence in that case. This second type of intuition plays a very important role in our methodology, so I want to say some more about it.

Intuitions about particular cases have several functions. To begin with, as we collect them, they can be used as evidence for new generalizations about rights, generalizations that are not themselves immediately intuitively evident. Thus, in my essays on abortion, I have used intuitions as the basis for a rather complicated (and certainly not intuitively evident) general principle about when A's right not to be killed is weakened, because his life is forfeited anyway, so that the right of others to be saved can take precedence. Secondly, these intuitions can be used as the basis for refining and making more precise general principles that are intuitively self-evident. In this way, we can use intuition to correct intuition. To refer again to my earlier essays on abortion, I found this use of particular intuitions extremely important in refining principles about pursuers and pursued.

There are, no doubt, many who will object to this extensive dependence upon moral intuitions. Moral intuitions, they will say, vary too much among people and change too much over time; such intuitions could not, therefore, be a reliable source of moral knowledge

I freely concede that there is a problem here, but I do feel that its importance can be (and often is) overestimated. To begin with, if there are disagreeing intuitions about a given case, one can always search out other analogous cases in which intuitions will be more in accord and use the intuitions about those other cases to resolve the questions about the disputed case. And if, at the end, one remains with disputing intuitions, one will have acquired at least a clearer sense of what are the sources of the moral disagreement. Secondly, that intuitions can (and often do) change should bother only those who are seeking a final and infallible source of moral knowledge. Others, who are seeking a more tentative experientially based source of moral understanding, may well welcome this fact about moral intuitions. In their view, that moral intuitions change is (at least often) a reflection of the fact that our intuitions are responsive to new situations and to better understandings that arise out of new experiences.

Let me end by freely conceding that both my account of this third approach to exception making and my defense of the intuitions it rests upon are very sketchy. I have, in this essay, only been able to outline this approach. In future, more elaborate studies, I hope to be able to do better.[10]

ENDNOTES FOR CHAPTER TWO

1 See Baruch Brody, *Abortion and the Sanctity of Human Life* (Cambridge: M.I.T. Press, 1975); Brody, ''Voluntary Euthanasia and the Law,'' in *Beneficent Euthanasia,* ed. Marvin Kohl (Buffalo: Prometheus Books, 1975).

2 Richard A. McCormick, ''The New Medicine and Morality,'' *Theology Digest* 21 (Winter 1973): 315.

3 Ibid., p. 311.

4 Most recently, this claim has been forcefully defended by John Rawls, *A Theory of Justice* (Cambridge: Harvard University Press, 1971), chaps. 1-3.

5 Henry Sidgwick, *Methods of Ethics* (New York: Macmillan Publishing Co., Inc., 1907), pp. 413-17; Nicholas Rescher, *Distributive Justice* (Indianapolis: Bobbs Merrill, 1966), pp. 25-41.

6   I will, in the final section of this paper, consider whether there are some exceptions to this rather sweeping claim.

7   R. D. Luce and H. Raifa, *Games and Decisions* (New York: Wiley, 1957), chap. 2.

8   Sir William Salmond, *Jurisprudence,* 12th ed. (Austin, TX: Sweet and Maxwell, 1966), section 89.

9   Fuller details can be found in my works mentioned in endnote 1.

10 See my forthcoming "Intuitions as a Source of Objective Moral Knowledge" in the *Monist* (1979) for a future elaboration, with some modifications, of this approach.

CHAPTER THREE

Incommensurability and Indeterminancy in Moral Choice

by

Paul Ramsey

The distinction between the *directly voluntary* and the *indirectly voluntary* has functioned to recognize a sort of ambiguity that cannot be eliminated from moral choice. It calls our attention to the unavoidable ambiguity which arises when we confront incommensurate goods or evils. Thus, the distinction between what is intended and what is permitted (or some other one-phrase summary) serves to clarify moral choice without suggesting that indeterminancy among the ends of action can be removed. In weighing commensurate goods or evils, there can be perplexity, uncertainty, and error, but never irreducible ambiguity. One can ask: Have I made the right calculation? Have I done my proportions correctly? Have I trammeled up all the consequences? But some sorts of choices are indeterminate. My contention is that the rule of double effect, which is often supposed to be a program for reducing ambiguity in moral choice until there is none, has served rather to sustain acknowledgment of an actual ambiguity that characterizes much of our moral experience and many moral judgments.

Nevertheless, Roman Catholic moralists in recent years, both in the United States and abroad, have been reexamining this traditional distinction, calling its meaning and significance radically into question. This literature has been reviewed in penetrating fashion by Richard A. McCormick, S.J. in his 1973 Pere Marquette Lecture entitled *Ambiguity in Moral Choice*. In this chapter I propose to contribute to this discussion by an analysis of that lecture. I shall pay principal attention to McCormick's own position—today it would be called his *metaethical* proposal concerning how we justify first-order *normative* ethical judgments—and only incidental to this shall I undertake to come to grips with the literature he surveys. Instead, to give a complete picture, other important writings by McCormick will be taken up. Since he is one of America's most distinguished ethicists, an overall report and analysis of the author's writings should be of importance to a reader's comprehension of the issues under discussion today.

So far I have used McCormick's term *ambiguity*. I ought to introduce my own here at the start. Ambiguity is a characteristic of statements people make. Doubt, difficulty, perplexity, uncertainty, quandary, dilemma, compromise, indecision are better words to use when talking about the moral choices we sometimes must make. *Indeterminacy* is the word I shall use in putting forward my own views when I have in mind the doubtful among the objective characteristics (the incalculable determinants) of moral decisions or actions—not ambiguity.

Incommensurability is another term at issue, or the term *commensurate*. The root meaning here is *measure,* some rather exact or determinate way, if not indeed a quantitive way, to settle upon the right moral choice. The *Oxford English Dictionary* defines incommensurable to mean "having no common measure" or "not comparable in respect of magnitude or value." Contrary to that definition, McCormick uses *commensurate* and *proportionate* interchangeably. I shall not do so except when expounding and analyzing his views, because one of the chief questions I have to put to him is whether *proportionate reason* means the same as *commensurate reason* in the sense that it leads to measurable choices, to determinate moral judgments. Or does *proportionate* encompass what I call the *indeterminancy* of many moral choices?

Traditional Christian ethics assumed that the greatest good for persons is friendship with God and that this is not measurable at all, whereas contemporary consequentialists assume that the greatest good means the "greatest net *measurable* good." During our lives on pilgrimage to the greatest good, there may be many goods claiming our allegiance that are not measurable at all. McCormick needs to be pressed to tell us whether by advancing "a form of consequentialism," he means to say that all goods are commensurate. Does he reject utilitarianism only because he is a *multivalue* consequentialist? Or as an alternative, is he a multivalue consequentialist only in cases of *conflict-resolution?*

My own view is that the distinction between direct and indirect voluntariety is pertinent and alerts our attention as moral agents to those moral choices where incommensurable conflicting values are at stake, where there is no measurable resolution of value conflicts on a single scale, where there are gaps in any supposed hierarchy of values, and therefore no way to determine the greater or lesser good or evil. It may still be that values are in some sense *comparable,* that some are higher than others. Values may be comparable qualitatively, yet there may be no way to measure addition to the one against subtraction from the other. Higher and lower values, more worthy and less worthy goods, may be known to us while still there may be gaps—incommensurability—in the scale, or perhaps there may be no clear single scale on which to measure the lesser or greater good or evil. The rule distinguishing between direct and indirect voluntariety helps us decide how to respond to values in conflict cases in which there is no clear single scale of higher or lower to enable commensurate reason to decide the issue, or where there are unbridgeable discontinuities in the hierarchy of values.

What, it may then be asked, is the meaning of saying that once actions are morally appraised in terms of the distinction between direct and indirect intentionality there must still be a proportion between the evil effect and the good effect? Those moralists who champion the cause of proportion *über alles* usually press this point: if proportionate reason has finally a decisive part to play, they say, then proportion may as well be the very meaning of the distinction in the first place between willfully doing and permitting an evil in a justifiable course of action.

Such an objection cannot be allowed; it traffics on the vagueness of the notion of proportionate reason. There is, of course, measurable meaning in some judgments of proportion; that is, when one takes (indirectly) one life to save the only one that can be saved (rather than lose two) in abortion cases, or when weighing 100,000 collateral civilian deaths against 125,000 in legitimately targeted acts of war. Obviously, one should choose the lesser of these commensurate evils. Such body counts are the only instances I can think of in which there is clear commensurate meaning in the final judgment of proportion under the rule of twofold effect.

Beyond that, judgments of proportion are extended to include choices lacking any clearly measurable criterion of greater good or lesser evil. To affirm this in no way weakens (it rather strengthens) the case for saying that where there is no single scale or common denominator, or where there is discontinuity in the hierarchy of goods or evils, one ought not directly turn against any human good. Beyond measurable criteria for determining the greater good or lesser evil (beyond commensurate reason) are decisions made in the midst of what I call "indeterminancy in moral choice." Commensurate reason deals with only a limited number of similarities or differences in the comparison of goods or evils. Moral reason must also deal with innumerable indeterminant comparisons and differences in morally relevant aspects of decisions to be made. Judgments of comparative overall similarity or dissimilarity are exceedingly difficult to execute, or to account for in moral reasoning. David K. Lewis writes:

> Overall similarity consists of innumerable similarities and differences in innumerable respects of comparison, balanced against each other according to the relative importances we attach to those respects of comparison. Insofar as these relative importances differ from one person to another, or differ from one occasion to another, or are indeterminate even for a single person or a single occasion, so far is comparative similarity indeterminate.[1]

In a similar vein the British moralist W. D. Ross wrote that we are "faced with great difficulties when we try to *commeasure* good things of very different types."[2]

Such indeterminate decisions are frequent in human experience. One chooses orange or apple or grapefruit juice for breakfast. One decides upon a vacation in the mountains rather than at the seashore. One picks a particular school instead of another for one's children, or this career rather than that for oneself. In all these cases, there are innumerable similarities and differences in innumerable respects of comparison among the goods presented for choice. There are also differences relative to persons and occasions. There is no clear single scale. So also in moral choice, commensurate reason choosing the greater over the lesser good cannot always decide the issue. Yet in many cases of such choices, all of us would defend their reasonableness, the *proportionality* (this is at least a possible use of the term) to actual or potential value-experiences. There are cases of indeterminancy in moral choice.

An illustration of indeterminancy in sufficiently well-grounded moral choice is the following. How can we decide whether the defense of Mother Russia against invasion and Hitler's plans to subjugate her people was worth the sacrifice of 20,000,000 Russian lives? That, I say, is an indeterminate decision. There cannot be a knock-down argument either way. It is reasonable to say Russia should have defended herself at that toll. It is also reasonable to say the cost was too great. Those who say all modern war is disproportionate make the latter sort of judgment. Either verdict rests upon a comparison of lives lost with the value of nationhood having a continuous history. This entails a comparison of innumerable similarities and innumerable differences and interconnections between the clashing values; a comparison of very different types of good things. The upshot is indeterminancy in moral choice, either way.

Such decisions still remain to be faced (not body counts only) even if, let us suppose, a just military defense of Russia requires that the death of no human being be brought about with direct intentionality, only obliquely. The grounds for this view would be the claim that the life of a human being is quite incommensurate with other values—Russian nationhood, for example. In pursuit of the latter, one ought never directly destroy a human being who is the image of God and is holy ground. Even so, it still would remain to determine how much death and injury obliquely caused is enough to offset, not other deaths and injury (that would be a commensurate aspect of moral judgments), but the value of continuing national traditions and unsubjected peoplehood. Such indeterminate decisions are often an obscure task of moral decision making.

The crucial issue is whether proportionate reason encompasses many indeterminate moral choices in addition to choices among commensurate goods. If so, proportionate reason *alone* is an insufficient guide to action when we face choices between quite incommensurate goods or values. Standing alone, an indeterminate choice of the good to be pursued is insufficient, even though it is arguably a choice that is not unreasonable. It is insufficient because, in the case given above, anyone who judges the cost of defending Russia to be disproportionate ought (in addition) not turn directly against the value of Russian nationhood (even if his action has detrimental effects on that), and he who judges the toll to be a proportionate defense should not turn directly against the value of human life even while exacting those deaths. Either way, an indeterminate decision was made with apparent good reason between "good things of very different types" (Ross). Decision in this and many other instances is just as fuzzy (indeterminate) and as clear as McCormick's prohibition of our ever willing the sin of another, which yet for proportionate reason we may *permit* in the public order and indeed *foresee* to be among the effects of certain sorts of legislation.

My thesis, then, is this: Insofar as proportionate reason refers to choice among commensurable goods, there is, of course, no need for the rule distinguishing between direct and indirect intentionality; one simply directly chooses the measurably greater good and the means thereto even if the latter are evils. But if proportionate reason encompasses also (and we need some term to refer to this sort of decision) choice among ends or goods that are indeterminate or not measurably comparable, then the rule of twofold intentionality has lexical priority in cases of important conflicted values in deciding what manner of action may *morally* be posited which, as a physical action, does evil to achieve good.

Perhaps proportionate reason should be reserved for choice among measurably greater and lesser goods or evils. Then we could say that choice among indeterminate goods needs to appeal to some "good moral reason." He who defends Mother Russia has acceptable moral reason for doing so. Nor can it be denied that the pacifist also has good reason for the primacy he ascribes to the inestimable value of human life. These are incommensurate goods; either choice is an indeterminate one. In addition to reasons for the good served, both need also to know that neither should intend the impairment of the incommensurate good he does not make the primary objective of his will.

However, the term *proportionate* has traditionally been used in the totality of the rule of double effect to refer also to what I now call indeterminate decisions and not for commensurate decisions alone. In just-war theory, I at least have always understood such proportionate reason to be a matter of taking counsel—not having the exactitude of a builder's orientation of means to ends. Moreover, the difficulty of comparing entire regimes in support of the teleological criteria for just war tends to the conclusion that in these respects there can be ostensibly just war on both sides (Vitoria and Ramsey, I am told). These are indeterminate decisions for which there can be good and acceptable reasons to conclude there is a just cause.

I shall continue to use the term *proportionate reason* for both commensurate and indeterminate decisions. The point is for us to understand clearly these two different usages; and to understand why, in the case of indeterminate choice of significant importance morally, a human agent ought not deliberately to intend evil or the impairment or destruction of the good he passes by on the way to his primary goal. If and only if proportionate reason always means commensurate reason should we, strictly speaking, ever *do* evil to achieve good.

In what follows I undertake to unfold more concretely the meaning of these analytic concepts, and in particular the meaning and multiplicity of indeterminate choices among incommensurate goods. Specifically, I try to show that the single instance in which McCormick believes indirect voluntariety to be requisite is, when unpacked, simply one among possibly many other instances of indeterminancy among conflicting values.

I

For McCormick the case of willfully helping to bring about the sin of another is a crucial test case supporting the view that there is a different descriptive account of the will (and likely as well some sort of significant moral difference) between when it intends and when it merely permits other sorts of evil as well. Bruno Schüller believes the former is the *only* case in which it makes sense to say that an evil occasioned (foreseen and in some sense done) should never be directly intended. In regard to the sin or moral evil of another, according to Schüller, and in this case alone, must the agent's will be thus distanced from the unavoidable evils brought about in justifiable courses of action (for example, establishing legal sanctions which tempt to bribery). The meaning of *indirectly voluntary* in all other cases to which that language was applied in past moral analysis is simply that the evil, if justified, must be proportionate to the good achieved in the totality of that course of action. So proportionate reason constitutes the entire meaning of the indirectly voluntary or the permitted evil, except in the one case of intending the sin of another. With that single exception in Schüller's proposed revisionism, the willful doing of evil is *reduced* to disproportionate reason in a comparison of greater goods or lesser evils. It is more honest as well as accurate to say we deliberately will and intend a lesser evil for the sake of a greater good.

I suggest he has *displaced* proportionate reason from the function it serves in the totality of moral analysis known as the "rule of double effect" and has *placed it in the position* formerly occupied by the indirectly voluntary—which then becomes a displaced person out of the boundaries of civil moral discourse.[3] I suggest further that Schüller has ignored the incommensurability that is actually constitutive of some sorts of choices among nonmoral goods and evils to which we are sensitized by the identification of evil done only with indirect voluntariety. He has replaced indeterminancy in moral choice by the simple uncertainty that attaches to many comparative judgments of greater or lesser evils or goods.

A way to approach an appraisal of this revisionism, and of Richard McCormick's more subtle version, is to examine first of all the area of agreement between him and Schüller on the matter of our accountability for the moral evil or sin of others. If their common analysis of why it is wrong willfully to intend the sin of another is inadequate or if their language expressing why this is so is misleading, then those flaws are likely to affect the account given of a moral agent's involvement in the production of other evils as well. In short, what is said about this crucial test case is itself a crucial test of the moral logic that tends to replace the indirectly voluntary by the proportionately reasonable.

In the first place, we need to come clear about the use of the terms *moral evil, nonmoral evil,* and *premoral evil.* This is a small point, but it should be made clear. It is also a familiar point I wish to make, since utilitarianism in general (and ideal or multivalue utilitarianism as well) holds that the *moral* right or wrongfulness of actions is based on a calculus of nonmoral goods that are premoral before that human judgment and choice is made. If we are analyzing the rightfulness or wrongfulness of the actions of a moral agent, *any* evil is *pre*moral to that. The same is true of anyone who is deliberating whether he should unite his intention with the sinful intention of another person. Whether he helps to bring about the moral evil done by another or by cooperation becomes an accomplice in that moral evil, those contemplated *moral* violations are "*pre*moral" to his own decision and action—as premoral as the (as yet uncaused) "nonmoral" evils of the pain, sickness, and death of others, or error in their minds. The distinction among physical evil, intellectual evil, moral evil, spiritual evil (the question which of these evils are moral and which nonmoral) is neither here nor there so far as the word *premoral* should be used in this discussion. Whether the sin of another or his ignorance or his death or his sterilization are deemed moral or nonmoral evils, all alike are premoral to anyone contemplating doing any of those things. *Any* accepted hierarchy or supremacy, even a physicalism, of values is premoral so far as the moral agent is concerned, and become moral in his human act.

This consideration prevents the minimizing of the premoral in appraising one's present or forthcoming decision and action. I believe that sometimes in this literature nonmoral evils are too far stripped of moral significance simply because they are described as premoral; and moral evil may be too far elevated, or the human act lifted from its anchorage in various nonmoral goods or evils by an unnoticed play on words. Doubtless death, injury, deception, ignorance, and sterilization are nonmoral evils; and sin is moral evil. But, as William E. May has pointed out, "the use of the gerund may be unfortunate''[4] (I should say it is) when speaking of killing, wounding, and deceiving as nonmoral evils in contrast to the moral evil of uniting one's intention with the sin of another. At the start of the discussion, it ought not to be implied that *killing* is any less of a moral evil (even if *death* is a nonmoral evil) than *intending* the sin of another, because in both cases a premoral evil becomes a moral matter for a particular human agent by his involvement in either the death or the sin of another.

The concept of moral evil or sin has for McCormick and Schüller this essential, constituent meaning, among others, that is, it is that evil which ought not to be willfully done. The conclusion that one should not intend the sin of another, therefore, is itself confessedly analytic and circular.[5] In any case, we are not told precisely why causing the sin of another should never be willfully brought about. Therefore, when more detailed feature-relevant justifications are brought forward for never willfully intending moral evil in another, it is possible that they can be shown to be applicable to other sorts of evil as well. In any case, simply to say *moral evil* says nothing at all about the reasons for reticence to barter that evil and compromise it with other sorts of evils or goods done in the course of action. To call the other *lesser* evils *nonmoral* is also to say nothing about the issue at hand. And to say confusedly that an evil is *premoral* is a statement about the course of the moral agent's decision; it is not a statement about the goods or evils themselves.

McCormick and Schüller believe that a sufficient explanation of the difference between intending the sin of others and causing nonmoral evils is that the former involves an *absolute* disvalue and all other cases of perplexity involve only *relative* disvalues. Again we may ask, is not the statement *"nonmoral* values = *relative* values = *proportionable* values" a circular stipulation, no argument at all, with no good reason yet advanced for the conclusion? "The absoluteness of the disvalue forces some such distinction" as that between direct and indirect voluntariety. Thus McCormick says it is the absoluteness of this one disvalue which forces the doubling in intentionality that produces the rule of twofold effect and sustains its moral significance. Other value-conflicts are among *relative,* nonmoral disvalues (error, pain, sickness, bodily integrity, death).

When McCormick writes that the distinction between willfully doing and unwillfully allowing "brings out the difference between the attitude to moral evil and that to nonmoral evil," in context he means to say it brings out the difference between absolute evil and relative evils. For no proportionate reason should we deliberately intend an absolute disvalue (the moral evil of another). For a proportionate reason, however, we may permit it. But "we may directly will and directly cause a nonmoral evil (any one of the relative disvalues) if there is a proportionate reason for doing so." A greater relative disvalue concurring among the effects of our action always justifies willfully producing the lesser relative evil instead. Most significant for the discussion to follow, McCormick and Schüller agree that the prohibition of willfully intending to destroy human life should control our decisions in, for example, the matter of abortion or warfare, if and "only if the death of a person is an absolute evil in the sense of a moral evil." This they deny.

My contention is that it is not the absoluteness of values or disvalues, it is not value-conflict involving an absolute such as sin, but the *incommensurability* of certain conflicted goods or evils that forces the doubling of intentionality in agents of actions in which these effects concur. It is the incommensurability of certain human goods or disvalues that nevertheless are locked in conflict which forces a significant moral distinction to be made between willfully doing the one and unwillingly permitting the other. The necessary and sufficient conditions for the *moral* significance of indirect voluntariety are two. First, if, in the concreteness of human decision and action, values are or may be in conflict (one must choose and he who chooses one good must *in some manner* turn against the other). And second, if the conflict is between incommensurate values or disvalues.

McCormick correctly says that the rule of the twofold effect is "a vehicle, not a principle," that it is "a vehicle as useful as its accuracy in mediating and concretizing (some) more general principle." It certainly is not an ultimate principle in Christian ethics, although the word *vehicle* is too disparaging. The sole question is, *what* more general principle does indirect voluntariety mediate and concretize? McCormick says it mediates and concretizes proportionate reason alone; that the latter is the one only principle of Christian reason in conflicts of nonmoral values. I believe rather that it does not so much mediate or concretize a principle as that it mediates and concretizes structures or varieties to be found in our moral lives and in our apprehension of articulated human values. This vehicle takes note of a radical difference between some value-conflicts and some others. It mediates and concretizes the fact that we are in some cases called to devotion to goods that are qualitatively incommensurate and yet are sometimes in irremediable conflict.

It mediates and concretizes the fact that the *ordo bonorum* is not a seamless *ordo,* at least to our perceptions of value.[6] It concretizes in fitting decisions and in actions the reality of genuine and irreducible ambiguity in moral choice (while yet not tolerating morally reducible ambiguity as some who "sin bravely" are wont to do).

The conflict may be between higher and lower values, but this need not be the case. McCormick assumes that indirect voluntariety in the production of nonmoral evil would be a requirement if and only if there are no higher values and nonmoral values never conflict with lesser ones. This shows, I believe, that McCormick simply cannot conceive (except in one case) of genuine moral ambiguity; he cannot conceive of conflicts of nonmoral goods or evils that are *not* resolvable by commensurate reason. The words *greater* and *lesser* are the siren songs tempting to this indulgence. Those words, however, also may suggest qualitative distinctions that cannot be negotiated. My contention is that indirect voluntariety does not so much bring out the difference between a proper attitude toward moral evil and a proper attitude toward nonmoral evils (or toward an absolute and relatives), as it brings out an important difference among the attitudinal postures of moral agents and the intentionality of their actions in cases in which incommensurable values or disvalues are conflicted, whatever these may be.

Of course, if goods and evils are commensurable one commensurates them; if they are measurably comparable one compares them, and chooses the lesser over the greater evil, or chooses the greater good. But if any human goods or evils are incommensurate, then there is genuine and irreducible ambiguity in moral choice. One cannot cut the Gordion knot by any calculus, however broad or deep or long-run; nor should he undertake to do so. While in some sense the moral agent must cause both if they are inseparable in action, still when choosing one he ought not to turn directly against either of the incommensurable human goods. I suggest that for McCormick and Schüller moral integrity is a good not measurably to be compared with the rest; sin or moral evil is not to be directly proportioned to other evils humans may do or may cause in others. This is the ground on which their agreement rests.

They say this by calling a single value and disvalue *absolute*. Even so, absoluteness is not predicated of the value or disvalue itself but of its *relation* to others. That relation, I suggest, need not in other instances be supremacy or height in the scale. To predicate conflict of value between higher and lower values is not enough to produce our problem (or to entail genuine moral ambiguity). Simply to call one "moral" and others "nonmoral" without predicating something about their relation would not be to the point. The proper predication in some cases is incommensurability. This would be to affirm that there are moral *chasms* at one or more places along the scale from lower to higher (if indeed there is such a normative scale known to us).

If then in the real world of action there occurs a conflict between a good on one side of the discontinuity and a good on the other side and both cannot be served, then one comes upon the moral relevance of the rule of double effect for cutting down but not removing the ambiguity that has become manifest. Then one should not resolve the moral dilemma by the device of ignoring the incommensurability of the values in conflict both of which claim the devotion of our wills and actions. This seems to me to be a better interpretation of the case on which McCormick and Schüller are agreed than that contained in the word *absolute*.

Schüller and McCormick are agreed that, as viewed premorally by the agent, intending the sin of another should never be something he willfully does; that can only be permitted as a necessary side effect of action in the social order. What, we may ask next, do they mean to include under the concept sin or moral evil? The answer to that question will show how extensive throughout the moral life is the one case in which they allow twofold intentionality to have a valid and commanding moral meaning.

The word *sin* has vertical connotations even when expanded to include going against an erroneous conscience. To intend the sin of another immediately calls to mind tempting him to violate an absolute, God himself. However, in expounding Schüller's views about moral values, McCormick listed also justice, truthfulness, and fidelity. These values, and their opposites, unlike sin, have for most people horizontal connotations as well; they belong to the texture of most moral dilemmas. If then one should never willfully intend the moral evil of another, he should never directly intend another's injustice, untruthfulness, or infidelity under any circumstances; nor himself do injustice, tell an untruth, or prove unfaithful to another. But these things can justifiably be in some sense done, provided no species of moral evil is ever directly encompassed within the agent's intention. This means that the distinction between intending and permitting moral evil has pertinence and moral significance in conflict cases along a whole range of moral dilemmas, far more than one might suppose when reading that sin as moral evil was without differentiation by these authors set over against all nonmoral evils. It seems, then, that one should never intend to do or intend for another to do an injustice in order to save life, for example; one ought not intend to tell an untruth or to foster untruthfulness even in order to save life; one ought not to advance knowledge by willfully intending infidelity in oneself or another.

That is a rather expansive list. Whether moral evil has only limited or has expansive relevance to conflicts of value in the decisions of daily life, the question to be pressed is: What characteristics of moral evil in relation to other sorts of evildoing supports the conclusion that one should never willfully intend moral evil?

Of course, one can say, with McCormick earlier, that it is not isolated values which generate norms—for instance: no violation of the expressive function of speech; no violation of integral sexual intercourse; no violation of private property; no taking of human life.[7] So one could continue on into the realm of moral values and say: no violations of justice, of truthfulness, or trust; no violations of fidelity, or in general of the moral good of another. In this sense only, every value, nonmoral and moral alike, is productive of norms that are analytic and so far exceptionless. But that is not what is meant by concrete behavioral norms. These, we can agree with McCormick, arise only when we formulate a law or norm after we reflect on two or more copresent and competing values and relate them as best we can. We can run through the list and say of only the so-called *nonmoral* values: no violation of the expressive function of speech without proportionate reason; no violation of integral sexual intercourse without proportionate reason; no deprivation of property without proportionate reason (against the owner's reasonable will); no taking of human life without proportionate reason (or in the revised version, no killing of the innocent without proportionate reason). Surely, it would be inadequate to stop at that point and refuse to continue into the range of *moral* goods and evils by saying: do not intend the sin of another without proportionate reason; it is unconditionally immoral to visit lack of truthfulness or infidelity on one's neighbor without proportionate reason; it is morally evil to will the injustice of another without proportionate reason (to intend a little injustice in order to put a stop to greater injustice).

At least, we need to know more precisely and persuasively the metaethical justification for metaethically cutting the universe of human values in half, especially because it is clear that moral evil is as interwoven with the nonmoral as the nonmoral values are relative to each other. I suggest that the claim must be that moral values and disvalues are incommensurate with the nonmoral, and therefore that there cannot be a more general preference-principle (proportionate reason) governing in cases of such conflicts from which concrete norms of action derive.

In any case, these authors do not *simply* say moral good and evil is set apart because *actus specificatur ab objecto*; that is, they do not simply say that moral good and evil have God as the object of choice, acceptance, or rejection; that we then are in the presence of a value or disvalue sharing in God's absoluteness. *They do mean this,* of course, but a nonreligious reader may not grasp all that includes. On a narrow construction of it (my vertical meaning), there could only be sin against the theological virtues or we might willfully tempt others to sin against the Holy Spirit, which we should never do. Nor is appeal made simply to God as object, implicitly, dimly, or confusedly apprehended in all truly human moral good or evil. Instead, as we have seen, some quite specific moral qualities are explicitly called moral goods—justice, truthfulness, fidelity—and their opposites, moral evils. This means that moral agents are together with God in most of their choices and actions.

Then one wonders why nonmoral goods and evils are not participatively linked to or subsumed into moral good and evil in almost all if not all of the actions of life, as the premoral is made moral in the course of a human choice. In particular, what argument can there be for classifying the slaying of one person by another as a nonmoral evil? Doubtless it is sensible to call *death* a nonmoral evil. But at issue here is the moral evil of killing a human being; he is the image of God and is holy ground. For this reason, it seems evident, our tradition of ethics distanced from killing to the same degree as from tempting someone to sin. The morality of doing either was not submitted to judgments of proportion alone or governed only by sufficiently worthy ends.

Indeed, an illustration of these authors' point about directly willing the sin of another shows how killing and sin are participatively linked together. Suppose nuclear deterrence for the worthy end of preserving the peace of the world required our political and military leaders to do everything possible to lead some troops under their command to make themselves conditionally willing to destroy whole populations as targets in retaliation. Our leaders themselves do not seriously *mean* to do this. They are only bluffing. But more troops are needed to operate the missiles than can be secured by enlisting only those whose (erroneous) conscience is free to do it. The whole scheme is a massive temptation to sin. I imagine these authors would say that such a system of deterrence ought to have put into it no more than the leaders' foresight that some participants (unlike themselves) will go against conscience, never a willful intention that they do so. Tempting to sin ought not to be judged solely by the proportionate good to come. Then in this instance is it not evident that leading into sin is inextricably linked with the moral evil of direct voluntariety in destroying civilians in warfare?

In the end I agree with McCormick and Schüller in what they say about sin or moral evil, only with the caveat that their view absolutizes a number of other moral values as well, subsumes more than they may think, and provides indirect voluntariety with more than one incommensurability to preside over.

I want now to pursue a more secularized version of their meaning (using *moral integrity* instead of the word *sin*) and to assume the role of someone who believes that that, too, ought sometimes to be bartered for (proportioned to) a sufficiently worthy cause. My goal is to clarify the metaethical reasons for setting moral integrity apart from the rule of proportionate reason. These authors cannot rest content with simply saying that anyone who knows the meaning of sin or moral evil knows immediately that he ought not directly to intend it; or, with Schüller, say simply that "moral evil is by definition unconditional disvalue" or that "the exceptionless validity of norms stating it are analytical." My thesis is that it is incommensurability between moral values and other values that dethrones proportionate reason in this instance; and, if the thesis stands, there may be other discontinuities in the scale as well.

Perhaps the term *absolute* should be banished forever from the discussion of moral questions. Also Latin expressions like *malum in se*. Only God has absoluteness and aseity; and even in his case we scarcely know the meaning of those attributes. In any case, reference to God as *summum bonum* of the human will tells us little about value conflicts.

So let us try to secularize the disvalue of sin or moral evil which McCormick and Schüller call *absolute*, in order then to try to see what alone can be the foundation for claiming that no one should willfully, that is, directly, intend the sin or moral evil of another. Surely, people who are not Christians, who indeed claim to be altogether nonreligious and who would not use the word *sin*, may agree with that moral verdict. Such people would propose that personal moral integrity is a value and its contrary moral evil is a disvalue which should not be measured, adjudicated, compromised, or balanced with other human values no matter what weights are assigned to each.

Professor Thomas Nagel writes that

the notion that one might sacrifice one's moral integrity justifiably, in the service of a sufficiently worthy end, is an incoherent notion. For if one were justified in making such a sacrifice (or even morally required to make it), then one would not be sacrificing one's moral integrity by adopting that course: one would be preserving it.[8]

It must be pointed out that Nagel was making a point that had to do only with the agent's own moral integrity. It seemed to him clear that if there were a "sufficiently worthy cause" demanding it, the sacrifice of moral integrity to that proportionately reasonable end would not be sacrifice but an expression of one's moral integrity. What he might say about willfully sacrificing the moral integrity *of another* to a "sufficiently worthy cause" I do not know. I suspect he might have been as reticent about that as are McCormick and Schüller.

Still his formulation, even though it speaks of "moral integrity" and not of sin in relation to a "sufficiently worthy cause," may help us to pinpoint the issue for metaethical analysis of why it is the case (if it is) that no one should ever willfully intend to injure the moral integrity of another for an alleged sufficiently worthy cause, why *no* cause can be sufficiently worthy to warrant that evil. This must be because moral integrity, or the moral integrity of another, is a commanding moral value incommensurate with other human values and therefore one that we should not attempt to pool with all the rest (or any other). In support of a discontinuity between personal moral integrity (or the disvalue of moral evil) and other sorts of values or violations that may be measured against one another according to their sufficient worth, one can of course appeal for backing to the eternal destiny of the human soul, to sin as a violation of one's relation to his supernatural end in contrast to other evils that impede one's attainment of a worldly common good or natural human goods. With McCormick and Schüller I believe these considerations also to be of moral significance. But they are significant only as backing for what they *back,* namely, the incommensurability of moral evil with other evils.

And I cannot deny that someone who does not make a religious absolute of that distinction or accept those backings may still believe there is a chasm fixed between *moral goodness* or *moral evil* and all other goods and evils. We then have a common problem, namely, whether there can be any proportionate reason for bridging incommensurate goods or evils; or whether, in case of conflict between incommensurate values both concurring and inseparable in the same action or course of action, simple moral wisdom does not say then that no one should willfully or directly turn against any of the human goods at issue in the case. To say otherwise, to invoke commensurate reason, would require the false judgment that all values have a common denominator when they do not.

One can also place in proper perspective the supposed absoluteness of moral evil by placing that in a fuller Christian context. One can go a long way toward the discreteness and discontinuity of realms of value as such (claims that have to be defended in ethical analysis) by reference to certain refinements in traditional Christian moral theology. Sin or moral evil has for Christians objective referents, both in morality within the limits of reason alone and also in morality that lives beyond reason within the expanded confines of God's revealed truth. But moral evil measured in terms of natural or revealed truth is not all McCormick and Schüller should have in mind when they speak of sin as an absolute evil. For sin also means any self-inflicted violation of subjective conscience as well. One should follow even an erring conscience. He ought, of course, to instruct his conscience, search out the truth, properly form his conscience. Still, when all is said and done, his conscience may be dim, confused, or even invincibly ignorant of the true course to follow. In all these cases, as well as in the case of a true conscience, to go against conscience is to violate one's moral integrity. That would be to make one's self good-for-nothing, not even good for any further, better instructions of conscience from nature, reason, or grace. To go directly against even subjective conscience is, then, to cut oneself off from life, from the appeal and claims of the good, from God. That would be a fundamental violation of our being human. Intending the sin or moral evil of another must, therefore, include also willfully meaning him to turn against his moral integrity as he himself conceives it. Neither Schüller nor McCormick would deny this to be the meaning of sin when they advance the claim that no one should ever willfully help to produce sin in another. In one of his expositions of Schüller's viewpoint McCormick wrote: ". . . one who wishes to seek the good of another never has a justifiable reason to lead a person to act against his conscience."[9]

Even when elaborated in terms of *subjective* rightdoing and not objective rightdoing alone, we can readily apprehend why McCormick and Schüller believe that sin against conscience is something no one should willfully and directly try to induce in another. I concur in that judgment, only demurring from saying that this is true because subjective moral evil is an absolute evil. Surely subjective moral integrity is not an absolute good. Yet the claim may be that subjective moral evil is incommensurate with other evils, and for that reason indirect permission of it is at worst the only positive attitude the will should take toward it in another.

Still it would not be outrageously unreasonable for someone to believe that directly to tempt a person to violate his subjective conscience and to do what for him is a moral evil could be justified because in some cases that had to be done for the sake of an overriding greater nonmoral good. An objector might contend that surely the authority of proportionate reason can extend to some violations of moral integrity, provided the good to be achieved thereby or the evil prevented are great enough. Perhaps instead our objector (to put in his mouth some of McCormick's themes to be brought out below) might say that the ultimate reason for never (or virtually never) willfully tempting another to sin ought rather to be *explained* in terms of proportion. That is to say, the reason must be because of the grave further "repercussions and implications" of deliberately doing any such thing, because of what will happen to the human good over the long haul if that became standard practice, and because to violate another's moral integrity will "make quite a difference" for all moral and nonmoral welfare to come.

He might also demand to know what is the consequence of one more mortal sin to a mortal sinner if inducing it was a necessary ingredient of an effort to save his life, with the opportunity that alone affords for repentance and moral reformation. In another example, the good of others may be at issue, if acting with a conscience that is clear to it someone is engaged in extensive and objectively evil deeds; and the only way to deflect him is to lead him into conscious sin, reveal to him his true state of soul with a view to contrition and reformation of life—a chancy course of actions to undertake, of course. Perhaps we ought to say it virtually never should be done, like directly attacking civilian populations in warfare. Still the reason for absolutely never joining our wills to the sin of another, for not directly intending his moral evil in any instance, and for exempting the sin of another from the rule of proportionate reason is made obscure by these examples.

At this point our objector could bring up additional McCormick themes yet to come. He might say: If I help to induce the sin of another to save his life for the higher end of fostering his opportunity for repentance, then *how* I do so is significant only because to do so willfully shows a greater willingness to have his mortal or actual sin occur than if I merely occasion it in the course of saving his life. The former action would require a *different* proportion to justify it than the latter. I should generally do no such thing because, but only because, of the repercussions and implications my closeness to that evil will have upon his righteousness, my own, and that of others in the long haul. Yet it remains true that if I am less willing to have complicity in his moral evil under these circumstances, I am also more willing that he die in a state of mortal sin. Someone else who is willing to stand closer to his present moral evil would undeniably also be more willing that he be saved and come to righteousness. On this view it would require a competent magisterium to tell me which is the truer expression of love for my neighbor in God.

Finally, an objector can use an argument to be found in this literature in rebuttal of those who affirm the moral significance of twofold intentionality in regard to some disvalues other than sin. You grant, he will say, that there may sometimes be proportionate reason for predictably occasioning the sin of others, for foreseeably permitting moral evil in the course of achieving a societal good. That is to deny the general disproportion at the heart of sin itself. If there can be proportionate reason for permitting moral evil, there can be, in principle, proportionate reason for intending it directly, provided only that the expected good is great enough. (Here *great* can only mean extensive, since we agree that qualitatively there is no more serious evil than sin.) You have already instated proportionality in relation to sin in the case of a permitting will. Then you need not search for some other explanation for withholding the will from intending the moral evil of another than can be found in proportionality itself. Probably, such a test will lead us still to believe that one should never, virtually without exception, willfully lead someone to sin.

When secularized, de-absolutized, and translated into violations of moral integrity, is it at all obvious that this alone of all values should be able to hold proportionate reason at bay? Why not also the inviolability of physical human life, which is the necessary precondition to all other values, including the value of personal moral integrity, which in turn is the necessary precondition of a right conscience, of moral righteousness, or of sin? If there is this incommensurability between moral evil and other evils which have in common that they can be weighed against one another and some of them directly willed for the sake of the greater good or lesser evil, there may also be other discontinuities in the scale of otherwise calculable goods. Perhaps the value of life is one such, conditional to all the rest though not value-supreme. Perhaps intellectual good is another.

Higher and lower in some value scale does not matter in the present issue, although higher and lower in some numerical scale would dissolve the issue. Higher and lower matter only if the values are measurable against one another, by comparison of a limited number of similarities and dissimilarities; but only if that is the meaning of those words. Concrete decisional conflicts between *equal* human values or disvalues that are incommensurable qualitative goods or evils would alone be sufficient and necessary for there to be an issue. Such indeterminate decisions among qualitatively equal but incommensurate values would call for directing the will toward one or the other, permitting impairment of the one not chosen. Where human goods or evils differ from one another qualitatively *and differ qualitatively in such fashion that they are incommensurate on any single scale,* then choice is irreducibly ambiguous. If, then, incommensurate rights to life come into conflict one confronts decisional ambiguity whose grammar can be parsed only by never doing any more than indirectly intending to take a human life if unavoidably the deadly deed must be done. The fact that one of the goods is of its kind higher in quality, ultimacy, absoluteness, and so on, than another, is not the principal issue. In fact, rank in some scale of very different types of goods is indifferent to the issue. At stake is rather the incommensurability of some sorts of goods with others.

If one can think of no demonstrably reasonable way to compare violations of the moral integrity of another with the violation of some other human good in decisional conflict with it, then it would be morally significant for him to distinguish in the manner of his action between willfully doing or indirectly allowing *either.* This, I suggest, is also the case when two lives conflict and one must be taken, the other chosen to live—as in some cases of choice between an unborn child and the life of the mother, however nonmoral or lower human life may be.

When McCormick elevates proportionate reason to rulership he begs the question of the commensurability of all nonmoral human goods—led to this move perhaps because the words *higher* and *lower* have both quantitative and qualitative meanings. When he writes that "to see whether an action involving evil is proportionate in the circumstances we must judge whether this choice is the best possible service to all the values in the tragic and difficult conflict,'' he begs the question of a possible radical discontinuity even among some nonmoral values.[10] He does not probe tragic and difficult conflicts to the bottom of the ineradicable indeterminancy in moral choice.

I have stated my agreement with Schüller and McCormick that moral goodness is a value and the sin of another is a disvalue that are *set apart,* and not to be located on a scale with other, measurable goods or evils. Such an ascription is relational (the relation of incommensurability). For all I know, a Calvinist might claim that no one should ever deny the Ten Points of the Synod of Dort; such *blasphemy* would be an intolerable violation of his soul's destiny and of the most absolute truth known to human beings. Still, admitting the complexities of behavior in the web of our earthly life, he might go on to say that one cannot altogether avoid helping to bring about that blasphemy in another or avoid all complicity in another's denial of the Ten Points. Then a proper acknowledgment of the *spiritual* value at stake would require him never to intend directly to do so, however much he sometimes may of necessity occasion that spiritual sin. To say this is to ascribe to adherence to the truth of Dort a significance incommensurate with any other.

To say that this is not so, to say that under some circumstances there could be proportionate reasons (however nuanced and *weighty* these are required to be) for willfully intending another to *sin* or to *blaspheme* Dort would be simply an analytical expression of one's belief that this is not one of those gulfs, or separate realms, to be found in human moral and spiritual experience. One must then offer good reasons of some sort in support of accepting either a smooth articulation or a discontinuity between the realms of worth. These reasons must be reversible *from* the case of causing the sin of another to other instances (perhaps ideal ''null classes'') as well, or else we have forsaken consistency in moral reasoning. Because the differences between *moral* and *nonmoral* or between *higher* and *lower* do not exactly *prove* that these are incommensurate claims upon us which proportionate reason alone cannot take the measure of, it is possible that sufficient, similar good reasons might also be offered for believing that not all nonmoral values are, in this sense, relative.

Our objector could go on to say that, appraising his choices premorally as an agent, he is of the opinion that causing error in the mind of another—any violation of the good of the intellect—should never be something he willfully does; that can at most only be permitted as an unavoidable side effect of something that for proportionate reason he ought to do. Or again one could say that destroying the physical, human life of another is an evil of such an order and such finality that it ought never to be deliberately and directly intended, even though killing must sometimes be done with indirect voluntariety in the course of actions of life that are morally tragic.

My point is that each of these proposals are prima facie equal claims. One has to justify Schüller's unique case and McCormick's prismatic case for morally distinguishing between the directly and the indirectly voluntary. Other sorts of cases can be advanced with equal-seeming legitimacy. It may be that the *substantive* good reasons for proscribing ever willfully intending the sin of another can be used as warrants also for never turning directly against other human goods besides moral integrity. In any case, simply to characterize sin as moral evil in contrast to other sorts of evil will not alone be enough to establish that intending sin is a unique case or a crucial test case exempt from an ordinary proportioning of lesser to greater evils.

Pertinent at this point are the views of the British philosopher W. D. Ross. An intuitionist, he is ordinarily recalled for what he had to say about our apprehensions of prima facie duties, and how in case of conflict these have to be resolved into our *actual* duties. It is understandable that philosophers who are not intuitionists, like McCormick and Schüller, should believe that proportionate reason is the instrument for resolving conflicted prima facie duties into actual ones. What is questionable is their casting the entire problem in terms of simple conflicts of value in the first place, such conflicts being complicated, perplexed, of uncertain resolution, but not basically incommensurable except in the case of intending the sin of others.

Often forgotten and lost from the thought of W. D. Ross is what he had to say about the discontinuity and incommensurability among human goods, between the good of happiness and intellectual goods and between intellectual goods and moral good. It was not simply that moral good is higher in the scale than intellectual goods, and intellectual goods than the good of happiness. Conflict of scaled goods can in principle always be resolved, whether higher or lower or equals, whether moral or nonmoral, personal or physical. Instead, Ross believed that there was one great gulf fixed between happiness and intellectual goods, and another between intellectual goods and moral goodness. He expressed this by saying that in a moral life worthy of humankind no amount of increase of happiness could justify *any* impairment of intellectual goods, and no augmentation of intellectual goods could justify *any* impairment of moral good or moral character.[11]

Now suppose Ross had recognized the complexity of actual moral choice to the further extent of acknowledging that some choices and actions reach across these divides and have effects on both sides. Suppose he conceded the necessity of some such choices. Then I suppose he might have said that while pursuing intellectual goods one ought not to turn directly against moral good, or for that matter that while pursuing the *higher* value of moral goodness he ought not to turn directly against the *lower* good of the life of the mind. I suppose he might have said that while pursuing happiness one ought not to turn directly against the claims of reason, or for that matter that while pursuing the *higher* intellectual values he ought not to turn directly against even the *lower,* still abundantly human good of happiness.

In short, if Ross admitted real indeterminancy in moral choice and some irresolvable conflicts of prima facie duties into actual duties, he would have had need of the morally significant distinction between willfully intended goods and the conscious or willing acceptance of the violations of other goods.[12] The reason for this is not the mere superiority of one value over another, much less its absoluteness, or the fact that some values are moral, others nonmoral. The reason rather is simply the discontinuities among values in the scale, their incommensurability along any clear single scale. That stops any primary appeal to proportionate reason alone to resolve the ambiguities in moral choice.

This, I think, is enough to show that the feature-relevant good reasons for finding "intending the sin of others" to require invocation of the distinction between willfully intending and consciously permitting that evil might also call for extending the same morally significant distinction as well to the cases of action that have bearing on other *incommensurate* values.

Human life, for example, is an inalienable right not because it is of supreme worth but because it is a basic good, conditional to all other goods. John Locke reasoned to an inalienable right of liberty on the grounds that a real threat to that is tantamount to a threat against an individual's life. "He who attempts to get another man into his absolute power," wrote Locke, should be understood to have "a design upon his life. For I have reason to conclude that he who would get me into his power without my consent, would use me as he pleased when he got me there. . . ."[13]

Not only do I have reason to conclude that he who would get me into his power would also deny my right to life (which was Locke's point in reasoning to liberty as a right). There is also reason to conclude that he might powerfully influence me to sin, and my children, and everyone else similarly situated. There is really not much sense in acceding to the contemporary Catholic bifurcation of the moral universe into moral and nonmoral values, or into physical and human actions or values. That trend of thought is likely skewed in that direction by its use of value-language instead of rights-language. Still it seems clear that if life is the necessary conditon of liberty and liberty a necessary conditon of moral goodness, and if one ought never willfully incline another to sin, then it is prima facie plausible to argue also that one ought never willfully or directly take away either the liberty or the physical life of another. He who directly attacks the necessary condition attacks also the conditioned value.

I have so far been using the value–language of the literature I am reviewing. That language seems to me to have been abandoned in the larger community of ethical discourse at least since Nicolai Hartmann and Wilbur Marshall Urban. It seems peculiarly inappropriate when we need to comprehend the claims of a human life, its singularity, uniqueness, and noninterchangeability. When we ask the meaning of *good* we are asking about the good for human beings, the good for their life; when we ask about *value*, we ask about the value for human beings, the goods they serve and may attain. It then is somewhat equivocal to ascribe good or value to life itself. Life is rather a gift or a given or even a surd—for which we seek goods and definitions of life's values.

We Christians say that life is a gift of God, to which other values accrue, including everyone's unrepeatable opportunity to praise and glorify God. From our creation, we say, human beings are by their natures oriented to love toward God and the enjoyment of him forever. A human life, and not only one's explicit moral choices, has God as the object of will and love. This means that a human life participatively belongs together with God and partakes of whatever inviolability derives from that no less than do moral good or evil. It is really quite as wrongheaded to compare the value of a human life with other values as to compare sin with nonmoral values. A human being and sin both have God as the object of the will, so long as creation remains. Every human being, simply because he is the image of the living and loving God, is priceless, incomparable, unrepeatable. Each human being, simply because he is, is a living symbol effectively imaging that God, no less than may his attitudes, volitions, or actions. So it can be theologically argued that to negotiate human lives against one another is an impossibility because that life's finality in friendship with God is utterly incomparable, imponderable, unnegotiable—no less than intending the sin of another.

Expressed in New Testament language, one's neighbor is a person for whom Christ died. More than that, whatever we do to or for him, we do to Christ (feeding the hungry, visiting those in prison). Killing Christ anew would seem to be entirely excluded from Christian volition and action. Killing may be tragically necessary in the fabric of life that restrains and sustains others for whom Christ also died (like passing laws that foreseeably tempt to bribery). Killing a human being must surely be classified with moral evil as something that Christians ought never to encompass with direct voluntariety. At most, either can only be indirectly intended or permitted. Neither should be the object of a directly intending will.

Christian moral discourse, and other ethical languages as well, suggest that human life is not a value simply to be located at some point on a scale of higher or lower values; that the value ascribed to a human life ought not to be relativized or compromised because of any of the values that enhance that life.

To destroy another embodied human life is at once to destroy in and for him the whole scale of goods and values, the whole world of worth he knows. The latter are commensurate; he is not. That seems to me to be good enough reason for the conclusion that one should never with direct voluntariety take any human life, although tragically it may be necessary to cause the deaths of others indirectly in course of actions which inseparably also save many other human lives. If any other verdict is to be deemed Christian, I rather think that we should avoid altogether, if that were possible, any taking of human life. Because a human life is so basic it is therefore set apart. To commeasure human life with other values deemed higher or to argue that this can be done because life is a nonmoral good and therefore relative and compromisable can find more support in philosophies other than Christian. Embodied human life ought not to be entered into teleological assessments of net measurable outcomes, no more than the sin or another.

Let me conclude this section with a current example of value-quality comparisons (within the class I call indeterminate choices) that are roughly corrigible with no prior reference to direct/indirect and the quite incorrigible incommensurability of life with life belonging to this same class of indeterminate decisions, where this distinction is needed in a complete account of rectitude in action.[14]

In the present practice of amniocentesis, intrauterine monitoring of the fetus can determine the *male sex* of a fetus of a mother who is a carrier of hemophilia or Duschene's muscular dystrophy, but not whether he is afflicted with the disease or not. Under these circumstances, both normal and afflicted males are aborted to avoid transmitting those defects to *one* (statistically). That seems to me to be like operating on the wrong patient, and excusing that because it would have helped the right one. A normal male is (unjustly?) aborted instead of the afflicted one which was not there. My judgment in this matter can be sustained if and only if one life is not to be pooled and exchanged or replaced by another. Moreover the lives in question are an order of value incommensurate with the quality (or disquality) of the disease to be avoided.

I am told that soon there may be a scientific breakthrough that will enable amniocentesis practitioners to identify *in utero* the three out of four fetuses who in the genetics of the disease cystic fibrosis are either afflicted or carriers. But physicians will *not* yet be able to distinguish between the two of the three who are normal and only carriers from the one that is afflicted.

A friend of mine, a practitioner of amniocentesis, told me that from hour to hour he goes to one side and then the other on the question whether, when that knowledge about cystic fibrosis is available to him, he should or should not abort three unborns (one afflicted, two carriers, indistinguishable) in order to enable the woman sooner or later to give birth to a child who is not afflicted. That was to him something of a moral problem, although aborting a normal male fetus of a woman carrying hemophilia trait was not.

The cases seemed identical to me, since in both the physicians destroy normal life in order to avoid the transmission of the disease in question, that is, for what they deem to be the greatest good altogether. When I asked him to distinguish the cases, his reply was as follows. He had no qualms about aborting the male unborns of hemophiliac mothers because, in the mathematical calculation of the genetics of that disease, he could expect or hope that he could enable her to have a normal (female) child after at most *three* abortions. By contrast, in the cystic fibrosis case, the statistical calculus predicts that a woman who starts on that course of action in order to have a normal child may have to endure *seven* abortions before a normal child appears (since in this case the *two* normal carriers must always be eliminated in order surely to kill the afflicted one).[15]

What my physician friend was shaking his head about was that it seemed to him to be a possibly reasonable decision to balance three abortion experiences against the joys of bearing a normal child, while he wondered whether giving birth to a normal child would be worth seven abortion experiences. His quandary was what I have called one sort of indeterminancy in moral choice, or the quantity of the quality (or dis-quality) decisions that ordinarily we manage to make, one way or the other, *with no other rule of moral practice.* We decide, whether the reasons are corrigible enough or not. So far proportionate reason *alone,* within the women's experience, can perhaps go.

The other moral issue was a different one, and I believe *quite* incommensurate, namely the right and claims of unborn human lives who in either genetic situation are normal (including the two carriers of cystic fibrosis) and who are nevertheless "given the treatment" (let us concede for the sake of the argument) that would have been justifiable in the case of a certainly identifiable defective fetus.

Those uterine situations are a microcosm of the human world. In either world, values or qualities may be governed by proportion *alone,* but lives are not. Human, embodied, physical, individuated life is the subject of all values and goods we know. The value or good of life itself should be acknowledged as not to be commeasured with all other or higher worths which for that life cannot be if it is not. Moreover, one life is not to be pooled or interchanged with another. Where human lives are concerned, the idea that they compose a net measurable good is a vacuous and a right dangerous notion. If such are the claims upon us of the incarnate image of God in everyone, who is holy ground, then the destruction of a human life ought not to be willfully brought about, no more than that individual's sin should ever be directly intended. The killing of an individual by another, when tragically necessary, can rightfully be done only with indirect voluntariety.

II

Beyond their agreement on the matter of intending the sin of another, McCormick takes a separate path from that of Schüller; or, as we shall see, he undertakes to take a separate path. He argues that the case involving the sin of another proves that "the will relates differently to what it intends and what it permits, in all cases," that this is generally true of voluntariety, and therefore that "there is a different relation to the will when it intends and merely permits even where nonmoral evil is concerned."

> The human action involving an intending will (of evil) is, or at least can be, a different human action from that involving a permitting will. To say anything else is to say that intentionality does not affect the meaning of human activity, a tenet that becomes inconsistent if one reverses it where *sin* is concerned.

The factual possibility of twofold intention toward nonmoral evil, however, does not yet prove that this is a *morally significant* distinction in such cases. Nor does it tell us *what that moral significance might be*. These questions McCormick undertakes to answer. Indeed, to spell out more precisely the moral significance of using twofold intention as one of our general action-guides in choice among nonmoral goods and evils would seem to be the only way to show that the psychological datum or description has any moral significance at all.

McCormick's answer is a complex and interesting one. If I understand him correctly, he wants finally to express the functional *moral* meaning of twofold intention in terms of teleological assessment, in terms of proportionality (the other principal part of the rule of double effect in its entirety), yet without allowing twofold intentionality as a correct description of human action to collapse altogether into the latter aspect of moral judgment in the case of all nonmoral goods, as Schüller does. Nor is McCormick content with the terminological game played by other contemporary Catholic moralists who simply allege that "proportionate reason" is all that ever was properly meant or should in the future be meant by the moral significance of the distinction between willfully doing and permitting nonmoral evil.[16] He seeks a *transforming* definition, not a *displacing* or *replacing* definition of twofold intention. Precisely for this reason *Ambiguity in Moral Choice* is worth careful study.

McCormick's quest is carried out, as I said, in vital relation with the other half of the theory, namely, proportionate reason. Granted that judgment must *finally* be made in terms of proportion in all these complex cases of doing evil, it does not follow, McCormick writes,

> that the same proportionate reason which would justify what is indirect (descriptively) would always justify what is direct. . . . There may be a

proportionate reason for doing something in one way which is not proportionate to doing it another way.

How deaths occur, for example, when they concur in our justifiable actions, does not affect their status as a nonmoral evil. "But *how they occur* has a good deal to say about the present meaning of the action ..." (italics added). And that in turn affects, in some way as yet unspecified, the proportionate reason required in a final teleological assessment to warrant one or another decision and action in these complex and morally troublesome cases.

In the foregoing paragraphs I have tried to state McCormick's position in the barest, most formal terms. In telling us materially and more fully what he means, there are two strands or directions in his thought, and I think I detect some wavering between them. Agreement or disagreement with McCormick may depend in the end on which of these roads or directions he has actually set out upon in his analysis of the relation between twofold intention and proportionate reason.

1. On the one hand, *the reason* different sorts or degrees of proportionate reason are required to warrant doing something one way (indirect) instead of in another (direct)—or, put another way, *the reason* how nonmoral evils are done (which tells us something important about the present *meaning* of the action)—functions morally in one's final judgment is because of "the relation of the evil-as-it-happens to the will" or of the relation of the will to the evil-as-it-happens. From the moral significance of the relation of the will to human evil, McCormick's first explanation runs to the difference this should make in nuancing judgments of proportion. (His other explanation, I believe, reverses this direction.) *If one asks why* all the "repercussions and implications" and why "what will happen to the good in question in the long haul" requires different assessments of proportionate reason to take account of whether the evil was willfully done or only permitted, McCormick's reply rings clear:

> I believe the answer is to be found in the fact that an intending will represents a closer relation of the agent to the disvalue and therefore indicates a greater willingness that the disvalue occur.

Schüller "fails to take seriously enough the real contribution of intentionality to the significance of human actions." That leaves him vulnerable in the case of nonmoral evils to the weakness of "a merely numerical calculus of proportion." McCormick affirms that Schüller should, logically, justify the judge who would execute one innocent man if that saved five from a lynch mob, since Schüller cannot distinguish that case from the incidental death of one in the course of saving five. So for McCormick there seems to be an important moral distinction at issue here even in the case of so-called nonmoral evil. His strongest formulation of that difference is:

> The intending will (hence the person) is more closely associated with the existence of evil than the merely permitting will. Furthermore . . . an intending will is more willing that the evil be than is a permitting will.

On the one hand, therefore, the *moral significance* of the (descriptive) difference between an intending and a merely permitting will is explained by the closeness of the will (that is, the person) to the evil. In the case of an intending will, a moral agent stands closer to willing that evil *be*.

On this interpretation, McCormick would seem to be moving in the direction not of an ethics of intention (of consequence), but rather of what William E. May calls "an ethics of intent + content," that is, plus the present meaning of the agent's closer involvement with concurring nonmoral evil effects. In that case, he here does not mean to say (as elsewhere he asserts) that the rule of twofold effect or intentionality mediates judgments of proportionate reason alone. It also signalizes the intimacy of one's involvement in causing nonmoral goods or evils. If that has moral significance in itself, then he joins May in concern not only for what a human action *does* but also for what it *says*.[17]

Moreover, if causing a nonmoral disvalue is not as such morally evil, then we may ask why is it morally significant *how* intimately involved the will is in that causality. Earlier I suggested that intertwining one's direct intention with the sin of others who are encouraged to become conditionally willing to destroy populations directly in warfare would be wrong only if the latter also is intrinsically wrong. In the present context, a similar issue arises. Unless agency in doing some nonmoral evil is morally wicked, then it could not be, as an excuse, morally significant how the will is intimately involved or distanced from that causality. Moving in this direction, McCormick must reinstate the moral significance of the distinction between direct and indirect voluntariety in the case also of nonmoral goods or evils, without decisive reference to proportionality. If there is moral meaning in what is "said" by the intimacy of one's involvement in the occurrence of nonmoral goods or evils, then proportionate consequences are not the only basis for the ethical assessment of actions.

2. On the other hand, however, McCormick derives the *moral signifi-cance* to be ascribed to the (descriptive) twofoldness of intentionality from proportionate reason alone. It seemed at first that proportionality was nuanced or attuned in significant degree to difference in rectitude of the intentions of agents and actions. It now appears that proportionality alone tells us whether moral significance should be ascribed to those *descriptively* different, *psychological* relations of the will to nonmoral evil. On the one hand, indirect voluntariety influences the composition of judgments of proportionality. On the other hand, proportionality composes the moral judgment, that is, whether and how far *the how* of human action, the present meaning of action, the closeness of the person to the evil done, are to be ascribed moral significance.

The move by which proportionality's "constitutional monarchy" within the kingdom of morality threatens to become a despotism is the following passage. McCormick summarizes his first account of the moral significance of the indirectly voluntary. "If someone is ready to bring the good into existence only by permitting the evil, it has been suggested that he is less willing that the evil exist." McCormick then turns that around when he continues in the next sentence: "Yet it must be said that he is also less willing that the evil exist, but *only because he is more willing that the good exist*" (italics added).[18] So, sadly, McCor-mick concludes (when as now indirect voluntariety must receive certifi-cation of its moral meaning altogether from proportionality) that what was formerly said about the intending will (the person) being more closely associated with evil than the permitting will "is somewhat circu-lar and considerably less than satisfying."

Why circular? Why unsatisfying? Because the facts in description of a person's intentions must now come before a morally unconstitutional monarch—proportionate reason—to find out from his rulings whether *the fact* of voluntary closeness or remoteness to evil-as-it-happens has any moral significance or not. That ruler can perfectly well decide that he who was formerly praised as "less willing that the evil exist" should rather be condemned because he is "less willing that the good exist." One who comes before that court admitting that by intending evil he is more willing that the evil exist can be completely exculpated from the charge of wrongful intentions or actions by a verdict which points out that he is the more praiseworthy because he is "more willing that the

good exist." Thus McCormick affirms that a person's greater willingness to have evil occur (by intending evil directly) is "morally acceptable only to the extent [why "only"?] that such an intention represents a
choice of what is the lesser evil." Except for the word *only* which shows
the influence of past ethics and affects the outcome of decision not at all,
why not then simply compose the entire moral judgment out of a comparison of greater or lesser evils? To call proportion's attention to the
bad results that may flow from allowing or encouraging people to will
evils deliberately (*when* the total evil they do is lesser) is only a caution
to be alert to *all* possible consequences, nothing more. It is also apt to
produce overscrupulous consciences.

   In any case, all possible consequences is the test in any consequentialism. That always included consequences flowing from intimate involvement in doing the nonmoral evil means, as well as any other
attitudes or corruptions of moral agents. Only someone backing half-
heartedly into a form of consequentialism from a former adherence to
the moral meaning of distinguishing direct from indirect intentionality
could suppose anything other than that the provable consequences of
those different agent-attitudes could never in principle be ruled out (or
failed to be noted) by any serious proponent of such a theory of ethics.

   I would say, therefore, that McCormick's disagreement with
Schüller, and his account of the moral significance of the directly and
indirectly voluntary, *crested* in his statements about an agent's will's
close or more distant involvement in the nonmoral evils he must sometimes do. In the foregoing passage we can feel the flow of the tide back
out to sea. All along there were strong undercurrents pulling in that
direction, and indications of a willingness to grant proportionality the
despotism. These need now to be noted.

   At one place McCormick remarks that "actions which are different
because of different intentionality have a different immediate meaning
and may lead to different social and long-term effects" (italics added).
The conjunction is significant in that then the sentence seems to indicate
two different or parallel reasons for certifying the moral importance of
the distinction, neither reducible to the other. The disjunction of two
possible grounds for ascribing moral significance to these two different
postures of moral agents toward evil-as-it-happens in the course of their
actions can also be read from the following statement:

> The relation of the evil to the will, how it happens, not only can tell us what
> kind of act we are performing, but can have enormously different immediate

and long-term implications, and therefore generate a quite different calculus of proportion.

Taking these and suchlike statements seriously, there are several options as to how to interpret McCormick's analysis, or options among the conclusions readers may draw for themselves from his work in place of the triumphalism of proportion suggested above. McCormick may mean to suggest some sort of double morality or double standard for morality, for example, a personal and a public ethic. When we are concerned with the virtues of the moral agent, with the rectitude of his attitudes and actions, then his intentional closeness to or remoteness from the evil done should be our benchmark. If, however, we are mainly concerned to do social ethics or to analyze political decision making, then the benchmark ought to be the agent's willingness to intend evil, his tolerance for doing it, as evidence of his greater willingness to see the good-to-come exist, provided only that the evil he wills is the lesser evil or the good he turns directly against is a lesser good. Protestant ambiguists in ethics might conclude from this account that here we have a case of "Christ and Culture in Paradox," in unrelieved tension.[19]

Instead of setting up a contrast between personal and public ethics, however, one could strain a bit and suppose that McCormick means to separate between an ethics of virtue and an ethics of action. He could mean that a person who stands distant from willing an evil is a better character than a person who directly does that evil for good to come. At the same time, an ethics of right action could draw a different conclusion: action is more right to the degree that it is best calculated to achieve good consequences. Then the goodness of a moral agent would go in a different direction from maximum rectitude in action. This incoherent suggestion will not work, however, because McCormick lays equal weight upon the fact that a person who does not distance himself from the immediate evil done is all the more willing that the greater good be achieved. Surely he must be the better person. Then the virtues of the moral agent and the rectitude of his actions are brought into accord. What then can be made of McCormick's waffling? Perhaps simply that a person who is unwilling to do evil directly is morally *scrupulous,* while the person who is more willing for good to come is more *daring* in behalf of causes external to his own soul. These too are attributes not without moral significance.

Since McCormick has a deeply Catholic mind with its profound confidence in the use of reason in morality, he may mean to suggest instead that while there are these two sources of moral judgment they will not ultimately be found to contradict one another.

Other readers who lack that confidence in the seamless robe of reason over the whole of Christian morality—and observing that a too zealous effort to maintain that this is so can only lead to a morally unconstitutional despotism of proportionate reason (and being Protestants, have better names for that regime)—may wish to conclude that, in giving us the foundation for a double morality of the kingdoms on God's right and left hands, McCormick helps us to see how nevertheless the former may "transform" the latter by sensitizing, perfecting, and elevating nuanced judgments of proportion where they necessarily reign in the public sphere.[20]

The foregoing are my constructions. I do not mean to impose any of these solutions on the material at hand. But these are several ways to clear up the confusion and block the road I believe McCormick has taken after some hesitation. For ordinarily McCormick does not nicely balance, between conjunctions, his references to indirect voluntariety telling us something about the present meaning of moral action and his turning the important moral meaning of that into estimations of long-run consequences. In numbered paragraph 1 above, I deliberately cut off quotations in the middle of sentences in order to show the crest of McCormick's disagreement with Schüller. (The crest of his independent ethical estimation of indirect intention still stands in the text before its back was broken later.) This needs now to be corrected for the sake of fairness in exposition, and other citations added in order to demonstrate the degree of McCormick's submission of every moral question to the rule of proportionality and to call into question that submission.

From first to last McCormick is concerned with "the *overall* implications and repercussions of human conduct." He simply observes that these repercussions are affected very much by whether a "certain evil is visited by an intending or merely permitting will." Therefore he concludes that the moral significance of distinguishing between killing one-hundred civilians directly in war or killing the same number incidentally is derived from the foundations we have in experience for believing that the former will "in the long run release more violence." So when McCormick wrote that *how* nonmoral evils occur has a good deal to say about the present meaning of action (as quoted above), he proceeds to add before concluding the sentence that this has much to say about "the effect on the agent and others, and hence about the protection and security of life in the long run." He does not say that it points us to that *also*. When stating that "the relation of the evil-as-it-happens to the will may say a great deal about the meaning of my action," he adds immediately, "its repercussions and implications, and therefore what will happen to the good in question over the long haul." Just above that statement, McCormick remarks in regard to proportion measured in terms of "long-term effects," that "whether one directly intends (or not) certain nonmoral evils he now does may *make quite a difference"* (italics added).

It is impossible to avoid the conclusion that, for McCormick, *making quite that difference* is the sole morally significant determinant of accountability in that agent's will. Why then should not *making that future difference* be the undifferentiated goal of attitude and action in such a way that the agent heartily embraces the present evil he must do (if it is lesser, and a necessary means), thus collapsing the intentional distinctions McCormick still wishes somehow to maintain? It is indifferent to ethical justification whether *making that difference* now requires willfully intending an acknowledged present evil or only permitting it. Or rather, one posits the moral significance of intentionability only because it is believed to make quite that difference. Any present greater unwillingness to have evil exist is either a surd or relic from past moral education and formation of conscience, or else it is the other side of the coin of a greater willingness to have the good-to-come come with calculable sureness and swiftness. Any present turning directly against human good, however immediately evil that may be, gains derivative justification (provided that evil is lesser) backward from the greater evil prevented or greater good-to-come. I must confess I cannot understand why McCormick disagreed with Schüller over the case of "judicial murder"—isolated as that fictional case was for purposes of thought from obscure long-haul consequences.

I submit, however, that at first McCormick correctly expressed the moral significance of the describable difference between the directly and the indirectly voluntary. In the course of his essay, however, he lost the thread. Unfortunately, however, the closer association of the intending will with the evil, a person's greater willingness for that evil to exist, began again to be described as a *psychological* difference only and not as an immediate moral meaning. The undercurrent carries McCormick away from his exhibition of the morally important issue back to its *descriptive* meaning or component alone. Then it is that the *ordo bonorum* for conflict situations, to choose the lesser evil, is introduced as the regnant principle, the rule of Christian reason. Without batting an eyelash, McCormick writes that if this is not true then "the *only* alternative is . . . that we should choose the greater evil." "Which is patently absurd," he adds. So it is; and so, too, is the argument. Before, I thought he allowed a third option even in the case of nonmoral evil. One can do the lesser evil with indirect voluntariety. And certainly in the case of causing the moral evil of another, McCormick and Schüller both teach that the *ordo bonorum* contains at least one discontinuity to which the will is not guided by simply reflecting upon lesser or greater goods or evils that can be compared, weighed, and compromised against one another.

In any case, it is at this point that proportionate reason is crowned. Indirect voluntariety becomes in no sense a principle, but a vehicle, a vehicle for mediating and concretizing the more general principle—indeed, it would seem the only principle—namely, greater good or lesser evil. This is not only the basic, it seems to be the only category for conflict situations, for resolving ambiguity in moral decisions.

These metaethical judgments concerning proportion are flanked and undergirded by an exclusive and complete *psychological* description of the twofold intentionality which before seemed to have some degree of moral significance in itself and therefore in a credible way could morally influence the nuancing of judgments of proportionality. McCormick now writes that to define the moral integrity of one's intentionality in terms of *psychological* indirectness would be "restrictive." Now, psychologically unintended evil effects are but an example of legitimate intentionality. Now, integral intentionality traces not to psychological indirectness but "*exclusively* to the proportionate reason for acting" (italics added). Why then, we may demand to know, can evil-as-means and evil-as-effect *morally* "demand different proportionate reasons"? Or do they? From the fact that evil-as-means and evil-as-effect are "different *realities*" (italics added), from the fact that they are different *psychological* states having as such no integral moral significance of their own, can directly flow *no* moral demand. Of course, from different psychological realities come different actions having different *effects*. Then it is the effects alone that are the source of difference in moral judgments of right and wrong.

Then, also, one ought to treat tenderly consciences which still ignorantly suppose that what they intentionally mean to do has something to do with moral character and the rightness or wrongness of their actions, and which are not yet mature enough to eat the strong meat of the gospel of proportionate reason as their steady diet.

III

Something is needed to complete McCormick's case—a capstone to his argument—for saying that the effects of action alone sustain moral significance in the distinction between direct and indirect voluntariety in the case of nonmoral goods or evils.

In his "Notes on Moral Theology" published over the past five or six years, Richard McCormick has traced the developments in contemporary theological writings that show Roman Catholic moral theology in this period to have "moved very markedly in the direction of a consequentialist methodology."[21] The path which McCormick traces is the path he also has followed. In 1969 he vigorously objected to the "all too familiar and pernicious dualism" in the understanding of sexual love, marriage, and of parenthood that must underlie, genetically or reproductively, engineering our offspring; and in that connection judged that "[Michael] Hamilton's uneven bout with [that] dualism brings him perilously close to a morality of goals."[22] Perilous or not, it now is exceedingly difficult to distinguish McCormick's own position from a morality of goals. In 1971 he agreed with Charles Curran's criticism of "Fletcherian consequentialism" for failing to explore how various consequences are to be appraised or for failing even to acknowledge the need for such appraisal because among consequences some are hierarchically more important morally than others. In that connection, McCormick wrote in a footnote: "I say 'Fletcherian' because I suspect that there is a rendering of consequentialism, as yet not systematically developed, with which many of us could feel at home."[23]

In any case, McCormick's progress toward that heavenly city of late twentieth-century moral theology is clear enough—despite his constant awareness of dangers to the right, obstacles to the left, the temptations in Vanity Fair, and the delusions with which the devil crowds people's minds in the course of such an earthly pilgrimage. McCormick has always rejected any "narrow consequentialism (that ignores the fact that my neighbor is everyone)" and an "individualism (that is insensitive to the communitarian dimension of moral knowledge and discernment)."[24] And certainly it is individualism and narrow-mindedness—even value blindness—that are chief characteristics of contemporary consequentialism other than that espoused in recent Roman Catholic ethical writings.

McCormick's insistence that our neighbor is everyone and his appreciation of community as the context of moral reflection and decision gives a decidedly conservative cast to the morality of goals at which he has arrived. These aspects of his thought, together with certain theoretical moves that he makes to contain individualism, may lead some readers to suppose that in addition to consideration of the consequences of actions there are additional sources of concrete behavioral norms or other guides to right action concurring in conflict situations. These metaethical moves or justifications generate some rather firm moral conclusions that resemble past moral teachings. They therefore are apt to lead to the supposition that McCormick has only proposed a somewhat novel interpretation of traditional wisdom, and has not rather poured some exceedingly fresh, weak wine into those old wineskins once filled with more heady substance and stronger medicine for the moral agent's stomach's sake.

I wish at this point to list a number of these justificatory procedures which seem to me to serve to preserve in the context of the sole test of proportionate reason some traditional norms that were generated from other sources of moral judgment and other perceptions of moral relations or claims in conflict situations.

1. In 1971, McCormick criticized Knauer's "sound description of proportionality" (to the effect that "a reason is commensurate if the manner of the present achievement of a value will not undermine but support the value in the long run and in the whole picture") by asking rhetorically, "Who can confidently make such a judgment? An individual? Hardly. It seems to demand a clairvoyance not granted to many mortals and would paralyze decision in most cases."[25] Feeling that reasoning to be weak when Knauer first advanced the claim, McCormick sought to *strengthen* the view that proportiontae reason determines right and wrong by appeal not simply to "the communitarian dimension of moral knowledge and discernment" but to a specific community of moral discourse. McCormick wrote:

> [The] moral prohibitions issued by the magisterium must be conceived as value judgments on the presence or absence of proportionate reason in certain concrete forms of conduct. But then one must ask whether the magisterium conceived its past prohibitions in this way.[26]

I suggest that the question remains to be asked not so much of the magisterium but about those past moral judgments themselves. Was that their meaning? McCormick explores the question with the judiciousness and balance with which he usually pursues issues, by asking whether papal teachings on artificial insemination by husband, for example, can properly be interpreted as value judgments in the sense of guidance provided by the magisterium to assist individual decision about the greater evil in the long run.[27] Again, I suggest that the question needs not first to be asked of the magisterium's conception of its task, but of the substantial form of the judgment itself and the reasons marshaled to back it.

Then it is that McCormick stated the "rule-strengthening" Catholic principle needed to complete with safety the shift to consequentialism.

> If individuals need the magisterium to rise above the limits of their own perspectives in assessing proportionality over the long haul, they will be appropriately hesitant to rely exclusively on their own perspectives in questioning these magisterial value judgments.[28]

In the following year, 1972, however, McCormick responded to Curran's contention that all consequences cannot be known in advance and their hierarchical evaluation is uncertain, by saying that this was not decisive in offsetting a consequentialist interpretation of principles in traditional ethics. Curran's doubts simply mean that moralists need to do their homework better, call on all sources of discernment, and so on.[29] Magisterial value judgments were not expressly appealed to.[30] By noting the latter fact I do not mean to suggest any slackening of McCormick's rule- or discernment-strenthening appeal specifically to church community. "It is precisely here," he wrote in 1973, to prevent our slipping into policies that are only symptoms of a desire to avoid discomfort or to get on too quickly to an immediate good, "that we need the wisdom and checks that a believing community led and challenged by a healthily functioning magisterium."[31] Finally, in *Ambiguity in Moral Choice,* in order to overcome the waywardness of judgments of proportionality in conflict situations, one should (among other things)

> . . . allow the full force of one's own religious faith and its intentionalities to interpret the meaning and enlighten the options of the situation. . . . To say these things is to say that an individual will depend on communal discernment much more than our contemporary individualistic attitudes suggest.

While the foregoing are intramural appeals to ecclesiastical backing to sustain and clarify an ethics of consequences, a non-Catholic can still wonder how there can be a healthily functioning magisterium if there is no limit to the revision of the deontological terms of ordinary moral discourse and in magisterial documents into the language of consequences.[32] At least one can ask the question McCormick raised at the

outset, whether the magisterium conceived of its past and present prohibitions in such fashion.

Finally, if the task of church moral teachings were demonstrated to be
simply the strengthening and clarification and supplementation of
doubtful individual judgments of proportion, would that not *weaken*
precisely the functional importance of church discernments to which
McCormick appeals to complete his case? It would seem so, because it
is prima facie more plausible for an individual to trust his own *prudence*
in conflict situations than that of his church (most moralists, especially
today, say he should do so), and for him to form his conscience in
accordance to the church's insight into the nonprudential aspects of
morality if church-community still claims to possess that sort of discernment. In this and other respects, the current revisionism is parasitic
on a past relation between church ethics and the believer. To the extent
that believers accept the proposed revision of Christian discernment
into long-run consequence judgments, to that same extent they will no
longer believe they have need of that source of instruction dealing with
their moral dilemmas.

2. The second point is pertinent to all people and to the human
community in general. It is strictly analogous to the first, however, in
providing foundation for assuredly resting all morality exclusively upon
judgments of greater good or lesser evil. An individual's decision in that
regard may be uncertain, but judgments of proportion are not exclusively individualistic.

Unless we allow exceptions to concrete behavioral norms there are
likely to be situations in which a higher human value will be compromised. But concerning this, McCormick wrote:

> To do this with intellectual rigor and satisfaction, we must grasp clearly two
> things: the reason why the behavioral norm is generally valid in the first
> place, and the particular conflicting value that puts a limit on this validity.
> Specifically, [he asks] why is it generally true that we should not directly
> terminate innocent human life?[33]

That seems a promising beginning. One way to answer that double-
barreled question is in terms of feature-dependent principles or behavioral norms in the first place (that is, qualitative sorts or classes of
commendations or prohibitions, specified justice-, fairness- or fidelity-
claims) and then to build in exception clauses that are also feature-
dependent in terms of the conflicting values that put a limit on that valid
principle or rule of behavior. This is the model most generally used in

philosophical ethics today (except for existentialists and those who prefer a more imaginative or story model for the moral life).

When McCormick first introduced the second in my ordering of his appeals that rebut the vagaries of an individualistic consequentialism he did so as an all-encompassing explanatory principle or metaethical justification of *all* moral norms and exceptions alike. This appeal was his answer to the foregoing twofold question; and specifically, his answer to the question, why is it generally true that we should not directly terminate innocent human life. As well it was the reason (if there is any) for holding that norm open to remotely possible exception or for in the alternative holding that norm to be closed to morally significant exceptions in the future.

"We must seriously examine," McCormick wrote, "the possible usefulness of the traditional notion of *lex lata in praesumptione periculi communis*." Perhaps a concrete norm like the prohibition of direct killing of innocent human life, he grants, cannot be proved. That would seem to be the case as well in the matter of establishing *any* "negative moral absolutes" (as they are called). McCormick's suggestion is that a concrete prohibition like the one in question—and thus his explanation of why any behavioral rule is generally valid in the first place — might well be the conclusion of prudence in the face of dangers too momentous to allow the matter to the uncertainties and vulnerabilities of individual decision."[34] As in "No outside fires!" during a dry summer, there is a presumption of universal danger if individuals are allowed to make decisions for themselves that may pose a grave threat to the common good. The same is true in regard to medical decisions concerning euthanasia. There is an enormous good at stake in finding the answers to a cluster of questions that together *might* warrant euthanasia by overriding right in an individual case. Since these "are unanswered questions and are destined to remain so," *for this reason* "it is more humanly reasonable to regard the [prohibition of] direct termination of any human life as a practical absolute."[35]

Another time when McCormick appeals to the presumption of common and universal danger is in the somewhat more limited context of showing that the prohibition of direct attacks upon noncombatants in warfare is, first, "teleologically established," yet is "virtually exceptionless." That would seem to have been virtually established as "a good human bet given our knowledge of ourselves and our history"— what McCormick now describes as "informed by our past experience and a certain agnosticism with regard to our future behavior and its long-term effects." From that he proceeds into an appeal to *lex lata in praesumptione periculi communis*. Since the illustration again is "No outside fires!" (and if that is capable of establishing no exception to rules governing official action—which it is not), it would seem that the principle of discrimination as a rule governing the conduct of war is more than virtually exceptionless. For in time of drought, *all* potential makers of outside fires are forbidden to do so; and they also are not permitted in *any* case to decide whether a theoretically and still remotely conceivable exception should be allowed. So I suggest that appeal to common and universal danger serves as an exception stopper that cinches the case for a metaethics of consequence justifications that was not complete without it.

In the moral logic of the issue I believe John Connery is correct when he says that "it is much easier to explain these conflicts if one postulates factors other than consequences behind these rules."[36] Otherwise one is bound to appeal to "hidden consequences," as Connery says, or to "good human bets" as McCormick does, or to agnosticism about future behavior, to conservative adherence to past moral norms once believed built on other factors but now alleged to be supported by probable but still hidden consequences. Into that gap comes appeal to common and universal danger to cover the hiddenness (and perhaps the absence) of justifying consequences, and to forbid individuals from acting on the belief that a single exception may lead to greater benefit.

In the practical order, one wonders what McCormick or any consequentialist will say when common and universal danger is generally believed to require universal obedience to the rule "No more than 2.1 children per marriage" or "No unwanted child should ever be born," or "No defective child . . ." as well as to the rule "No outside fires!" Even to distinguish these proscriptions from one another, and to allow that one but not the other may be a fit subject for the enforcement of morals, requires an understanding of the human common good (and so of common danger) that is composed of immediate behavioral meanings and norms that are not exclusively judgments of proportion or conclusions from future consequences.

3. In addition to the communitarian dimension of moral knowledge and discernment within the Christian church, and in addition to well-founded appeals to overriding public danger, there is a third way to correct the uncertainties of variable individual choices and to help complete the case for virtually exceptionless rules drawn from experience as conclusions from consequences. This is by appeal to the wisdom

deposited in the moral experience handed on to us in the human community generally, or through specific societies. So McCormick reasons:

> If long experience and reflection have built the conviction that the profound human values involved in sexual intimacy are best protected and enhanced by conditions describable as marriage, then this means precisely that the values and disvalues of other options have already been sifted over the centuries. Must it not be supposed that the values the individual unmarried couple might find for initiating sexual relations are, by and large, the very values experience has weighed and rejected as sufficient to outweigh the eventual disvalues? To ask the couple to do this all over again is to suggest that reasons similar or identical to theirs had no part in the establishment of the norm.[37]

In short, if *all* moral judgments are derived from experience and all are expressed in social ethical judgments of proportionate reason, that still does not mean that everyone needs to do the sums over again. The contrary is in fact the case. McCormick writes:

> . . . if a couple are to except themselves from an accepted norm, they bear a double onus: (1) to show that the values and disvalues they adduce are *different* from those which gave birth to the original value judgment, and (2) to show that these different values would outweigh the disvalues in this instance—in terms of both long-term individual and societal considerations.[38]

I think we must agree with the wisdom in many of the foregoing exception-*stopping* considerations, or indeed agree to telling aspects in each case, perhaps calling for alternative formulations that may be given. I myself have made such appeals, calling them rule-strengthening rules or principles, some drawn from general moral experience, some based on specifically Christian teachings.[39] However, their presence in the ethical writings of Richard McCormick is apt to disguise the function for which he needs them. He needs them for a basic theoretical reason, namely, to complete the proof that one can derive from experience of consequences or from proportionate reason alone some firm behavioral norms. The work these exception-prohibitors do is to establish that it accords with our experience of moral obligation to believe proportionality alone is generative of proper decisions in conflict situations.

The state of the question is rather to be compared with the lapsed-link theory so important in the arguments of classical utilitarianism. The utilitarians believed that the only *reason* for judgments about right and wrong is to be found in usefulness to the end of the greatest happiness altogether. (Other values can be substituted for happiness.) Yet they could not deny that ordinary moral discourse contains many seeming *terminal* appeals besides happiness; to justice, for example, to fairness, and to virtues such as courage or temperance. The explanatory and justificatory scheme of the utilitarians would collapse unless it could be shown that these apparently terminal warrants were not truly final. To accomplish this task a theory of lapsed links was devised, a psychosocial history of morality.[40] According to this account, humankind, once abundantly experienced the conduciveness of justice, fairness, courage, temperance, and so on to the end of the greater happiness. That is to say, teleology justified and established the respect we have for virtues, moral roles, and relationships. Then human beings forgot about their connection with happiness, the linkage lapsed from vivid memory, and so moral language was filled with deontological terminology.[41] For purposes of social reform in nineteenth-century England, it was necessary to connect the links up again with the greater happiness in order to dispel false limits to be found in traditional morals and law. Of course, the claim was that sound reasoning about good consequences is sufficient to sustain and account for the moral substance in all the intermediary terms that falsely were believed by many to have meaning and some normative weight in themselves.

Roman Catholic revisionists make a similar move. They too fly in the face of a good many traditional moral meanings, and run against the meaning of terms in a great deal of ordinary moral discourse (not to mention papal teachings). Then the task is to show that all norms really *do* mean (or *should* mean) proportionate reason. The lapsed links need to be connected up again to the principle of proportion. Past moral teachings, then, are simply false if proportionate reason does not sustain them; or in the alternative, their meaning can be traced home to that source and certification. Consider the following contention by McCormick in the light of the lapsed-link way of discounting the ordinary meaning of moral language:

> The moral formulations of the Church are, above all, practical guides for the formation of conscience and direction of the faithful. Since they are teaching statements, moral reasoning and various forms of persuasion will be, indeed must be, used. And moral reasoning does imply ethical structure. But because a structure or system may be implicit in the way a teaching is formulated, this should not be taken to mean that this system is being taught or approved. . . . In this sense it is incorrect to refer to nonconsequentialist ethics as gaining "explicit ecclesiastical approval."[42]

In this section, I have pointed out the usefulness for this undertaking of certain exception-prohibitors: these moves effect more linkage and firmer connection between proportionate reason and past moral teaching and norms not, at least not ostensibly, based on such reasoning. Thus a greater continuity is ostensibly maintained with past and with nonteleological justifying reasons.

The extent of McCormick's use of a form of the lapsed-link theory, and its signal importance for his thought, can be shown by the following illustration. McCormick had been criticized for an earlier statement to the effect that

> human sexual intercourse has a sense and meaning prior to the individual purpose of those who engage in it, a significance which is part of their situation whether or not the partners turn their minds to it.[43]

McCormick's defense against criticism of that statement was to beat a *logical* and *psychological* retreat. He asks how was that judgment of his derived? To that he replies:

> It seems that it is a conclusion of long experience and reflection, especially about consequences. In other words, the experience of centuries has led us to conclude that unless this type of intimacy is restricted to the marriage relationship, the integrity of sexual language will be seriously threatened. Such a judgment is clearly a form of consequentialism.[44]

Then and only then can one speak of the marriage act or of the nature and meaning of human sexual intercourse (whether or not the partners turn their minds to it) in a value-laden sense. But given the experience of centuries, one can use those terms independently in a value-laden sense. Clearly, McCormick needs not only the experience of centuries, but a lapse between that experience and the freight borne by those terms as they become quasi-terminal justifications or counters to be used in moral discourse.

And what, we may ask, is the source of the value-laden meaning of "the integrity of sexual language" which already expresses a concrete normative resolution of at least some conflicted options (for example, rape, promiscuity, plural marriages that seem necessarily exploitative or less than humanly expressive), and which presumably men and women need to know something about before the experience of the centuries can tell them anything about which consequences are or are not threatening to it? Is another linkage lapse to be located between the expressive integrity of human sexual relations and the brightest and best proportionate reason? Unless that interpretation is to be adopted, McCormick's question "that must be put to our generation" (In what circumstances should the sexual experience of intimacy occur if sexual language is to retain its viability as truly human language?[45]) appeals to a terminal norm (even if the marriage act does not), and one that is independently generative of obligation as we press to the point of application and of institution building, and on to moral dilemmas that may or may not generate certain sorts of reasonable feature-dependent exceptions to the rule that always and everywhere sexual expression as an equalitarian, truly human language should never be violated.

In McCormick's first extensive treatment of the question, Are there exceptionless moral norms?, he acknowledged that "at its heart is the discussion about the deontological or teleological character of normative statements."[46] What was then at the heart of the matter has now been dropped from McCormick's own account of "virtually exceptionless rules." And when summarizing the view of Donald Evans, from whom that expression derives, McCormick listed the possibility of further "feature-dependent" exception clauses along with quantity of benefits (QB) exceptions as among Evans's reasons for holding most moral rules open to further qualification while still finding some to be virtually closed.[47]

No serious objection can be raised, of course, against lifting an expression from one context and using it in another. Still, before concluding this section, it may be instructive to notice the radical difference between McCormick's "virtually exceptionless rules" and the several grounds generating obligation in the discussion in which Donald Evans conceded there are some binding moral rules for which he coined the expression "virtually exceptionless."[48] While McCormick borrows the term, he does not mean by it the same thing as Evans. In fact, their meanings are in important respects opposed.

The moral reason for McCormick's willingness to call some prohibitions virtually exceptionless traces home ultimately to our estimate of long-term consequences, to proportionate reason. Such moral constraints are precipitates of and warranted by the moral experience by which humankind has learned that breaches of them lead to worse evil in the effects of action.

By contrast, teleological assessment is for Evans simply one reason for holding already established and seemingly exceptionless rules to be only virtually so. Such teleological assessment is simply one reason for holding moral rules open to exception. It is not the only or even the chief ground and meaning of moral obligation in conflict situations. Reference to proportionate reason or long-run consequences is, also, merely one reason for conceding exceptions still to be remotely possible. Other possible exceptions are feature-dependent. The grounds or moral reasons generating the obligation or prohibition in the first place, for positing an exception or for holding some concrete behavioral norms to be virtually exceptionless, may all be quite other than the reason for writing into every moral rule what Evans called a "QB (quantity of benefits) exception clause." McCormick needs PR (proportionate reason, or QB) as the metaethical justification of specific normative judgments. But for Evans there may be *deontological* exceptions as well as *deontological* rules. In short, there may be a showing of binding moral obligation that is virtually exceptionless based on fairness or justice or fidelity claims—to which Evans adds that *in extremis* appeals to PR (QB) could override them.

Typically, Evans's formulation for a "calculative exception" is as follows: "Never lie except when lying, as compared with not lying, will promote at least quantity Q of benefit, as it does in this situation SI. (If the comparative benefit of lying is less than Q, don't lie.)" This is a *universal* quantity of benefits exception, the reasons for which are presumably calculable in some sense or can be bartered against one another. The quantity has yet to be specified. In any case QB would need to be of great degree to override; and it need *not* be *continuous with* the moral reasons for positing the rule "Never lie . . ." in the first place, or for positing the other sort of exceptions, feature-dependent exceptions, to that rule. Evans agrees, in fact, with the present writer that some sort of QB exception clauses, like "We should not commit adultery except when it would do more good on the whole to do so," has the effect of *replacing* the moral rule with a maxim—a maxim that reads:

> Usually adultery results in less good than nonadultery (since it usually causes considerable evil), so usually it is wrong to commit adultery; but in each and every case we have to decide solely on the basis of which alternative will, in the particular case, produce more overall good.

Evans clearly states his opinion that every moral rule needs a QB-exception clause; he *states* this view, but does not argue extensively for it. This was not his concern in that essay. The noteworthy point for our present purposes, however, is that Evans believes that "certain species of action have an inherent moral relevance, weight, and significance apart from consequences." QB (or PR), even if capable of overriding the observance of *all* moral rules in some remotely possible cases, does not or need not constitute the reasons or moral meaning of all concrete behavioral norms themselves that are valid in conflict situations. When Evans says "virtually exceptionless," he means deontological rules, fidelity rules, and promissory rules as well as *rule*-utilitarian rules. And when he says there may always be exceptions, he means qualitative or feature-dependent exceptions (like "except to save life") and *rule*-utilitarian exceptions. Then for completeness' sake, he affirms the possibility of universal QB-exceptions as well. He does not fully discuss the point.

Incidentally, Evans advanced a counterprinciple against each of the rule-strengthening rules or principles I stated.[49] That debate was chiefly over how far and how early to ward off QB or PR exceptions. If there are virtually exceptionless rules, these are established on feature-dependent evaluations of actions or moral relations (that is, nonteleologically), however much adherence to them should be strengthened also by consequentialist exception-stoppers.

The question is, What do exponents of regnant proportionate reason mean by *virtually exceptionless?* Does PR mean QB? The question is whether McCormick has not reduced the moral immunity of noncombatants from direct attack and the prohibition of direct euthanasia, for example, to maxims. For him, in conflict situations, there need be no independent moral significance or immediate meaning in the attitude of the will toward the taking of human life. Clearly Evans *could* say there is, even while still believing that QB (or PR) is sufficient on occasion to override, either as a rule exception or in an act. I therefore must conclude that use of the expression *virtually exceptionless* tells us little or nothing about the substantive moral analysis behind that usage.

IV

The foregoing exposition and critique has been properly metaethical and at times abstract. This can be remedied by taking up in greater detail two special moral problems: the principle of discrimination in warfare and the prohibition of dispatching terminal patients.

Holding noncombatants immune from direct attack is "a practical absolute," according to McCormick, "a practically exceptionless imperative" governing conduct in war, "virtually exceptionless." He believes this basically because of the radical difference between the intentionalities involved in killing innocent civilians deliberately and in bringing about their deaths as one attempts to repel an enemy's war machine. Why, the reader needs to ask, is this difference *morally* significant?

The *manifest* reason, the reason based on the wisdom of accumulated human *experience,* is contained in McCormick's judgment that

> . . . taking innocent human life as a means removes restraints and unleashes destructive powers which both now and in the long run will brutalize sensitivities and take many more lives than we would now save by such action.

He acknowledges, of course, that he cannot prove this assertion "with a syllogistic click." However, it is "a good human bet given our knowledge of ourselves and our history. . . ." He quotes Joseph L. Allen on why not obliterate a city to shorten a war, who argues that military policy ought not to be based on a too narrow calculation; one should take into account also "the increased callousness to creaturely beings that tends to accompany such acts."

Why, we may ask, will increased callousness, the removal of restraints, the unleashing of destructive tendencies, the brutalizing of sensitivities result *more* from willfully causing the deaths of the innocent than from unwillfully but foreseeably accepting those deaths as among the effects of action? After all, it is a good human bet that all acts of war also tend to be brutalizing. Why more in one sort of taking life than in another? What evidence strengthens the prohibition of indiscriminate attack up to the point of "a practically exceptionless imperative" whose final certification is and must be that it alone assures that lesser evil will be done in warfare?

McCormick's answer is a good one; and it is a good *moral* reason. For it is here that he repeats in substance the crest about the intending will (the person) being more closely associated with the evil, more willing to have that evil occur. In short, *because* an intending will is, so to speak, *more evildoing,* taking the lives of noncombatants *that way* is bound to be more brutalizing, more destructive of restraints and productive of greater evil in the long run than, say, the same deaths brought about by a permitting will which is *less evildoing.* That, I should say, is a good moral justification; and if that is McCormick's view, he has provided us with an independent moral source for sensitizing and nuancing judgments of proportion.

But on the next page McCormick sets down the passage that, as I have pointed out, undercuts any independent moral significance among the intentions to evil, and which again constitutes the bridge to the ascendancy of an only psychological or descriptive difference. A person who is less willing that evil exist is also less willing that the good exist (shortening the war), while a person who is more willing that the evil exist (the deaths of the innocent) has that attitude because he is more willing that that good exist.

If that is true, we now must ask, what becomes even of the manifest, experiential reason for holding the prohibition of direct attack on civilians to be a "practically exceptionless imperative" grounded in proportionate reason's recognition of radical differences in the increased callousness and lack of restraint that may result from how acts of war are intended and carried out? The *moral* reason for believing that greater brutalization will flow from killing civilians directly than from merely foreseeably permitting, for example, *the same number* to be killed in discriminate military action has been completely evacuated. When that is removed, also removed is any manifest reason for supposing that one sort of killing in war is likely to be more brutalizing than any other. Then one can only resort directly to judgments of proportionate reason to tell us, without moral prejudice or relic from past moral teaching or the laws of warfare, which way or manner of warfare leads to the lesser evil.

The laws of warfare, imperfect as these may be as constraints, and the principle of discrimination in codes of military justice and in past moral teaching, have now been reduced to an action-guide one abides by if lesser evil results, and an action-guide one breaks if it is expected not to do so. McCormick says as much:

> Such a willingness (a willingness to have evil occur by an intending will) is morally acceptable only to the extent that such an intention represents a choice of what is the lesser evil.

Again the word *only* seems strange; the explanation of the use of it must be the weight of past moral teaching and emotional reluctance to draw the conclusion *drawn*. One can also say that willingness to have that evil occur from a permitting will is acceptable only to the extent that the choice is of a lesser evil to come.

Lesser evil is the sole operative test; independent rational moral significance has been withdrawn from the distinction between direct and indirect targeting of acts of war, from the relic of these limitations in international law or in military codes, in the sentiments and moral impulses of commanders and soldiers and still in people generally.

The latter can only be described, in the language of military analysts a few years ago, as an irrational or *nonrational* boundary, barrier, and "fire break" still exerting its influence even without a rational moral core to control and justifiably impose those contours on political resorts to violence. In this era of unlimited potential for military destruction any limitation whatsoever, however nonmoral or nonrational it may be, is a very precious thing to be cherished and shored up—pure and undefiled judgments of proportionate reason in given military circumstances to the contrary notwithstanding. Nonrational limits are to be cherished because *they are there* in the conventions and conscience of humankind, because they have the power of traditional acceptance behind them, or simply because they are clear enough for people to count on one another to agree to resort to them at least in some crises, to agree to judge one another's behavior and to be judged by them (like an implicit mutual agreement to fight only up to a certain river).

Still we ought to be clear that, if revisionists of the rule of double effect have good reason on their side and are persuasive, there remains no *moral reason* for backing discrimination as a limit upon warfare, unless it is the lesser of possible destructive options toward a good victory. Except, of course, for purely practical considerations that support shoring up the principle of discriminating because, like Mt. Everest, *it is there*. Like "No outside fires!" such prohibitions are by no means to be despised. Still, these in no way depend on even a purely descriptive or psychological difference between intending and permitting. For it can be said with equal correctness that if President Truman had refused to order the atom bombs to be dropped on Japanese cities, that was because he was less willing for the good to come, namely, shortening the war and saving the lives of a greater number of Japanese and American combatants than the number of civilians deliberately attacked.

Much the same thing can be said about the constraining effects of the presence of the "moral immunity of noncombatants from direct attack" as a *datum* in subjective consciences. Or in general about a factual, descriptive, or merely psychological difference between willfully intending evil and permitting it. Someone who *believes* that that is a morally significant distinction apart from greater or lesser evil in the result, *and he alone,* is likely to be corrupted, calloused, desensitized, unleashed in destructiveness by acting in violation of that subjective conscience. If he were better instructed about the teleological right-making and wrong-making features of action, he would not thereby be morally corrupted. Nor *should* he be, no more than now by deaths brought about in the course of repelling an enemy's war machine if the dead number the same. Therefore, to the degree that McCormick's analysis ultimately tends to make "somewhat circular and considerably less than satisfying" as a *moral reason* the closer relation an intending will has to evil than that of a permitting will, his analysis also has this practical upshot: to that very same extent are manifestly undercut the *manifest* grounds one has for taking any such distinction seriously because of the corruption and brutalizing of moral agents. Unless there is independent moral significance in distinguishing these two directions of the will toward evil, McCormick's "good human bet" is off, except as a relic of past moral teachings and until this revisionist literature has had its way with the consciences of humankind.

It is a confusion to suggest that the need not to corrupt or brutalize ourselves or others can be the *source* of obligation. For if by murdering civilians one engages in a brutalizing activity, that can only be because there is *already* something wrong with murdering them; because such actions are already *morally* different from killing combatants in war. The general reason against committing indiscriminate acts of war cannot be merely that such acts desensitize everyone in the human community and weaken restraints in the time to come. For if one were ever justified in committing such indiscriminately violent acts (or even morally required to do so for sufficient reasons), then one would not be sacrificing one's moral integrity or corrupting the youth by adopting such a course. Instead he would be preserving his moral integrity and instructing the consciences of others. Thus the notion that the *reason* for not doing a morally corrupting action lies in its impairment of a sufficiently worthy end is an incoherent notion. Deliberate, direct attack upon civilian populations is either a brutalizing violation not to be compared with other evils on a single scale, or else it is subject to the rule of proportionate reason alone whose office it is to compare and adjudicate relative values and disvalues and to bring forth the greater or lesser.

The foregoing themes can also be rehearsed by considering an article in which McCormick applied his method of ethics *in extenso* to arguments, respectively, for direct euthanasia and for letting die.[50] That "suicide and killing are generally wrong," he writes, "we grasp spontaneously and prethematically." These are "our basic commitments" and are "not the result of discursive reflection." These "always-and-everywhere principles root in our spontaneous inclinations toward basic human goods and remain, therefore, somewhat mysterious. . . ." Concerning that foundation of the moral life, it remains only to ask: Does McCormick mean in his method of ethics to espouse "multivalue consequentialism"?

McCormick avoids or obscures his answer to that question by moving directly to a consideration of the here-and-now issues of exception making, which can be done in ethics, as we have seen, in a number of other ways besides multivalue teleology.

The article just referred to seems to me to be one in which McCormick holds consequentialism in closest embrace, without the reservation usually indicated by his use of expressions like "a form of consequentialism." At the same time, paradoxically, I am constrained in this context to ask whether his consequentialism is not simply a linguistic mistake, whether it is simply an inept way of saying that some values (which may be deontological relations or claims no less than ends) override others; and to ask him whether he has explained the meaning of proportionate reason adequately and may not have fuzzed the meaning he has in mind by that thoughtless embrace.

He embraces consequentialism: "It is not the end that justifies the means, as Fletcher contends, but the ends." The ends, in the plural, justify the means. I do not know where Fletcher puts forward a single value-end that justifies the means. Neither have the defenders of proportionate reason as a principle encompassing every moral decision. In his consequentialism, Fletcher has never made entirely clear that his view is a simple utilitarianism and not multivalued. And McCormick does not clearly embrace multivalue teleology, in contrast to other modes of ethical reasoning in making exceptions or dealing with conflict cases. So what is the difference? And when defenders of proportionate reason say clearly what feature-dependent action (what value-enhancing or value-violating actions) override what others, it will turn out that they are not consequentialists in the ordinary meaning of that theory of ethics—unless such defenders of all-encompassing proportionate reason mean to become consequentialists by linguistic stipulation.

So, while saying that the ends justify the means (one has to count all the costs, not some only), McCormick still seeks to distinguish his position from that of Joseph Fletcher. The latter has "failed to show us why and in light of what criteria and values direct termination [of dying patients] is truly proportionate." Fletcher has failed to examine "those aspects, values, and dimensions that would alone inform us whether certain forms of behavior are proportionate." "Aspects, values, and dimensions" of moral actions, and "criteria," are a quite good start in the development of a nonconsequentialist, nonutilitarian ethics. If *proportionate reason* means such an ethics, we should be told so more clearly and told how this is so.

This is to say, one can suggest a return to the point in the fashioning of this method in ethics where Schüller simply said that when "put before two concurring but mutually exclusive values, men should discover which merits preference."[51] That suggests an ethics consisting in significant measure of "preference rules."

An ethics elaborative of this point differs significantly from one that follows the lead of Schüller's other observation, to the effect that behind specific norms (like the preference-principle in the case of theft to save life) there is "a mere general preference-principle from which these norms derive," which is proportionate reason.[52] That is a vacuous generalization unless its content is given by preference-principles themselves. McCormick seems to say something quite feature-specific when he writes that there is no proportion between "avoiding shame and burden and destroying fetal life," and when he objects (because it is lacking in guidance) to Van der Poel's projection of human action "against the background of the whole of human existence in this world" with a view to "community-building." What is proportionate reason as a preference-principle governing all concrete preference-principles if not as vacuous as "human flourishing" or "community building"? Perhaps all that is meant in this school of thought is the resolution of prima facie into *actual duties* when put before clashing, hierarchical goods; and that such a situation generates preference-principles. This would mean the analysis of action in terms of its morally significant features. Exceptions, too, would be feature-dependent, and not direct appeals to proportionate reason, if that means simply quantity of benefits. Then, also, it need not be denied that some value-conflicts are between incommensurate goods. Thus the *nisus* toward *telos* would be curbed, that is, the effort to explain all possible preference-principles in terms of proportionate reason or to derive them from it. The latter—at least, the language—suggests that only some ultimate teleological preference-principle, like the greater good or lesser evil, is generative of obligation. "Human flourishing" is at least more poetic.

I am encouraged to believe that McCormick may mean feature-dependent preference-principles, by one of his latest characterizations of past Christian casuistry. He writes:

> The permissible exceptions with regard to life taking (self-defense, just war, capital punishment, indirect killing) are all formulations and concretizations of what is viewed in the situation as the lesser human evil."[53]

Verbally or in the context of prosecuting the case for a vacuous proportionate reason, that would unavoidably mean "a form of consequentialism." It would also be a false account of past teachings. The actual context of the foregoing words, however, was a searching inquiry for the moral justification for destroying a fetal human being. For that to qualify as the lesser of two evils, McCormick wrote, it would be required that there be at stake another "human life or its moral equivalent." Here *lesser evil* means building up from below, as it were, preference-principles like theft to save life. Features of action and clashes of concrete values generate real obligation. These need not be derived (from above, as it were) from any more general and vacuous preference-principle, which verbally begs the question in favor of a morality of ends.

Returning to the *Theology Digest* article cited above, McCormick opens his discussion of dispatching terminal patients or letting die by affirming that we may "cause or permit" evils in our conduct only when the evil is, all things considered, the lesser evil in the circumstances, that is, when there is a truly proportionate reason.[54] Why the option between caused or permitted should even be mentioned is not at all clear. It is mentioned at this point in the preamble only to say in effect that the distinction may not need to be mentioned so far as the final justifying reason is concerned.

McCormick seeks to establish that (1) there *is* a proportionate reason for not using every means to save or prolong the life of a terminal patient; and that (2) there is *no* proportionate reason for directly dispatching a terminal patient. Proportionate reason rules; but, a different proportion would be required to warrant direct killing than in the case of letting die, for action than for refraining. Proportionate reason assessing *all* the goods or evils consequent upon those two courses of action validates, as it turns out, the traditional distinction. That apparent validation, however, is actually a replacement, if it is the case that the original distinction between direct and indirect voluntariety meant something of signal moral importance about the virtue of moral agents and the morality of their actions before ever it could be right to count the costs in terms of consequences in a final appraisal under a morality of ends.

I venture to suggest, in order to facilitate future discussion, that the class name *proportionate* will become adequately informative only when it is fully spelled out which evils are greater than the merely great, which goods greater than the lesser, what values override what other values in case of clash, and so on. I also suggest that such an ethics, if completed, will not resemble an ethics in which the *ends* justify the means. It will look rather remarkably like the ethics elaborated by many a philosopher today who does not imagine he is putting forward "a form of consequentialism."

It is important for McCormick to believe that "those who argue the immorality of positive euthanasia by appeal only to the inherent value of all human life, even dying life," are appealing *"therefore to the general disproportion* at the heart of killing and suicide in general" (italics added).[55] He earlier described our always-and-everywhere apprehension of life to be a value as a prethematic and mysterious claim upon us. The present rendering of those value-claims when in conflict in terms of proportionate reason seems to me to be a circumlocutory misinterpretation of past moral discourse. It makes the meaning of disproportion even more obscure than I thought. Yet it is important to McCormick's case because he wants to argue that such persons simply "forget that they have already abandoned this evaluation when they have provided for passive euthanasia." Who, we may ask, admits the correctness of the translation: the general disproportion at the heart of direct killing? Who among those who have reasoned that the inherent value of human life, coupled with the analysis of right action in terms of direct and indirect intentionality in the case of conflict among incommensurate values, would accept that interpretation of what he said? Who, therefore, among those who distinguish as a cardinal aspect of morals between killing and letting die in the cases in point, is in need only of a mere reminder and not of a knockdown demonstration, if one is possible, that he already abandoned this evaluation when he provided for passive euthanasia? McCormick assumes what needs to be proved, namely, the all-inclusiveness of proportion as a vehicle mediating a moral agent's attitude toward human goods in conflict. Rather like the lapsed-link argument that considerations of justice, fairness, and the virtues of courage, temperance, and so on, in ordinary moral concern and discourse are actually only forms of the prudent pursuit of the greatest happiness altogether.

Of course, it need not be denied that decisions to withhold or withdraw treatment may be described as *proportionate* in some sense of that multifaceted term. These are choices of the greater good or lesser evil. They are reasonable (proportionate) choices. But not choices among lives. On the part of the patient, they rather are decisions about "how to live while dying."[56] On the part of the physician, they are decisions whether a treatment is indicated or not, or determinations whether treatment to cure is any longer useful or whether the helping professions should now only care for the dying. I suppose prudence is the aptitude exercised in all such judgments in the course of medical care. However, one who allows that decisions to let die are *in this sense* based on proportionate reason need not in any way concede that his objection to directly dispatching terminal patients is based on general disproportion.

It is quite incorrect to say that proponents of letting die have already abandoned, under certain circumstances, the negative evaluation ("general disproportion," McCormick calls it) at the heart of the prohibition of direct killing. They have rather decided how to live or how a patient should live while dying. That compares one state or condition of dying with another, one treatment with another, or treatment with no treatment. *These* are judgments of proportion if the latter encompasses indeterminate decisions. In no way do they bring the human life itself into those evaluations. To the contrary: choices having to do with "how the last days of the dying person are to be spent," or about "what is the most meaningful way to spend the remainder of life" are, as Dyck says,

> no different in principle from the choices we make throughout our lives as to how much we will rest, how hard we will work, how little or how much medical intervention we will seek or tolerate, and the like.[57]

These are all reasonable (proportionate?) decisions about goods *for* life. They are indeterminate choices. But they in no way raise any question about the good of life itself, or call in question the equality of lives in conflict situations. Nor do we have grounds for saying that one life should be commeasured with another, or the same life measured in value with itself at a later stage in its declining trajectory.

McCormick, however, seems to say that human life is evaluated differently at different stages. Clearly, however, it would be incorrect to press him into that mold. The fact is that his use of the words *evaluated* or *evaluation* are poorly chosen to convey his meaning, as I shall try to show. When we say that at a certain point medical means no longer ought to be used which in other circumstances we would be obliged to use, McCormick writes,

> we are putting *in some sense or other* a different evaluation on that life than we would if it were nondying life; [we] evaluate dying life differently *(in the above sense of evaluation)*. . .(italics added).

What is that "above sense," that "some sense or other" which McCormick means by "evaluation"? He tells us plainly. " 'Evaluation' here refers to the delineation of our duties to protect and support a good."[58]

That does seem rather peculiar usage. It is like saying that when we decide under one set of circumstances not to put a patient on a machine that in other circumstances we would be obliged to use, we are putting in some sense or other a different evaluation on that life than we would if it were not a damaged life. Then comes the explanation: evaluation refers to the delineation of those machines or medications that are indicated, that is, the delineation of our medical duty in this case to protect and support the good of human life. Life itself is in no way thrown into that balancing act, nor is it submitted to varying evaluations (in that word's ordinary meaning). Not unless we are going to say that when we put a person upon a machine we necessarily put upon him a different evaluation than if we do not. A "delineation of our *duties* to protect and support" life are clearly compatible with ascribing an equal, incommensurable right to life, regardless of a patient's age or condition. Rights and duties or obligation are the terms ordinarily used correlatively in ethical analysis. In letting die one makes a judgment concerning whether he can any longer support life; he chooses among conditions.

By using *evaluation* as a term of art McCormick gains an increment of persuasiveness for the rule of proportionate reason over decisions about direct killing (positive euthanasia). He tries to persuade proponents of misnamed passive euthanasia that they have already abandoned any *steady* (I do not say absolute) "evaluation" of human life regardless of its state or conditon. When, then, they return to the question of directly killing terminal patients, he wishes to argue that they would be inconsistent if they decided that question by reference to the equal, steady, and unvarying value of human life regardless of its state or condition. (I do not say inherent value, if that makes any difference.)

I believe that in the foregoing I have correctly interpreted McCormick's meaning, and to his credit. McCormick made that meaning clearer in another recent article in which he discussed the morality of "letting die," by itself and not, as here, as a transition to including that along with directly dispatching terminal patients under the same rule of prudence. It must be emphasized, he wrote, that:

> allowing some infants to die does not imply that "some lives are valuable, others not" or that "there is such a thing as a life not worth living." *Every human being, regardless of age or condition, is of incalculable worth.* The point is not, therefore, whether this or that individual has value. Of course he has, or rather *is* a value. The only point is whether this undoubted value has any potential at all, in continuing physical survival, for attaining a share, even if reduced, in the "higher, more important good" [Pius XII]. *This is not a question of the inherent value of the individual.* It is a question of whether this worldly existence will offer such a valued individual any hope of sharing those values for which physical life is a fundamental condition.[59]

In other words, in the ethics of letting die quality-of-life decisions mean choice from among the conditions under which we shall live while dying. However, that does not entail comparison of the relative value of human lives as such, or of the same life at different times. How a human being had better live while dying (Dyck) can be weighed and weighed without lessening by a feather's weight the value of that life, which remains incalculable and inherent; it simply *is* an irreducible good.

It is open, of course, for someone to try to *reason to the conclusion* that prudent respect for comparative life conditions supports direct termination as readily as letting die (or to join McCormick in the belief that prudent grounds can be found for the latter but not, all things considered, for the former). It is not cogent, however, to charge that someone who espouses an ethics of letting die (because *there* a prudent comparison of life conditions is appropriate) is somehow inconsistent if he also believes that suicide is wrong and terminal patients ought not be directly dispatched (because as long as a human life is and there *is* a value, that inherent, incalculable, mysterious good commands our respect and care and should not be weighed against any more or less). If the first sort of evaluation is correct, it does not follow, logically or otherwise, that the second needs as well to be a conclusion of proportionate or comparative evaluation. Therefore, so far the claim remains undefeated, untouched: the proper moral attitude toward doing or hastening the death of another should be that of indirect voluntariety.

It remains to indicate how the moral reasoning of these subsequent articles parallels the logic of ethical reasoning methodically set forth in *Ambiguity in Moral Choice*. McCormick presupposes that proportionate reason, and that alone, mediates every morally justifiable response to values in conflict. Therefore he must try to show that the *moral* difference between omission and commission, where the dying are concerned, is adequately accounted for and grounded in the different proportion of greater and lesser evils or goods in the consequences flowing from procedures dealing with the dying that directly intend their deaths in comparison with procedures that merely intend to care for them without further curative treatment. This he must show if proportionate reason is the sole intermediary action-guide and if he is to maintain that there is proportionate reason for letting die but no proportionate reason for direct dispatch.

An unhesitating way to advance this claim would be to affirm that omission and commission manifestly have different consequences. Instead McCormick asserts that omission and commission (*descriptively* different in intentionality), "are not *morally* identical, at least insofar as the moral significance is traceable to, *or revealed by,* effects" (final italics added). He points out that there may be effects, long-range implications, fearful consequences which should be taken into account, if only suspected or unknown, "that would spell, *or at least reveal,* the *moral* difference between omission and commission where the dying are concerned."[60]

The words "or revealed by" and "or at least reveal" show McCormick to be a reluctant dragon. He does not assert simply that the *moral* distinction between omission and commission is established by tracing it to their different long-run effects for greater or lesser evil. He says also that the difference in the consequences, reasonably to be expected, *reveals* a *moral* difference that was there all along between direct dispatch and letting die.

This is the same ambiguity we found in *Ambiguity in Moral Choice*. In direct volition of the evil, the person stands closer to it, he is more willing for that evil to occur. That was why, in order to warrant the intention of evil co-present with some greater good among the consequences of action, a proportionately greater good is required than in cases in which the concurring evil is unintended. So here greater evils in the long run reveal that prior closer embrace of evil in the immediate action.

On the other hand, it can be reasoned that a person who is less willing to do an immediate evil is also less willing that some good result, and that if he were more willing to accomplish good in the ends he would be more willing to directly intend evil among the means. In that case, the only thing to be said in support of drawing any distinction between direct dispatch and letting die would be that the former spells more resulting evils in the long haul. One could say only that the moral significance of that distinction is traceable to effects. Then nothing in the resulting corruption of human behavior reveals or establishes that there was anything morally wrong or followed from any wrongness in the original intention.

We may now rapidly conclude. McCormick marshals the evidence that "when death is the immediate result of disease rather than direct human intervention, its associated implications are different, and so is therefore the calculus of proportion." If a physician's explicit purpose is to kill, "there would be a profound difference in the way one would grasp the syringe, the look in the eye, the words that might be spoken or withheld."[61] Granted.

And grant also that such considerations are important supporting evidence for the proscription of direct medical killing. Certainly, however, much the same can be said about letting die: the way one pulls the plug may be in desperation or flight, the look in the eye may be guilt, caring words may also be withheld. Many of the same qualms of conscience afflict nurses and physicians in letting die.

Again, if the primary actors in such all-too-human situations become morally corrupt, and grave consequences flow from that, it must be because their actions were wrong in the first place, or were conscientiously and erroneously believed to be wrong. The actions cannot have been wrong simply because those persons were morally corrupted by doing them. The idea that one can sacrifice his moral integrity by doing the right thing is an incoherent notion. If directly dispatching patients is the right thing to do, physician integrity and the ethics of professional practice are expressed by so doing, not threatened. The consequences to which McCormick points can only reveal the wrongfulness of directly dispatching terminal patients; those consequences cannot be the reason that the act is wrong. He who believes, and only he who believes, that it is inherently wrong to turn directly against the life of a dying patient and his quietus make will tend subjectively toward disintegration as a moral person or an ethical physician. For this reason McCormick's method in ethics, his all-inclusive appeal to proportionate reason, depends for its evidence upon past formations of conscience.

Even so, the capstone in the arch is again the argument from overriding, common, and universal danger if individuals were allowed to decide that it might reasonably be the lesser evil to kill. *Even if* the action in question does not threaten the persons concerned with more evil than good, to allow individuals to make that decision may pose a threat to the common good. So McCormick summarily concludes:

> There are enormous goods at stake, and both our past experience of human failure, inconstancy, and frailty, and our uncertainty with regard to long-term effects lead us to believe that we *ought* to hold some norms [namely, the norm prohibiting direct killing] as virtually exceptionless, that this is the conclusion of prudence in the face of dangers too momentous to make risk tolerable.

If these are the reasons for holding that terminal patients ought not be directly dispatched, I suggest that those reasons probably should be kept secret. If the grounds for saying that directly dispatching terminal patients is unexceptionally forbidden is overriding danger to the common good, there may still be some usefulness in a deontological ethics of right and wrong forbidding direct medical killing. That could be issued as a noble lie, a needed fable, on which to erect the ideal republic of proportionate reason upon somewhat more enduring foundations.

The need for such a noble lie can be accented in the following way. At about the same time as the publication of *Ambiguity in Moral Choice,* Daniel C. Maguire published a passionate defense of positive euthanasia, *Death by Choice.*[62] That book was reviewed by William E. May, who criticized its reasoning for, among other things, its abuse of the traditional distinction "direct/indirect intention."[63] In response Maguire affirmed the purely psychological significance of that distinction, and for support he quoted McCormick: "the immorality must be argued from lack of proportionate reason."[64] So here we have two true believers in the sole decisive moral significance of proportion, both morally sensitive men, reaching opposite conclusions on the gravest moral matter. I suggest that the reason is that, indeed, there is little moral guidance in proportion alone. That being so, I suggest further that when McCormick reads back from proportion to support conservatively the traditional teaching against direct killing and Maguire reads it to jettison that prohibition the difference between them is a function of temperament or some other factor and not of moral reason in exercise.

Perhaps we do need a magisterium or laws like "No outside fires!" or a believed fable on which to base the incomparable value of human life in the present day.

V

The conclusion of McCormick's essay is puzzling. His theme is "The notion of proportionate reason is analogous." Now, analogy is a superb gulch, as the man said when first viewing the Grand Canyon, in which to get rid of all one's old razor blades, the blades used up in ethical analysis. McCormick wishes to show that proportionate reason is a profounder notion than casuistry supposes and more fruitful and Christian than deontologists imagine. (Here again we seem prevented from interpreting proportionate reason and value judgments in terms of nonconsequentialist moral rule making.) I suggest that the theme "proportionate reason is analogous" should read "proportionate reason encompasses indeterminancy in moral choice," in the sense explained above. Most of McCormick's cases fall under that rubric.

For example, McCormick discusses heroic charity and he wishes to bring that, too, within the provenance of proportionate reason. There is proportionate reason for a soldier to throw himself on a live explosive to save the life of a fellow soldier. There is proportionate reason also for him not to do so. So also in the cases of defending oneself against an assailant. McCormick does not simply say there is good or sufficient reason for these alternatives, but that there is proportionate reason. What does that modifier add to the substantive that is not conveyed by good reason in indeterminate cases?

He is not content with saying that it is a good or right decision for a bystander, who cannot swim, not to try to save a drowning man he cannot save; or for a fetus to be aborted when it will die and the mother die as well if that is not done. He says rather that these decisions are alike "proportionately grounded decisions." But these are very dissimilar cases. The second, indeed, contains a judgment of proportion if the sole reason was that it is better to save one life than for two to perish; and it was altogether the right decision if the fetus was not ascribed lesser worth to complete the proportion favoring the mother, and if the lifesaving action was correctly describable as stopping the fetus's lethal action upon the mother or removing an obstacle in the way of a necessary lifesaving operation upon the mother (who was the only one of the lives in conflict that could be saved).[65] The first case, however, need not invoke proportionate reason in any sense comprehensible to me at this point. The solution of it need appeal only to the good reason that no ethics requires the impossible, and no individual is obliged to try the impossible.

McCormick writes also that because of human sin, weakness, and immaturity, there can sometimes be "proportionate reason for not aiding my neighbor in distress." I see the good reasons that can be offered as backing in these instances of indeterminancy in moral choice; but I confess I do not understand McCormick's use of the language of proportionality to explain both heroic charity and attitudes and actions lacking in charity, and along with those extremes to encompass also an ethics of compromise as well.

Above I suggested that the *ordo bonorum* is not a seamless robe or a hierarchy of commensurate values (and that the heuristic relevance of direct and indirect voluntariety is at points where there are good reasons to believe there are significant discontinuities). It is interesting that when McCormick is discussing analogous proportionate reason he faces as a Christian ethicist another significant divide. Here the incommensurability of charitable actions and actions lacking charity could be deemed so great that the question of direct and indirect voluntariety hardly arises. This is surely a greater discontinuity than that between moral and nonmoral evil, which sustained a moral difference between intending or occasioning the sin of another. Still McCormick uses the language of proportion and *ordo;* he speaks of the *ordo bonorum* that before was under consideration and the *"ordo bonorum* viewed in Christian prespective" as if the latter made no vast difference.

We may agree with and, I think, dismiss as irrelevant his contention that, of course, sacrifice must be inordinate in the sense that *if useless* (as in the case of the landlubbing bystander), an effort to save the drowning man out of *benevolentia* would not be *beneficentia;* it would no longer be governed by the *ordo bonorum,* no good would flow from charity unless it is "controlled by the possible."

No ethics requires the impossible. One can say the same of a selfish system of ethics. A hedonist has lost touch with reality if he selfishly wills actions for his own sake that cannot possibly be done or which cannot deliver the expected benefits. So also in the case of heroic charity. That too can be disproportionate in the sense that some of the attitudes and actions of any moral outlook may be failed attempts from the beginning, and *therefore* are inordinate.

It is the use of the expression "proportionate reason" when explaining the works of love that seems strange indeed. I confess I may not fully understand what is the meaning of saying that, when the good of another is *equal* to mine and my sacrifice is the only way of securing his good, to do so would have proportionate reason. It is singularly unpersuasive to say that heroic sacrifice

> is *proportionate* not because his life is preferable to mine—they are equally valuable as basic human goods—but because in case of conflict, it is a human and Christian good to seek to secure this good for my neighbor at the cost of my life (italics added).

That may be the Christian thing to do, perfecting and transforming proportionate reason. That may be a Christian good, and in that light a redeemed human good; but I do not see how it can be called a proportionate good, unless his life *is* preferable to mine or unless heroic sacrifice is simply another instance (passionately expressed) of indeterminancy in moral choice whose indeterminancy is removed by the example of Christ. Indeed, the denial that another's life is preferable, the affirmation that in the *ordo bonorum* our lives are equal, is the only way to give backing to or good reason for the view that I may save my own life instead of his. If there is sufficient reason for either decision made amid indeterminancy, then proportion means indeterminancy not only because there are innumerable similarities and innumerable dissimilarities in the comparison but also because, as David Lewis wrote, relative importances differ from one person to another and from one occasion to another for the same person. In this case, the moral judgment turns upon whether we are talking of a Christian person or not, and what sort of Christian.

Surely it is inconclusive, if not even foolish, for McCormick to write that

> . . . to deny that such sacrifice could be proportionately grounded would be to deny that self-giving love after the model of Christ is a human good and represents the direction in which we are moving.

Surely there is another alternative, namely, to deny that self-giving love after the model of Christ can be or need be proportionately grounded in order to be the human good. To claim that the direction of the human good, as Christians are given to know it from knowing through Christ the heart of God and the heart of human beings, is *not unreasonable* is one sort of claim or conviction. But to say that such insight into the human good is "not disproportionate" makes a more restrictive claim, one that requires proof up against an *ordo bonorum*, preestablished and otherwise known, however indeterminately.

I suppose we could say in face of the discontinuity between Christian and natural morality (as was said of the sin of another) that no one should ever willfully intend another to fall short of the call of charity (no, never) for the sake of any goods that are lesser, as all are. Still there is a difference between floor-prohibitions in morality and the "obligations of charity" (if indeed the latter is not a contradiction in terms) because of the reasons McCormick cites: human sin, weakness, immaturity, and the fact that we live between the times of God's redemption.

Some remaining issues here may be somewhat unraveled if not entirely clarified by Philippa Foot's suggestion that "direct intention" and "oblique intention" can helpfully be replaced by the distinction between avoiding injury and bringing aid, between negative and positive duties.[66] Indirect intentionality works, she believes, in the case of the negative duty to avoid one of comparable injuries. Thus, the driver steering a runaway tram should at the switch go in the direction that involves death to one person rather than in the direction that would kill five. Perhaps, also, conflicts of positive duties require us only to pass by the duty not done, never willfully to turn against it. But the distinction between avoiding injury and giving aid, between negative and positive duties, is far more important for morality; and this is shown in cases where there is conflict *between* positive and negative duties. Our negative duties are more binding. We ought not willfully kill an innocent man in order to save five in the case of the lynch mob (even if the numbers are the same as in the case of the runaway tram). Never inflict injury is a prohibition. Bring aid is a counsel.

When McCormick writes of the counsels of perfection, of heroic charity, he makes use of some such distinction. Positive Christian duties or ideals, he rightly insists, are not obligatory for all *urbi et orbi*. Yet he seems to believe that such actions *as well as their contraries* are proportionately reasonable. Bringing aid in Foot's sense is a *positive* duty, in contrast to the negative, avoiding injury. Bringing aid in self-giving love according to the model of Christ would seem to be for McCormick a positive duty. The puzzle is that he seems to say that not bringing aid according to the model of Christ may also be a proportionately reasonable good, and for the Christian as well as the natural man.

In actuality, McCormick has discovered here such a discontinuity in the *ordo bonorum* (between morality within the limits of reason alone and morality within the broader confines of God's grace) that there is not the slightest suggestion that he even thinks of invoking the clarifying distinction between direct and indirect voluntariety which was serviceable in the case of moral and nonmoral evils or goods. Still, for reasons I cannot fathom, he wishes to encompass the whole of the Christian moral life within the principle of proportionate reason which was all along limited to conflicts among nonmoral goods or evils. Why he should raise any question about Philippa Foot's use of the equivalent of proportionate reason in connection with her more secular or philosophical distinction between negative duties and giving aid I cannot comprehend.

There may, however, be a simple explanation. Sins against charity are essentially sins of simple omission, of not doing, of failure to will or do or care enough. There is conflict enough in that: he who does one thing (defend himself) does not do another. Choice here, as always, is decisive. But simple omission and commission, and the concomitant tragedy and failure, are then not the fundamental ambiguity in moral choice. Omission is not *wrongdoing,* directly or indirectly. With one exception, none of the cases McCormick discusses under the heading of the quandaries about charity involves evil positively *done* irremediably locked in objectively with the good that is primarily chosen and also *done*. That is, where *both* are commissions, and not one merely an omission. In short, he is using a Christian version of Philippa Foot's distinction between negative and positive duties, which are agonizing enough judgments to resolve but not fundamentally ambiguous.

The single case in which the good and the evil are interwoven in the texture of a single (justifiable) action, which McCormick discusses in these last pages, is the case where mother and unborn child will *both* certainly die unless by abortion the mother's life is saved. At this point McCormick is undertaking to show that "one who cannot save another but still tries is no longer governed by the *ordo bonorum*." A mother in such a case who would sacrifice herself is not governed by a reality principle controlling her benevolence. She is a well-wisher, but she does no good. McCormick assimilates this case entirely (and that is the point of it) to the case of the bystander who cannot save a drowning man. He does not bring into account, nor need he do so, the fact that the bystander does nothing while in abortion something is done.[67] McCormick's discussion at this point is clearly limited to the sole formal purpose of illustrating that no ethical principle or outlook requires the impossible.

For the most part, "proportionate reason is analogous" is an effort to enfold charity within proportionate reason. Here would seem to be the place to use Foot's distinction between negative and positive duties, between causing injury and bringing aid. McCormick, however, wishes to stress that "self-giving after the model of Christ is a human good and represents the direction in which we should all be growing." That would be denied, according to McCormick, if we "deny that such sacrifice could be proportionately grounded." Here, then, is the puzzling point: human good for McCormick, even that human good toward which the redemption and sanctification of humankind is directed, must be dubbed proportionate.[68] Surely that stretches the category beyond the breaking point; or else by meaning all things it means nothing.

To conclude briefly. Catholic moralists prior to the Second Vatican Council had extended the distinction between direct and indirect voluntariety from cases from which it originated and actually did apply as an action-guide (intending the sin of another, and killing another human being) routinely to other cases, for example, sterilization and conception control, to which it did not validly apply. During the ethical debates since Vatican II it has been sufficiently established that, in the latter realms, commensurate values are at stake; or if not altogether commensurate values, still value-conflicts permitting smooth enough indeterminate choices to be made between, for example, the communicative good of marriage and the good of procreation. In these matters, it is widely believed (I think correctly so) that there are no moral judgments for which proportionate reason alone is not the guiding preference-principle. Will not the manner of protecting the good (procreation) undermine it in the long run by serious injury to an associated good (the communicative good)? That was the question searchingly asked. Issues of sterilization and artificial conception control were thus brought within the reign of proportionate reason alone.

That victory having been won in interface with reason if not with the official ecclesiastical teaching, these moralists went on to generalize proportionate reason to sorts of cases to which it never did and does not apply, for example, the killing of another human being (stopping only at intending the sin of another).[69] The momentum of this impulse carries McCormick so far as to say that acts of charity are somehow proportionate (also their opposites).

I can only conclude that a vice of Catholic moral analysis is the other side of its great virtue, namely, to seek always for a universal understanding of the moral life. Therefore, before Vatican II, the rule of double effect held sway where it did not apply and where it did not originate. After Vatican II, proportionate reason is believed to hold sway where it does not apply. Our moral lives are more various than either generalization.

ENDNOTES FOR CHAPTER THREE

1   David K. Lewis, *Counterfactuals* (Cambridge: Harvard University Press, 1973), pp. 91-95. Jeffrey Stout drew my attention to this citation and to its significance for my discussion of McCormick's writings.

2   W. D. Ross, *The Right and the Good* (Oxford: Clarendon Press, 1930), p. 144 (italics added). "Such compromises are a part of everyday morality," Donald Evans observes, "but they raise serious problems for ethical theory, for their logic and rationale is obscure." Donald Evans, "Paul Ramsey and Exceptionless Rules," *American Journal of Jurisprudence* 16 (1971): 191; reprinted in James T. Johnson and David H. Smith, *Love and Society: Essays in the Ethics of Paul Ramsey* (Missoula, MT: Scholars Press, University of Montana, 1974), p. 25.

3   See Grisez's remark: " [Knauer's] redefinition of ' directly intended ' . . . bears no relation to any previous use of the expression." Germain Grisez, *Abortion: the Myths, the Realities and the Arguments* (New York and Cleveland: Corpus Books, 1966), p. 331. Daniel C. Maguire agrees. Concerning Knauer's replacement of "directly intended" by "commensurate ground," Maguire writes: "If this statement confuses the reader, it is because the reader is thinking clearly. Knauer is changing the meaning of direct so much that it has no relationship to its previous meaning." Daniel C. Maguire, *Death by Choice* (Garden City, NY: Doubleday and Co., 1974), p. 68.

4   William E. May, *Becoming Human: An Invitation to Christian Ethics* (Dayton, OH: Pflaun Publishing, 1975), pp. 91-92. In the matter of killing or letting die, to be taken up below, choice between a heart bypass operation at great risk and unrelieved chest pains may be another example of an indeterminate decision. But with such an indeterminate decision between *conditions* of life we come to the outer limits of proportion, that is, obscurely reasonable choices.

5   Richard A. McCormick, "Notes on Moral Theology," *Theological Studies* 34 (March 1973): 62. The point Schüller made, in referring to sin, injustice, untruthfulness, and infidelity as moral evils was, as reported, that "since moral evil is by definition unconditional disvalue, the exceptionless

validity of norms stating it is analytical.'' To this, a proper reply surely is: (1) that the exceptionless validity of moral norms is analytic in the case of nonmoral values as well, for example, knowledge, health, happiness, and life, *before* they come into conflict with other value-claims; and (2) the same sort of indeterminate choice may have to be made if (a) rightousness, justice, truthfulness, and fidelity ever come into irremediable situational conflict with one another where one must be taken, the other left aside, and (b) if there is a question of compromising those moral values with the claims of nonmoral values such as life.

6   For all the edification in the Latin language, *ordo bonorum* means greater or lesser evil or good, no more and nothing other, as one's final test.

7   Richard A. McCormick, ''Notes on Moral Theology,'' *Theological Studies* 33 (March 1971): 80-97.

8   Thomas Nagel, ''War and Massacre,'' *Philosophy and Public Affairs* 1 (Winter 1972): 132-33.

9   Richard A. McCormick, ''Notes on Moral Theology,'' *Theological Studies* 33 (March 1972): 69.

10 McCormick quotes with approval Charles Curran's words: ''. . . all the moral values [this expression has not the restricted meaning of our text so far] must be considered and a final decision made after all moral values have been *compared*'' (italics added). But what if that were impossible? If no ethics demands the impossible, no metaethical justifications ought to include it among its structuring of the way to go about making normative ethical judgments. Moreover, to advise oneself or others to try to do the impossible when making moral decisions is apt to produce some quite undesirable moral consequences.

11 Ross, *The Right and the Good,* pp. 142-53. Because Ross's analysis and terminology lend considerable support to the thesis of this chapter, perhaps I should quote several statements of his position. Ross writes: ''With regard to pleasure and virtue, it seems to me much more likely to be the truth that *no* amount of pleasure is equal to any amount of virtue, that in fact virtue belongs to a higher order of value, beginning at a point higher on the scale of value than that which pleasure ever reaches; in other words, that while pleasure is comparable in value with virtue (that is, can be said to be less valuable than virtue) it is not commensurable with it . . .'' (p. 150). His statement about the second great discontinuity is: ''When we turn to consider the relative value of moral goodness and knowledge as ends, here again I am inclined to think that moral goodness is infinitely better than knowledge. . . . When I ask myself whether any increase of knowledge, however great, is worth having at the cost of a willful failure to do my duty or of a deterioration of character, I can only answer in the negative. The infinite superiority of moral goodness to anything else is the clearest in the case of the highest form of moral goodness, the desire to do one's duty. But

even of the lesser virtues the same appears to be true" (pp. 152-53). Ross concludes this chapter by an example. Suppose a person in whose life there is exactly the amount of happiness in "proportionment" to the degree of virtue, yet that some of that happiness derives from a bad disposition, for example, pleasures of cruelty. Who would not approve an amendment of life in which there is a "much less proportionment of pleasure to virtue" brought about because he was both more virtuous and less happy? (pp. 153-54). Yet he acknowledges that "the suggestion that there are two orders or classes of good things such that those in one class are not commensurable, though they are comparable, with those in the other, is obviously not free from difficulties" (p. 154).

12   Instead, in his chapter on "Degrees of Goodness," Ross was concerned to show that his view does not lead to a puritanical moralism or severity, and that ordinarily the three levels of goodness *can be readily harmonized.*

13   John Locke, *Second Treatise on Civil Government,* chap. III, par. 17.

14   Paul Ramsey, "Screening: An Ethicist's View," in *Ethical Issues in Human Genetics:Genetic Counseling and the Use of Genetic Knowledge,* eds. Bruce Hilton, Daniel Callahan, et al. (New York: Plenum Publishing Corp., 1973), pp. 146-67. I spoke of the "quantity of the qualities" problem which renders problematic every judgment concerning the "greatest good altogether." That article also argues, more decisively than here, that utilitarianism does not solve the problem of just distribution because "those concerned" are incommensurable human beings, some or many of whom need not (except for some other principle in ethics) be included and could be positively excluded from participation in the good that is "greatest." The reader will understand that the class of "indeterminate" decisions includes (a) trivial choices, like orange or apple juice, (b) choice among incommensurable *qualities* that are doubtless important but to which indeterminate decisions direct/indirect bears no relation, and (c) *fundamental* human goods, inseparably conflicted in action, between which there is a gulf commensurate reason cannot bridge.

15   I do not vouch for the figures.

16   Beneath seeming "descriptive metaethics" in this revisionist literature one can readily detect a "normative metaethical" proposal—a proposal calling for agreement about how the normative ethical terms *should mean* or be employed. See William K. Frankena, "On Saying the Ethical Thing," *Proceedings and Addresses of the American Philosophical Association, 1965-66* (Yellow Springs, OH: Antioch Press, 1966), pp. 21-42.

17   See May, *Becoming Human,* pp. 81-82.

18   McCormick begins with a weakened form of the rule of double effect. A counter-statement to his starting point would be the following stronger formulation: "If someone is ready to bring the good into existence only by permitting the evil, it can be and ought to be suggested that he is not *willing*

or choosing that evil to exist at all. Evil is not what he is ready to bring into existence. He is simply bringing into existence a good whose 'bringing into existence' entails an evil.''

19 See H. Richard Niebuhr, *Christ and Culture* (New York: Harper and Row, 1951), chap. 5.

20 Ibid., chap. 6.

21 McCormick, "Notes," *TS* 33, p. 90.

22 McCormick, "Notes on Moral Theology," *Theological Studies* 30 (December 1969): 690.

23 McCormick, "Notes on Moral Theology," *Theological Studies* 32 (March 1971): 7.

24 McCormick, "Notes," *TS* 34, p. 55.

25 McCormick, "Notes," *TS* 32, p. 94. A position McCormick now says he agrees with in substance. Knauer's opinion has now become McCormick's "good human bet given our knowledge of ourselves and our history."

26 That is, value judgments are judgments of proportionate reason. This suggestion would replace the claim in papal documents that the church is commissioned to teach the whole moral law, including the clarification of the natural law accessible in principle to human reason, with the claim that it has the competence accurately to teach specific judgments of proportionality which are also open to rational moral judgment.

27 McCormick, "Notes," *TS* 32, pp. 95-96.

28 Ibid., p. 97.

29 "If we moralists seriously propose exceptions as possible (and they are), our most basic task is to discover those values which do or do not justify causing the disvalue. Unless we do, are we not inviting people to except themselves without providing any hierarchy which would make such a decision rational, and therefore promotive of greater humanization?" [McCormick, "Notes," *TS* 33, p. 77.] On its face, that calls for the elaboration of feature-dependent sorts of exceptions to feature-dependent action-guides. These would be nonteleological moral rules and exceptions. Instead, the dominant tendency of McCormick's thought is to appeal directly to proportionate reason to explain every exception, even though the basic norms that are in conflict arise prethematically from the individual's sense of value. Such direct appeal to proportionality—left unarticulated as it is—moves in the direction of writing a QB (quantity of benefit) exception clause (see below) into every moral principle or rule. This is so, even if in some unexplained way, proportionality (greater good or lesser evil) is not exactly the same thing as quantity of benefit. If benefit is a value-term, what in fact is the difference?

30 McCormick, "Notes," *TS* 33, p. 79. At issue was the principle of discrimination in the conduct of war, which McCormick wanted to reduce to a long-run consequentialist judgment.

31 McCormick, "Notes," *TS* 34, p. 84.
32 Deontological is almost meaningless because it covers a host of moral norms and relational claims that have in common only the fact that they are to be understood nonteleologically. McCormick gives the only definition at all useful or needed in the current discussion: "A deontological norm is one that evaluates an act by a characteristic that cannot be gathered from its consequences." ["Notes," *TS* 34, p. 62.] What right–making characteristics emerge, and by what warrant, is certainly not conveyed by the word *deontological* in its current usage for many sorts of nonteleological theories of ethics or of ingredients in ethics.
33 McCormick, "Notes," *TS* 34, p. 72.
34 Ibid., pp. 72-73.
35 Ibid., pp. 73-74. See p. 69, in exposition of the views of P. R. Baelz: ". . . the general good will be better served by a proscribing rule than by permitting alternative decisions."
36 John R. Connery, S. J., "Morality of Consequences: A Critical Appraisal," *Theological Studies* 34 (September 1973): 413.
37 McCormick, "Notes," *TS* 33, p. 85.
38 Ibid., p. 86.
39 Paul Ramsey, "The Case of the Curious Exception," in *Norm and Context in Christian Ethics,* eds. Gene Outka and Paul Ramsey (New York: Charles Scribner's Sons, 1968), pp. 114-19, 128-29.
40 John Gay, *Concerning the Fundamental Principle of Virtue or Morality* (1731), in Edwin A. Burtt, ed., *The English Philosophers from Bacon to Mill* (New York: Modern Library, 1939), pp. 769-85.
41 *Deontological* is only an uninformative class name meaning nonteleological. What the species mean has yet to be explained; and when explanations are given there is usually about as much diversity among the accounts as between any one of them and a teleological ethics.
42 Richard A. McCormick, "Notes on Moral Theology," *Theological Studies* 35 (June 1974): 344-45.
43 Richard A. McCormick, "Human Significance and Christian Significance," in *Norm and Context in Christian Ethics,* eds. Outka and Ramsey, p. 252.
44 McCormick, "Notes," *TS* 33, p. 83.
45 McCormick, "Notes," *TS* 34, p. 90.
46 Ibid., p. 61.
47 Ibid., p. 63.
48 Evans, "Paul Ramsey and Exceptionless Rules," pp. 184-214, reprinted in Johnson and Smith, eds., *Love and Society,* pp. 19-46.
49 Ibid., pp. 210-14; pp. 41-45.
50 Richard A. McCormick, "The New Medicine and Morality," *Theology Digest* 21 (Winter 1973): 308-21.

51 According to McCormick, "Notes," *TS* 32, p. 90.
52 Ibid., p. 93.
53 Richard A. McCormick, "Notes on Moral Theology," *Theological Studies* 35 (June 1974): 354.
54 McCormick, "New Medicine and Morality," p. 316.
55 Ibid., p. 317. By the same argument, McCormick and Schüller have placed disproportion at the heart of one's relation to the sin of another. By providing for "passive" occasioning the sin of another *for proportionate reason* (legislation that may lead to bribery), they admit that "active" willing the sin of another could be justified for greater proportionate reason—or that proportionate reason alone distinguishes between the two ways in which the sin of another may be brought about. The formal argument has weight, or it has no weight, in both cases. I believe it is a debater's point that can be turned back upon anyone who fails to use it consistently for all cases of conflicted incommensurate values.
56 Arthur J. Dyck, "An Alternative to the Ethics of Euthanasia," in *To Live and To Die*, ed. Robert W. Williams (New York: Springer-Verlag, 1973), pp. 98-112.
57 Ibid., p. 105.
58 McCormick, "New Medicine and Morality," p. 317.
59 Richard A. McCormick, "To Save or Let Die," *Journal of the American Medical Association* 229 (July 8, 1974): 176 (italics added).
60 McCormick, "New Medicine and Morality," p. 318 (first italics added).
61 David W. Louisell, "Euthanasia and Biathanasia: On Dying and Killing," *Linacre Quarterly* 40 (1973): 234-58.
62 Maguire, *Death by Choice*.
63 William E. May, "Euthanasia, Bene Mortasia and the Dying," *Linacre Quarterly* 41 (1974): 135-40.
64 Maguire, *Death by Choice,* pp. 141-43.
65 See Paul Ramsey, "Abortion: A Review Article," *The Thomist* 37 (January 1973): 174-226. McCormick's irenic penchant for finding proportionate reason sitting under every vine and fig tree leads him to put that interpretation not only on all past Christian teachings but to ascribe it to contemporary moralists as well. Concerning the analysis of justifiable abortion by the present writer, McCormick asks—in the teeth of evidence—"whether the really operative factor is the intention of the action," whether the nub of the argument is not proportionate reason instead. His answer: "It seems clear that directness and indirectness do not really function critically in Ramsey's analysis." ["Notes," *TS* 35, p. 349.]

Why does he say this? Because I was discussing the case in which only one life, the mother's, can be saved. Save that one or both die. Therefore, McCormick tells me, proportionate reason must be the sole justificatory principle. He dismisses the fact that I was discussing cases in which the unborn child is either naturally aggressing on the life of the mother or is an obstacle (or shield) that must be removed before life-saving action can be extended. I suggested that the objective of the first (lethal) action is stopping the aggression or removing an obstacle, and not directly killing the unborn. That specific action–guide he dissolved into the preference–principle (proportion) he finds lurking behind every choice.

McCormick need not be convinced, but we should keep the state of the question clear. Perhaps my analysis of the intentional objective of death–dealing surgical action in those cases is only another form of the argument from necessity in the law of justifiable homicide. I think it is more than that. Let us suppose that I only described those conditions of necessity. Still those specific conditions are needed before the moral imperative to save one life rather than let both die (proportion) becomes operative.

Why not simply say that proportion alone functions critically in this analysis? Precisely because by that reasoning—the choice of the lesser evil—I would be justified in killing the child or threatening to kill the child of a criminal in order to stop him from killing my wife and child. One for two. Reasonable enough, except for the fact that the child I might kill is in no way connected with the death of my loved ones except through its father's evil will. The child itself does not stand in the way of my lifesaving action. The good results I could accomplish would be even greater if I save four men from a lynch mob by selecting a fifth for "judicial murder" to quiet their fury. In these cases, also, we must assume there is necessity enough, the characters mean what they say, the psychological deterrence is likely to work, there is no other recourse and two or four lives saved would be proportionately a greater good than one life taken. Still I judge we would say such direct killing would be wrong despite the good consequences.

66   Philippa Foot, "The Problem of Abortion and the Rule of Double Effect," in *Moral Problems,* ed. James Rachels, 2nd ed., (New York: Harper and Row, 1975), pp. 59-70.

67   McCormick needlessly fuzzes the issue by going on to speak of, as a parallel, uttering falsehood as a means to protect reputations.

68   The endeavor to bring charity within the ambit of proportionate reason seems to be related to the no less puzzling debate among contemporary Catholic moralists about whether there is a *distinctive Christian ethics*–to which question the majority answer in the negative. For many decades Protestants also (without debating about it) have been engaged in identifying Christian ethics with a generally humanistic morality.

69   Even after the encyclical *Humanae Vitae* there could still be for Roman Catholics a "veritable conflict of duties," as the French bishops expressed it. And Catholic moralists gained freedom of maneuver by paying special attention to a seemingly restrictive statement in that encyclical: "It is not licit, even for the gravest reasons, to do evil so that good may follow

therefrom, that is, to make into the object of a positive act of the will something which is intrinsically disordered." Since the intrinsic disorder of contraception was mentioned and doing evil so that good may come was ruled out, the discussion among moral theologians centered upon the meaning of "making into the object of a positive act of the will" *(in id voluntatem conferre)*. This should control the resolution of moral dilemmas rather than "intrinsically disordered" *physical* acts. Those words became the springboard for reinterpreting the meaning of direct intentionality, that is, the *human* action. So much so that it is said that the will does not *"in id conferre"* with pieces of physical behavior ranging from contraceptive interventions to killing a human being, so long as there is proportionate reason. This is the genesis of the revisionist views we have been discussing. Catholic moralists generalized beyond the case. Thus, McCormick is apt to say that "turning directly against" nonmoral good *means* doing evil or violating that good without proportionate reason. It is not farfetched to suggest that his notion of intending a disvalue *in se sed non propter se* is applicable principally to questions of intending the disvalue of contraceptive intercourse or the disvalue of sterilization *in se* but not *propter se*. When that analysis is moved to conflicts of incommensurate disvalues and the sin of another or killing a human being is intended *in ordine ad finem proportionatum,* the life and destiny of the human person are wrongly turned into pure means

CHAPTER FOUR

McCormick
and the
Traditional Distinction

by

William K. Frankena

In *Ambiguity and Moral Choice* McCormick reflects on the doctrine of double effect or, as he prefers to call it "the traditional distinction" between "what is directly voluntary and indirectly voluntary." He sees the whole matter simply as a subject of debate among Catholic moral theologians (except for a few pages on Foot), noting that there has been a traditional position in which the double effect is or was a "staple" (which I shall call the Position) and a recent reaction to it (the Reaction), and presenting his own view as a "tentative" critical "synthesis" not identifiable with either of them. The book consists of a review of six authors belonging to the Reaction (Knauer, Van der Marck, Van der Poel, Foot, Grisez, and Schüller) and a presentation of his own conclusions; what he thinks of the Position comes out only in the course of doing this, not in any separate or systematic study of it. My interest in the subject is not due to any wish to crash a Catholic party—which my father would have forbidden me to do—but to the fact that I see it in the context of a more general debate in moral philosophy that has been going on for some time, a debate ignored by McCormick, the Position, and the Reaction alike, but very relevant to their discussion, and, if I may say so, further advanced philosophically and carried out in clearer and more rigorous terms. I mean, however, primarily to try to learn from this encounter with Catholic moral theology; if at the same time I can do something that is of some use to McCormick and others who are interested in these matters, so much the better.

I

I shall not concern myself very much with the Reaction, about which I know little except what McCormick tells me in terms I do not find very clear, which may not be his fault. My interest is mainly in the Position, in McCormick's views about it, and in his own ethical theory or moral theology insofar as it is presented in his book (and in some relevant passages in one or two articles). As will become manifest, my sympathies are with him and the Reactors rather than with the Position.

As McCormick's title suggests, the discussion is about conflict situations and the relation of evils to moral choice—about the issues involved in that part of traditional Catholic morality that centers around the doctrine of double effect. Anything more comes in, if at all, only incidentally to the treatment of these topics. The problem is about situations in which an agent foresees or foresaw that an action open to him will or would have an evil effect along with others that are good or indifferent. Is such an action ever morally good, permissible, right, or tolerable? The question is one of moral guidance in such cases, and the emphasis is on not doing wrong, not acting ill, not being bad or culpable—on being morally in the clear in one's actions. Is one responsible for all foreseen or foreseeable effects? Are all and any evil effects relevant to a moral judgment on one's actions? Should one simply do what will give him the best score in terms of goods and evils added up? McCormick is deeply aware that there is or should be more to the moral life, but here he concentrates on this part of it, which certainly needs thinking on.

At once I must say that there is one aspect of McCormick's discussion that makes me unhappy. Like most moral theologians, Catholic and Protestant, he carries his discussion on almost entirely by the use of words like *good, bad, evil, evil in se, value, moral evil, immoral, morally acceptable;* he makes little or no use of *right, wrong, ought, duty, obligation,* or *a right.* That is, he mainly uses what I call aretaic terms and only occasionally deontic ones. As a result, I shall have to fall in with his usage more than I would like. But I must say it seems to me important and even necessary, as V.J. Bourke has recently recognized, (1) to distinguish moral goodness, virtue, and so on, as a predicate both of actions and of agents, their motives, character traits, and so forth, from moral rightness as a predicate of actions; (2) to take aretaic predicates of actions as dependent on facts and/or aretaic judgments about agents, and so on; and (3) to see deontic predicates of actions as depending, not on the agent's character, intentions, motives, and so on, but on an action's nature and/or consequences, that is on what it consists in, does, or sets in train.[1] For actions may be right—do the right thing or what one ought to do—and yet not be morally good if the agent's motive were morally bad or indifferent; or they may be morally good because of the agent's motives and other dispositions, and yet be wrong or do what one ought not to do. When one is asking what action one morally ought to do in a certain situation, one is not asking about one's motives, and so on, but about what one should set in train. All of this is relevant when one is assessing the Position, as I shall indicate, and when one is trying to interpret the force of expressions like *morally tolerable, justified, acting morally well, immoral,* and *malum in se,* in statements or criticisms of the Position.

II

Now that I have entered this complaint, let me try to state the Position as I understand it after readingMcCormick, Anscombe, Ford, Ramsey, and others.[2] While it is held mainly by Catholics, though losing ground among them, it is at least approximated by some Protestants, for example, Ramsey and Mortimer, and could be subscribed to in some form by secular and atheistic moralists.[3] Whatever its genesis and history, there is nothing necessarily Catholic, Christian, or theistic about it, though it may be less plausible in a completely natural and secular framework than in a religious or Catholic one. It might be intuitionistic in the British sense, regarding its basic norms or value judgments as logically and epistemologically autonomous; on the other hand, it might reject the "natural law" doctrine in all of its forms, and hold them to be positive divine laws, as theological voluntarists do. All that is essential to the Position, as I see it, at least for the present purposes, is the following set of propositions:

A. That there are, in the case of voluntary or willed actions, real, tenable, and important distinctions (all of which I am sure McCormick has in mind when he speaks of "the traditional distinction")

1. between actual effects, foreseen effects, and aimed at or desired effects,

2. between foreseen effects and intended effects, and

3. between intended effects and permitted effects (or between directly willed and indirectly willed effects), where under intended effects are included both those that are aimed at or desired, and those that are

not but are taken or willed as means to some other effect that is aimed at or desired, and where by permitted or indirectly willed effects is meant those that are indeed willed but not taken either as ends or as means.

B. That there are a number of kinds of evils, some moral and some nonmoral, which are such that it is absolutely or always morally bad or wrong (not just prima facie in Ross's sense or *ceteris paribus,* but *actually*) to will directly or bring about intentionally.

C. That among these *evils* are: death, or at least the death of an innocent human being; sterility; the sin of another; the state of being in adultery.

D. That, therefore, the following kinds of *actions* are absolutely bad or wrong, when directly or intentionally done: the killing of human beings, or at least of innocent ones; abortion; euthanasia; adultery; sterilization; contraception; apostasy; scandal, and cooperation in another's evildoing, in short, all kinds of actions in which any evil of the sorts in question is taken or intended either as an end or as a means.

E. That evils of the sorts listed may not even be permitted or allowed to happen voluntarily (that is, are not morally tolerable) except in certain conflict situations, but *may* be permitted or tolerated in such situations, *provided* that:

1. One's act of commission or omission in permitting them is not morally bad or wrong in itself or on other grounds;

2. One *both* intends a good effect *and* does not intend a bad or evil one of the sorts in question either as end or as means, that is, a good effect is intended and the evil effect foreseen is really only permitted;

3. The good effect intended and the evil effect permitted must arise simultaneously or equally immediately in the causal sequence (or be causally independent of one another) or, in other words, that the evil is not only not willed as a means to the intended effect, but actually is objectively not a means to it; and

4. Permitting the evil effect is justified by "grave proportionate reasoning"—for example by the fact that the only alternative is intentionally to produce one of the proscribed evils, or by the fact that all the alternatives would have much worse effects.

Some further remarks:

a. The stipulations immediately above under E summarize the rule of double effect.

b. It is not essential to the Position to hold any one view about what makes the evils listed absolutely evil or what makes intentional acts effecting them absolutely wrong or bad, or to hold any particular theory about how we know that death is such an evil or that intentional killing is so intolerable. But, of course, proponents of the Position do usually bring in the theory (or *a* theory) of natural law, whatever that is, at this point.

c. It is implied in the Position as stated above that the traditional distinction among effects is *morally relevant,* that is, the distinctions it includes are relevant to determining what moral judgment is to be made on an action or agent in situations in which an evil effect is voluntarily brought about.

d. It is also implied that those distinctions are *necessary* in such situations and may even be *decisive* or *sufficient* without further ado in bringing us to a valid moral judgment. In some cases, for example, knowing that an action or agent will or did directly intend, perhaps among other things some good, an evil effect of one of the kinds listed is enough to tell us that the action or agent is morally bad, wrong, or culpable without any further consideration of proportionate reasoning.

Thus, it is morally bad or wrong voluntarily and intentionally to kill an innocent human being, whatever the consequences, no matter what else happens; but it is not morally bad or wrong voluntarily to let or permit any number of innocent human beings to die, no matter what the consequences of this may be, if the only alternative is to kill one intentionally.

It follows that the questions at issue in the debate between the Position, the Reaction, and McCormick are these: whether distinctions are to be made between foreseen effects and effects aimed at, between intended and permitted effects; whether these distinctions are morally significant and, if so, in what ways; whether there are some kinds of evils or some kinds of actions that it is always wrong intentionally to bring about or do; whether the doctrine of double effect is a valid way of determining what it is morally right or wrong, good or bad, to do or forbear.

There is also a question about precisely which things are absolutely evil and which actions absolutely wrong, if any, but this is not crucial to the debate. The Reaction, I take it, either denies the validity of the distinctions between foreseen, intended, and permitted evils (A above) or their moral relevance (necessary, decisive, sufficient, and so on), or both. McCormick asserts both the validity of these distinctions and in some sense their moral relevance and importance, but agrees that they are not necessary in all cases and that they are never decisive or sufficient by themselves. Both he and the Reactors, as I understand them, deny that there are any absolutely exceptionless moral norms such as the Position (A-E) posits (and even Milhaven), excepting maybe the prohibition of scandal (intentionally causing or trying to cause another to sin, a moral evil).

III

As for McCormick's own position; it seems to have changed somewhat since 1968, possibly under the influence of Schüller and other Reactors. Even then he wrote in one article that

> . . . if man's being . . . is the basis for and the law of his becoming, and if we are now more sharply aware than ever of the historicity of his being, we will be forced to take a long second look at those norms formerly proposed as absolutely invariable.[4]

And he made it clear that he subscribed to the antecedent clauses in this statement. In the same year, however, in another essay, he seems to defend the absolute inviolability of precisely "those norms formerly proposed" against Milhaven, who maintains that, while some norms like love and courage are absolute, others like adultery and respect for life are not.[5] He only adds, in a somewhat puzzling way, that the problem of absolute prohibitions

> is not much of a problem; for even traditional theological categories—when properly understood—admitted very few absolute prohibitions.[6]

I say puzzling, because absolute prohibitions have been enough of a problem for him to feel it necessary to reply to Milhaven and to return to it in the present book.

In the same paper, McCormick says most Catholic moral theologians believe in "the primacy of charity (agape)" and are "love-monists" in Gustafson's sense (agapists in mine), holding "that reason's task within theological ethics is [merely] to discover the demands of Christian love."[7] This also puzzles me. For McCormick must be thinking that his statement is true of most Catholic proponents of the Position (and not just of himself and the Reaction), and yet, as I see it, they hold, not only that there are other absolute norms besides the law of love, in the sense of holding to absolute norms that make no reference to love, but also that these norms can be established without using the law of love as a premise—which is what pure agapists deny. I do not mean to suggest that any Catholic proponents of the Position would reject the New Testament summary of the moral law in the law of love; this would be un-Christian. But Christian moralists outside of Catholicism have often subscribed to this summary and not been agapists or love-monists, for example, Clarke, Butler, and, I take it, Gustafson, and I suspect this is true of insiders too, and in particular of Aquinas.

The point is that "Love is the fulfillment of the law" can be read in two ways: first, as saying that loving is our one and only basic duty or the one and only cardinal virtue; second, as saying that loving consists in fulfilling the law, where the content of the law is not found simply by using reason to discover the demands of love, as Fletcher thinks (and even rule-agapists), but perhaps by intuition or by an inquiry into the laws of nature or of nature's God. McCormick emphasizes the first way of reading but the second is indicated by one of his sentences:

> The following of Christ . . . will mean loving God *by keeping his commandments* . . . and loving one's neighbor as Jesus loved us. . . .[8]

I am not convinced that Catholic exponents of the Position would not favor the second reading—with the further understanding that God's commandments may be discovered in natural law as well as in revelation or in an inquiry into the demands of love.

IV

Be these things as they may, it looks to me as if McCormick has moved away from the Position and its absolute prohibitions, however few, toward a more clearly agapistic and monistic one—more or less in the direction taken by the Reaction, though probably without giving up his 1968 belief in "the existence of natural law." In a way this movement was anticipated in 1968 when he quoted with approval the following sentence from Ramsey: "The real issue is whether there are any agape- or koinonia-embodying rules, and, if there are, what these rules may be. . . ."[9]

The general conclusion of McCormick's present book is that "the traditional distinction between direct and indirect is neither as exclusively decisive as we previously thought, nor as widely dispensable as some recent studies suggest." His first main contention is that the distinctions made among effects (A above) are real and important, though he actually discusses only the intending/permitting distinction. I agree that all of the things distinguished in A can and should be distinguished. More debatable is the question which kinds of effects are to be said to be intended, those taken as ends, those taken as means, or both, or all that are foreseen and in some sense willed. This is a more disputed matter than McCormick here recognizes, but the answer depends partly on what one believes to be relevant to moral judgment, and the really interesting question is whether said distinctions are morally significant, and if so, how. As Anscombe puts it, "is one responsible for all the effects one foresees, or, better, are all the results one foresees relevant to any or all moral judgments made on one's action or on one's self?"[10]

I have myself always thought them all to be relevant to any judgment of the objective or material rightness of one's action but not to a judgment of its or one's own moral goodness or virtue, which is more a question of one's motives or ends, that is, of the effects one aims at or desires. If one prefers "ethics of virtue" talk one might express this by saying that all foreseen effects bear on a judgment about whether one is doing *what* a good person *would* do but not on a judgment about whether one is doing what one does *as* a good person would do it.

This view is, I believe, the usual view outside of Catholic and Protestant moral theology. But, in connection with the Position, the question is about the moral bearing of the fact that one intends certain effects either as ends or means as compared with the moral bearing of the effects one does not so intend but does voluntarily bring about. Faced with this question, I am still inclined to maintain that all foreseen (or even all actual) effects are relevant to the question of what I objectively ought to do or have done, while what I take as an end, what I take as a means, and what I permit are more relevant to judgments about the moral quality of my character or will. As McCormick himself says, what I intend and what I permit do tell something about me and my posture toward good and evil. If I am correct, then the Position is mistaken; but I am not sure that McCormick would agree with me, because, as I mentioned before, he seems not to employ any distinction between moral rightness and moral goodness any more than the Position does. In any case, I welcome his insight when he points out that a will that intends an evil effect, whether as end or as means, has a different moral quality from one that does not, and, particularly, from one that never does. It does not follow, however, that there is any difference in the material or objective rightness of their actions. Thus, while I agree with McCormick that the distinction between intending and permitting has moral importance, I am not sure he agrees with me about what this importance is.

V

More crucial for McCormick is the matter of the role in moral judgment of the traditional distinctions among effects and the rule of double effect. As we saw, for the Position both are necessary for dealing with conflict situations and often decisive in doing so; the distinctions among effects express the basic structure of such situations and the doctrine of double effect is our chief guide in making moral choices in them and in making moral judgments about choices made in them. Proportionate reason (PR) has a subordinate, though important, role—that of determining which acts of permitting evil, among those that meet the other qualifications, are justified and morally acceptable. The list of absolute prohibitions and the traditional distinctions among effects do the rest. McCormick rejects all this, though rather tentatively.

> The basic structure . . . in conflict situations is avoidable/unavoidable evil, the principle of the lesser evil . . . in situations of this kind, the rule of Christian reason, if we are governed by the *ordo bonorum,* is to choose the lesser evil . . . or proportionate reason.

I take this to mean that, even in the problem cases with which the distinctions among effects and the rule of double effect were designed to deal, the true solution is to weigh the goods and evils foreseen and to choose the best or least evil course, that is, the course of action or inaction that has the best or least bad effects, because this is what PR consists in for McCormick. If one does this, and acts accordingly, then one's action and the posture of one's will are morally satisfactory even if one *takes as a means* some evil effect like death or sterility, even if one intends to bring it about and is not just permitting it. One may not be a moral saint, but one is morally in the clear in all respects. (To bring about death or sterility cannot, on any view, be morally acceptable if one takes such evils *as an end.*)

McCormick thinks there really is no "reasonable, defensible alternative to this [view]," and this may be; but (apart from the abortion case in which without killing the child directly both the child and the mother will die) he does rather little to show that the Position is unreasonable and indefensible. He does argue that "the only alternative is that in conflict situations we should choose the greater evil, which is patently absurd." But it surely will not do to suggest that the Position can be polished off so easily as this. McCormick also ignores the possibility of a reasonable antiteleological or deontological alternative; in fact, like other Catholic moral theologians, he simply assumes that PR must take a teleological form—that ethical reasoning is entirely a matter of weighing good against bad effects (except perhaps if scandal is involved). It should at least be noted, therefore, that there has been in moral philosophy a long and honorable tradition rather different from the teleological one McCormick belongs to, one which is also opposed to the Position and has recently mounted some sharp criticisms of the line of thinking he espouses.

One can, in fact, take a deontological line in analyzing and dealing with conflict situations, without falling into a situational ethics with principles no stronger than rules of thumb, even if one gives up both the traditional distinctions among effects and the rule of double effect. This was, if I am not mistaken, the view of the British deontological intuitionists from Clarke to Ross, excepting maybe Prichard and Carritt in some of their writings, as well as of Kant. On such a view, the fact that an evil effect follows from a voluntary action is not necessarily, if ever, decisive, since it holds that the goodness and badness of an act's consequences, actual, foreseen, or aimed at, are not the only considerations that matter, as they are for the Position in its Catholic form, for the Reactors, and for McCormick. Such a view may still posit "deontologically exceptionless" norms, as Kant did, but it need not; Ross, for example, holds a number of general truths about prima facie rightness and wrongness (and no general truths about actual duty) to be self-evident and stronger than rules of thumb, including principles of beneficence and of nonmaleficence, but also others that may take priority over them.[11] This view entails regarding as ultimately decisive some kind of weighing of alternatives such as Anscombe, speaking for the Position, claims to be "corrupt";[12] but it is rather a weighing of rightnesses and wrongnesses than of goods and evils, and hence is not utilitarian—whether that is bad or not.

If one believes in unconditional evils, it may be possible to maintain that there are absolutely inviolable norms without being a deontologist, even if one gives up both the traditional distinctions among effects and the rule of double effect; but then one must live with the conflict cases they were designed to deal with. Now, as Foot points out, some of these cases are such as to lend favor to the doctrine of double effect, for example, those involving what has been called "judicial murder" and "cooperation with another's sin." Others, however, as she also points out, are such that the "Catholic doctrine on abortion must here conflict with that of most reasonable men," for example, "the situation in which nothing that can be done will save the life of child and mother, but where the life of the mother can be saved by killing the child.''[13] The Position must maintain that in this situation one must permit both to die. It is, I think, this case that convinces Ramsey and McCormick and the Reactors—not just reasonable men but Christians—that something is wrong with the Position. Foot concludes that we must give up the rule of double effect and replace it with an emphasis on the distinction between positive and negative duties. I think I agree with McCormick that this move is not adequate for dealing with all the cases or for saving something like the Position.[14] In any event, if I understand him, McCormick is here giving up both the rule of double effect and the belief that there are any absolutely exceptionless norms (other than the prohibition of scandal) except that of love or the *ordo bonorum* (I take it that he equates these). He also relegates the traditional distinctions among effects to a secondary, if important, role in the process of proportionate reasoning (that is, of weighing goods and evils).

Possibly he does not give up the doctrine of double effect entirely. One passage at least suggests that he may mean to retain it, not as a principle, as it is in the tradition, but as a vehicle, useful in "mediating and concretizing the more general principle [of choosing the lesser evil]." I take it that Ramsey also uses the doctrine of double effect to mediate and concretize a more general principle: Christian love.[15] Still, it seems to me that McCormick has in mind retaining the distinction between intended and unintended effects only in the secondary role just referred to (and still to be explained). If one gives up exceptionless principles, there is not much reason, if any, for retaining the doctrine of double effect in any capacity.

VI

So far, McCormick's position is like that of Fletcher and Robinson as well as that of Ramsey, but now comes an important parting of the ways.[16] Fletcher and Robinson, act-agapists and act-utilitarians, go on to propound a kind of "situation ethics" that allows general principles only in the form of maxims or rules of thumb generalized from previous cases.[17] Ramsey goes on to argue for exceptionless moral rules after all—for a rule-agapism that generates such rules, not on some independent ground as natural law doctrine does, but out of the law of love itself. The logical possibility of doing this was made clear by Berkeley in

Passive Obedience (1712), when he reasoned from the well-being of humankind—"the end proposed by God"—to "certain universal rules of morality," including some absolute prohibitions, one of them forbidding active disobedience to rulers. The question is what McCormick does. It looks as if he means to steer a course between the situationalists' Scylla and Ramsey's Charybdis, but to see better we must review what he says about PR, that is, about ethical reasoning.

It must consist for him in a predicting and weighing of goods and evils. In conflict situations he says, it involves showing three things, namely, that

> (a) a value at least equal to that sacrificed is at stake; (b) there is no less harmful way of protecting the value here and now; and (c) the manner of its protection here and now will not undermine it [or block the maximization of good?] in the long run.

McCormick is rightly insistent that PR entails the fullest possible consideration of long-run and indirect effects of alternative courses of action, not just of direct or short-run results, but this is a point that has long been observed by utilitarians, if not by agapists. He is also insistent, of course, that the only adequate kind of teleological reasoning is one that goes on in a fully Christian perspective, which has not been usual among utilitarians, who have tended to be more this-worldly.

Coming to cases, McCormick plumps for a straightforward application of teleological PR of the sort just described to the questions of capital punishment, self-defense, deception to preserve professional secrets, self-sterilization to prevent pregnancy by rape, indirect sterilization by a physician, and taking innocent or noncombatant lives in war—all whether the intentionality is direct or indirect. Here he cites with apparent approval the teleological (and I would say utilitarian) kinds of arguments used by Zalba and Allen, and he specifically agrees that direct or intentional deception and self-sterilization is justifiable teleologically in the cases mentioned. What is more interesting at this point, however, is the fact that McCormick thinks the principle of noncombatant immunity, or of not taking innocent lives as a means in war, can be established as a "practical absolute" or "virtually exceptionless principle" by such teleological arguments, and, especially, that taking their lives intentionally can be plausibly shown to have much worse effects in the long run than only permitting them to to be killed—and that this is true "because of the [kind of] intentionality involved," that is, *because* one is intending their deaths and not merely permitting them.

> Taking innocent human life as a means removes restraints and unleashes destructive powers which both now and in the long run will brutalize sensitivities and take many more lives than we would now save by such action. We cannot prove this type of assertion with a syllogistic click, but it is a good human bet given our knowledge of ourselves and our history—at least good enough to generate a practically exceptionless imperative. . . .

This is interesting because it shows how McCormick thinks the distinction between intending and permitting is of importance in ethical reasoning, even if the Position is given up in favor of a straight teleological approach. I find his point here plausible but also unclear. It may well be that it is useful in the long run to discountenance certain kinds of intending dispositions while not discountenancing certain kinds of permitting dispositions, if this is what McCormick is suggesting. But what does this show? That the distinction between intending and permitting is relevant to judgments about what actions are objectively right or wrong, or that it is relevant to judgments about the moral goodness or badness of some postures of the will as against others?

In any event, we also see here that McCormick is seeking a *via media* between Fletcher or Robinson *and* Berkeley or Ramsey. What he says is cryptic and none too clear, but he seems to be thinking that a teleological and agapistic method of ethics can establish moral principles that are not just maxims or rules of thumb but are also not exceptionless. This is where one wants to hear more. In particular, one wants to know just what McCormick's conception of the nature of those principles is. In his brief answer to this question he alternates between saying that such norms are to be "held as exceptionless" and saying that they are to be "held as virtually exceptionless"—in either case on the basis of "nondemonstrable calculations" or "prudential [that is, teleological] judgments based on both the certainties of history and the uncertainties of the future." Now, this suggests to an outsider like me that what he has in mind is rules of the kind favored by rule-utilitarians like Berkeley and Brandt, except that McCormick vacillates a little between thinking they should be held as absolutes and thinking they should be held as virtual absolutes, which is different.[18] That is, he seems to envisage a utilitarian line of argument for the conclusion that, in our positive morality, we should adopt as actually or virtually exceptionless certain norms or rules like—well, I suppose, almost exactly like the absolutes of the Position. If he means "adopt as actually exceptionless" his position is essentially like Berkeley's or Ramsey's, otherwise it is only practically or virtually like theirs. I assume he would choose the latter alternative—if he means to be a rule-teleologist at all.

This last I say, because most of the time McCormick's actual sketches of his kind of PR make it look like an application of what on the outside is called act-utilitarianism.

> To see whether an action involving evil is proportionate in the circumstances we must judge whether this choice is the best possible service of all the values in the tragic and difficult conflict. What is the best possible promotion of all the values in the circumstances will depend on how one defines *in the circumstances*. A truly adequate account of the circumstances will read them to mean not just how much *quantitative* good can be salvaged from an individual conflict of values, but it will also weigh the social implications and reverberating aftereffects insofar as they can be foreseen. It will put the choice to the test of generalizability ("What if all men in similar circumstances were to act in this way?"). It will consider the cultural climate, especially in terms of the biases and reactions it is likely to favor in a one-sided way. It will draw whatever wisdom it can from past experience and reflection, particularly as embodied in the rules people of the past have found a useful guide in difficult times. It will seek the guidance of others whose maturity, experience, reflection, and distance from the situation offer a counterbalance to the self-interested tendencies we all experience. It will allow the full force of one's own religious faith and its intentionalities to interpret the meaning and enlighten the options of the situation. This is what an adequate and responsible account of the circumstances must mean. So informed, an individual is doing the best he can and all that can be expected of him. But to say these things is to say that an individual will depend on communal discernment much more than our contemporary individualistic attitudes suggest.

Except for one sentence, this is just what a good act-utilitarian would say, as is the line of argument McCormick borrows from Joseph L. Allen. The one sentence is, of course, that which mentions "the test of generalizability," and, if he really means that in our PR we must always (or at least sometimes) apply this test, then McCormick's method of ethics begins to resemble Singer's general utilitarianism, rather than either act- or rule-utilitarianism.[19]

VII

McCormick himself denies that PR is "reducible to a simple utilitarian calculus," and of course it is not, if one puts the emphasis on the word *simple*. But, as was noted, good rule- and even good act-utilitarians do not regard their *calculations* (McCormick's own word) as simple. And on the basis of what we have seen *thus far* I see no alternative but to interpret McCormick as a utilitarian of some sort, though presumably not a hedonistic one—and I do not mean this as a criticism, though I am not a utilitarian myself. My question has been, "Of what sort?"

At this point, however, McCormick says, "The notion of proportionate reason is analogous" and argues that it takes three different forms. He cites the case of the soldier choosing between throwing himself on a live explosive to save the life or lives of others, mentioning that moral theologians (of the Position?) have regarded self-sacrifice in such a situation as heroic but not obligatory; there is a PR reason for doing it and a PR for not doing it; it is right or good to do but not wrong or bad not to do (that is, it is not wrong or bad to permit the others to die). Then he adds that, if one is attacked by an assailant, PR will likewise justify either one's killing the assailant or allowing him to kill oneself, unless more can be said about it. To deal with this case (and others), McCormick again insists that "the criterion of proportionality is [the] *ordo bonorum* viewed in Christian perspective," for this is what is determinative of what one should do, that is, it is "the criterion of the objectively loving character of one's activity." But then he argues that this criterion operates in different ways in three kinds of situations.

1. Take the abortion dilemma in which, without killing, both will die; or other situations in which the only alternative to causing or permitting evil is greater evil, for example, that of the bystander who cannot swim but sees a man drowning. Here, McCormick holds, it would be immoral for the bystander to try; in the abortion case it would be immoral not to save the mother. I agree about the latter example; but I am very doubtful that we should judge the bystander to be immoral or acting badly if he were to jump in and try to rescue the drowning person. We certainly should not judge his character or motives to be bad and would probably think it desirable to foster such dispositions as he manifests. McCormick may reply that his jumping in is still objectively wrong, but then he must distinguish between rightness and goodness in the way I have advocated.

2. Now consider other cases in which I lay down my life for another (one other), for example, my friend or my assailant. Here there are ostensibly equal goods at stake, my life and his life; I must choose, and a "simple utilitarian calculus" will yield either conclusion. But, if I understand him, McCormick himself holds that I *should* sacrifice my life, even for the assailant. Apart from raising the question whether it is *bad* or *wrong* not to sacrifice oneself or let oneself be killed in such instances, this is interesting because it suggests two ways of interpreting McCormick's position. One is to say that he is here finally rejecting utilitarianism and straight teleologism, in all their forms, in favor of an agapistic ethics of Christian love that does not ultimately answer moral questions on the basis of "prudential calculations" or weighing good and evil, however long-run or indirect—an ethics of love, in other words, which transcends even the *ordo bonorum*. However, McCormick also refers to securing my neighbor's life even at the cost of mine as "a human and Christian *good*," though only in "a world of conflict and sin," and this suggests that it constitutes an added value to be considered in our "prudential calculations," one which (always?) throws the balance to the side of self-sacrifice. Then he may still be a straight teleologist of a utilitarian kind, subscribing to a type of "ideal" or nonhedonistic and "impersonal utilitarianism" or "extended rule-utilitarianism" (depending on McCormick's choice between these).[20]

McCormick could help himself in dealing with these two kinds of cases if he were to distinguish more than he does between two questions: (a) What action is it objectively right (or wrong) to do in a certain situation? and (b) What action is such that in doing it the agent would be good, heroic, or saintly (or bad, and so on)? He could then say that I am not doing wrong if I lay down my life *or* if I do not lay it down, but I am being good, heroic, or saintly if I do—if he can marshal an appropriate piece of PR to show this.

3. In yet another kind of case, McCormick contends with "scholastic tradition" that an action or omission may be said to be proportionately grounded when and

> because the preference of a good for or in another at the cost of that good in or for myself should not, in view of human weakness and immaturity, be demanded.

One could argue for this view in a straightforwardly utilitarian way (either act or rule), by trying to show that our *demanding* such self-sacrifices is itself not finally for the greatest good, though *praising* them may be. Sacrifices might then still be good or even obligatory in themselves, as McCormick seems to hold in discussing the previous cases, but in our positive social morality we should not insist that omitting them is bad or wrong, even if we do teach that sacrifice is better. Is this what McCormick is thinking? I am not sure. What he says is that in this world the ideal of love is best advanced if we proclaim it but do not press its demand too hard. Is this another way of saying that the good is most promoted if we praise self-sacrifice but do not demand it? Or is Christian love somehow more than a concern for good that can be poured into some utilitarian bottle? In any event, what McCormick writes here once more seems to imply the idea of a positive morality in which some norms are insisted on as exceptionless or virtually exceptionless and some "ideal rules," as they have been called,[21] are taught but not insisted on—all somehow on the basis of an ethics of love or of concern for good of which this positive morality is a "vehicle," but which, being itself absolute, knows "nothing of 'excusing causes,' 'extraordinary measures,' 'excessive inconvenience,' etc.," as McCormick says Jesus did not. That is, basic morality is simply a matter of love or of concern for the good of persons and other sentient beings, but there is or should be also a positive morality, social and/or ecclesiastical, which on the one hand may insist on the letter of a rule when the spirit would not, and on the other may ask less than the spirit would when the flesh is weak. As I indicated earlier, such a view would be a kind of rule-agapism or rule-utilitarianism, one about which one would also like to hear more. It would at least imply making a clearer distinction between basic morality and positive social morality than McCormick makes, which could also be used in handling the cases in 1 and 2 above. It would probably also require dividing positive social morality into two parts: one in which certain things are demanded or forbidden and another in which certain things are praised or dispraised or even blamed, that is, into a deontic and an aretaic part.

VIII

Since McCormick may yet be what we outsiders call a utilitarian of some sort, it should be pointed out, as was intimated earlier, that deontologists have advanced some objections to all forms of utilitarianism. Like many others, I myself have contended that a principle of justice is needed for an adequate morality *in addition* to any principle of beneficence or utility (or love, for that matter).[22] Donagan has also argued very forcefully that, whatever is true of our world (and this is not clear),

> it can hardly be doubted that a world in which the good of the people sometimes would require [judicial murder] is *possible,* and that, in such a world, [even] rule-utilitarians would be committed to the position of Caiaphas.[23]

McCormick himself uses the case of judicial murder in criticizing Schüller but he seems to think that such a taking of an innocent life, which he calls "appalling," can always be shown to be wrong in this world by a consideration of its long-run effects (which he seems to think Schüller would not take into account). But, if Donagan's kind of argument is cogent, it shows that a consideration of long-run consequences, whether done in act-utilitarian or in rule-utilitarian style, cannot serve to make any form of utilitarianism credible. One must, if Donagan is right, posit as absolute the principle of never treating an individual merely as a means, in addition to or as part of any other principle one may hold. Something like this, of course, is what the Position did in the first place, and McCormick may want to reply by claiming that Donagan must use the traditional distinctions among effects and the rule of double effect if he is to make his own view credible. On the other hand, McCormick may just concede, as I think I would, that what is appalling may sometimes, or in some possible worlds, be morally tolerable as the lesser of two evils.

McCormick might, however, answer that love, or at least Christian love, is more than a concern for the good (and the *ordo bonorum?*), and that an ethics of love can rule out treating an individual as a means even if a utilitarian or teleological ethics cannot. Some Christian writers have, I think, conceived of agape in such a way, but I see nothing in what I have read of McCormick to prove that he does.[24] Moreover, as was just intimated, to conceive of it as proscribing absolutely every action of treating oneself or another as a means only is to return to something like the Position, and brings one back again face-to-face with apparently irresolvable conflicts of life with life as in the abortion case—which, in a sense, is where this discussion began.

My impression has been that Catholic moral theologians have thought harder about practice and cases than secular moral philosophers, while the latter have thought harder about ethical theory. It follows that each group has much to learn from the other, and, perhaps this paper does something to show this. At least it shows that some members of the two groups, all too unknowingly, may be moving in the same direction.

ENDNOTES FOR CHAPTER FOUR

1 V. J. Bourke, "Aquinas and Recent Theories of Right," (Washington: Proceedings American Catholic Philosophical Association, 1975).
2 See the essays by G. E. M. Anscombe and J. C. Ford in *War and Morality,* ed. R. A. Wasserstrom (Belmont, CA: Wadsworth Publishing Co., 1970); Paul Ramsey, *War and the Christian Conscience* (Durham, NC: Duke University Press, 1961), chaps. 3-4.
3 See R. C. Mortimer, *Christian Ethics* (Atlantic Highlands, NJ: Hutchinson's University Library, 1950), chap. 8.
4 Richard A. McCormick, "The Moral Theology of Vatican II," in *The Future of Ethics and Moral Theology,* eds. D. Vrezine and J. V. McGlynn (Niles, IL: Argus Communications Co., 1968), pp. 7-8.
5 J. G. Milhaven, *Toward a New Catholic Morality* (Garden City, NY: Doubleday and Co., 1972), chaps. 9-10.
6 Richard A. McCormick, "Human Significance and Christian Significance," in *Norm and Context in Christian Ethics,* eds. Gene Outka and Paul Ramsey (New York: Charles Scribner's Sons, 1968), pp. 252, 260.
7 Ibid., pp. 234-35.
8 Ibid., p. 234 (italics added).
9 Ibid., p. 243.
10 G. E. M. Anscombe, "War and Murder," in *War and Morality,* p. 50.
11 W. D. Ross, *The Right and the Good* (Oxford: Clarendon Press, 1930), chap 2.
12 G. E. M. Anscombe, "Modern Moral Philosophy," reprinted in *Ethics,* eds. J. J. Thomson and G. Dworkin (New York: Harper and Row, 1968), p. 207.
13 Philippa Foot, "The Problem of Abortion and the Doctrine of Double Effect," in *Moral Problems,* ed. J. Rachels (New York: Harper and Row, 1971), pp. 28-41.
14 See also J. J. Thomson, "Killing, Letting Die, and the Trolley Problem," *The Monist* 59 (1976): 204-17.
15 For Ramsey's position, as referred to in this essay, see his *War and the Christian Conscience* (n. 2 above); his essay in *Norm and Context in*

Christian Ethics; and *Deeds and Rules in Christian Ethics* (New York: Charles Scribner's Sons, 1967).

16 See Joseph Fletcher, *Situation Ethics* (Philadelphia: Westminster Press, 1966); J. A. T. Robinson, *Honest to God* (London: SCM Press, 1963), chap. 6.

17 On act-agapism, rule-agapism, act-utilitarianism, rule-utilitarianism, general utilitarianism, and so on, see William K. Frankena, *Ethics,* 2nd ed., (Englewood Cliffs, NJ: Prentice-Hall, 1973), chap. 3.

18 For Brandt's views see R. B. Brandt, *Ethical Theory* (Englewood Cliffs, NJ: Prentice-Hall, 1959), chap. 15; "Toward a Credible Form of Utilitarianism," reprinted in M. D. Bayles, *Contemporary Utilitarianism* (Garden City, NY: Anchor Books, 1968), pp. 143-86.

19 See M. G. Singer, *Generalization in Ethics* (New York: Alfred Knopf, 1961).

20 See Brandt, *Ethical Theory.*

21 See G. E. Moore, *Philosophical Studies* (Atlantic Island, NJ: Humanities Press, 1951), pp. 320-23.

22 See Frankena, *Ethics,* pp. 41-43.

23 Alan Donagan, "Is There a Credible Form of Utilitarianism?" in Bayles, *Contemporary Utilitarianism,* pp. 187-202.

24 See Gene Outka, *Agape* (New Haven: Yale University Press, 1972); F. S. Carney, "On Frankena and Religious Ethics," *Journal of Religious Ethics* (Spring 1975): 7-25; D. Z. Phillips, "The Christian Concept of Love," in *Christian Ethics and Contemporary Philosophy,* ed. Ian Ramsey (London: SCM Press, 1966), pp. 314-28.

CHAPTER FIVE

The Double Effect in Catholic Thought: a Reevaluation

by

Bruno Schüller, S.J.

The moral rightness or wrongness of any human action or omission is determined by the principle of double effect. That is P. Knauer's view, expressed some years ago in several articles. This is a highly original thesis, no doubt; but it is also a thesis quite apt to provoke skeptical reserve. The so-called principle of double effect, at least as a set of formulated rules, appears to be the exclusive property of Catholic moral theology. It serves the purpose of morally assessing certain actions fairly complicated in their structure. To many non-Catholic ethicists this principle is the upshot of a dubious casuistry. Would it be reasonable to presume that by a principle like that the moral character of all human actions is determined? Scarcely.

On closer inspection, however, it becomes clear that Knauer is referring not to the principle of double effect as understood by Catholic tradition, but to the principle as understood *correctly*.[1] A statement like that attracts attention. If traditional moral theology was mistaken, one is anxious to learn what is the proper understanding of the principle of double effect. To put it briefly, the principle, if interpreted correctly, means consequentialism or a teleological theory of normative ethics. Knauer does not employ these terms. Apparently they were unknown to him when he wrote his articles. Nevertheless, there cannot be the slightest doubt that Knauer's thesis is to be counted among the teleological theories.

Knauer continues to use the specific vocabulary used by traditional theology to formulate the principle of double effect. But he thoroughly

165

redefines the key terms. To someone familiar with the traditional doctrine it may be fascinating to observe Knauer's argumentative strategy.
Step by step the traditional doctrine is transformed into a consistent
teleological theory. However, this finally leaves me with certain regrets.
Knauer puts consequentialism, a new wine to Catholic theology, into
old wineskins. By doing so he unnecessarily exposes himself to many
misinterpretations.

Some years ago I attempted to show that within a teleological theory
the principle of double effect, as used by tradition, is virtually superfluous.[2] I admitted one exception. From a teleological viewpoint the principle seems to hold good when we are to appraise actions apt to induce
other people to sin. In this regard I believe I am in agreement with
Knauer, who, in redefining it, also makes the principle of double effect
virtually redundant.

After a thorough and penetrating analysis of our arguments, R.
McCormick comes to the conclusion that he must disagree with us at
least with regard to one crucial point. There is little doubt that he too
endorses a teleological theory of normative ethics. He too, therefore,
thinks it necessary to reinterpret the principle of double effect in some
ways I am inclined to consider very momentous. But after doing that he
attempts to prove that precisely on teleological grounds the principle of
double effect is morally significant in some areas other than those where
actions inducing to sin are concerned.

McCormick expresses himself very clearly. Nonetheless, it is not
clear to me exactly at what point our disagreement begins. Perhaps this
statement seems somewhat odd. The reason for my difficulty is apparently the principle of double effect itself. It is comparatively easy to
apply this principle correctly, but extremely difficult to give a satisfactory account of its meaning and validity. As for myself, for many years
as a teacher of moral theology I have had to handle the principle very
often. I have had to handle it also in the course of discussions with my
colleagues. I cannot remember one single case in which I was criticized
for making an incorrect use of the principle. But it was only a few years
ago that it first dawned upon me how the principle is to be understood.
However, while considering how to respond to McCormick's criticism,
I became more and more doubtful whether I had really grasped the
proper meaning of the principle. I find the matter highly intricate. As of
now, it strikes me that the principle, when applied to actions inducing to
morally wrong behavior, differs remarkably from the principle as commonly employed to interpret such a norm as the prohibition of killing. At

any rate, before commenting on McCormick's criticism, I think it very advisable to try to explain the role that in my view the principle of double effect plays in traditional moral theology.

The Principle of Double Effect According to Traditional Theology

Anglo-American moral philosophers generally divide normative theories into two classes: (1) teleological (utilitarian, consequentialist) and (2) deontological (formalist) theories. Teleological theories are said to assert that the moral rightness of any action is *exclusively* determined by its consequences. The expression *deontological* in this context is defined as "nonteleological." Consequently, anyone who holds that at least some actions are morally determined *not exclusively* by their results has to be counted among the deontologists.

Such a division in the form of a flawless disjunction possesses a sort of logical elegance. However, this elegance has its price. The class of deontological theories comprises members so different in character that dangerous ambiguities could be precluded, were they called by different names. Reflecting on the discussions held in the past few years among moral theologians, I believe it necessary to draw a distinction at least between the two following views, both deontological in character: (2a) The moral rightness of any action is determined always *also,* but not always *solely,* by its consequences. (2b) There are at least some actions whose moral quality is completely independent of their consequences.

Obviously traditional Catholic theology holds a deontological theory of the stronger type (2b). And as is evident to those who have followed the recent controversies, an increasing number of Catholic theologians doubt or even bluntly deny that their own tradition is right in believing some actions morally wrong irrespective of their results. Many of them seem to regard a pure consequentialism (1) as the only alternative open to them. Apparently they overlook the weaker form of a deontological theory, even though by adopting it they would find their main problems solvable in a way satisfactory to them.

Yet suppose these theologians, probably unfamiliar with Anglo-American ethics, would be reminded of the difference between a pure consequentialism (1) and the weaker form of a deontological theory (2a). I venture to say that the vast majority of them would consider the difference as academically interesting to people like professors of philosophy and theology, but virtually irrelevant to someone preoccupied with concrete moral questions. I share this view myself.

The formulation of teleological theories is put also as follows. In the last resort there is only one principle to determine whether or not an action is right, the principle of benevolence. Now, if a theologian is allowed to understand "benevolence" as "love" in the sense of agape, in all probability he regards himself as a teleologist. For he accepts as certain that the second tablet of the decalogue is "summed up in this single command: You must love your neighbor as yourself."[3] The deontological theories of the weaker form are also described as assuming two or three or even more moral principles in no way reducible to one single principle. A Catholic theologian will probably be amazed when told that, for instance, justice and fairness as moral principles can in no way be accounted for by the commandment of love. In 1953 R. Carpentier, a Belgian Jesuit, wrote that the problem of teaching moral theology essentially consists "dans la formulation, concrétisée, 'spécifiée' de mille manières, de la charité, mère et racine des vertus."[4] To my knowledge no one objected to such a statement as this. It is quite possible that the exact manner in which justice or fairness are to be conceived of as ultimately founded on love (benevolence and beneficence), has not yet been established by Catholic theologians in a wholly satisfactory way. But that need not embarrass us much for the moment. I suppose Catholic theologians take it for granted that in appraising the results of an action we have to apply the principles of justice and fairness. The controversial issue, then, is only whether justice and fairness are to be regarded as specific mediations of love or as independent principles forming with the principle of benevolence a coalition to govern persons' morally right behavior. From this it should be clear what I mean when I say of McCormick or Kanuer that they have adopted or favor a teleological theory. They hold view 1 which they, as I strongly presume, consider materially identical with view 2a, at least *grosso modo*.

The main problem in the field of normative ethics, however, that has been commanding moral theologians' attention since about 1964 is the traditional claim that there are some actions whose moral wrongness has nothing to do with their results. The problem may be put into the excruciating question of how a "love ethic" can consider as morally wrong any course of action that would spare human beings harm and suffering. For convenience sake let me introduce the expression *deontological norm* and understand by it any action or omission that is thought right or wrong whatever its consequences.

As far as I can see, traditional Catholic theology holds deontological norms of two different kinds. (1) An action is believed to be illicit because it frustrates the finality of a natural (God-given) faculty. Thus telling a lie is said to be forbidden because it is contrary to the natural purpose of human language; contraceptive devices are considered wrong because they are contrary to the natural purpose of sexual intercourse. (2) An action is thought of as morally unlawful because performed without the required authorization *(ex defectu iuris in agente)*. Suicide is illicit because God alone is entitled to give and take life. If we prescind for the moment from an evaluation of these two ways of establishing deontological norms, it appears to me very important that moral theologians of former times were also aware of the peculiar problems deontological norms may produce. They took pains to mitigate these problems or even to remove them altogether. In pursuing this aim they made use of a procedure which I would like to call "restrictive interpretation." In a way it reminds one of the rule laid down for the interpretation of ecclesiastical laws. *"In odiosis interpretatio stricta, in favorabilibus interpretatio lata locum habet."* (A strict or narrow interpretation is in place where afflictive matters are concerned; a broad interpretation is called for in favorable matters.) Because in my view the principle of double effect in the most important and most debatable cases of its application serves precisely the purpose of a restrictive interpretation of deontological norms, I think it apppropriate to illustrate by way of two examples what this interpretation, when practiced, looks like.

The first example is well known. Suppose it is illicit to tell a lie (an untruth) whatever the consequences. Immediately the question arises about our duties if telling an untruth is the only means to keep an important secret or to shield other people from serious harm. Immanuel Kant and J. G. Fichte do not hesitate to claim that even in such cases as these telling an untruth would be far from morally justified. Catholic moral theologians, especially of the older school, insist with no less emphasis on the invariable illicitness of lying, but do not fail to add that telling a lie is never the only and, therefore, necessary means to keeping an important secret. In conflict situations like the one just mentioned, one is always in a position to employ ambiguous phrases or the so-called "broad mental reservation." The meaning of the expression *telling an untruth* circumscribes the scope or range of the normative proposition "telling an untruth is invariably unlawful." By defining telling an untruth in a way that excludes ambiguous phrases and the like, one narrows the scope or reach of the deontological prohibition. The result is that the clause "whatever the consequences" becomes completely harmless even in the eyes of a teleologist. Not quite satisfied with the fairly subtle distinction between telling an untruth and making use of a "broad mental reservation," moral theologians have for many years been making other proposals as to how the unlawfulness of lying is to be interpreted. All proposals have in common the aim of avoiding the conclusion that observance of the deontological prohibition of telling an untruth could ever lead to social harm.

In the recent past this same procedure of restrictive interpretation is applied by many theologians who on the one hand think it necessary to uphold the absolute indissolubility of Christian marriage, but on the other hand are anxious to ensure that extreme hardships are avoided. Only for those couples who are confronted with the disintegration of their marriage is the institutional impossibility of a second marriage of a really existential concern. Now, in examining the reasons why marriages often fail, one concludes that certain factors precluded the validity of marriage from the beginning, for instance lack of mental maturity. And there is no doubt that a marriage, if null and void from the beginning, cannot be indissoluble.

According to tradition only sacramental and consummated marriages are indissoluble absolutely. A marriage is regarded as sacramental if husband and wife are both baptized persons, and as consummated if the act of sexual intercourse has been performed. Both institutional regulations, many theologians argue, should be reconsidered and deepened. Simply being baptized, they say, cannot be sufficient for attributing sacramentality to marriage. Personal faith and Christian commitment are additional requirements. In the same way sexual intercourse, as a mere physical occurrence, could not make marriage absolutely indissoluble. In order to have this effect it ought to be the expression of conjugal love. It is immediately evident that by enlarging in this way the number of conditions under which marriage is to be taken for sacramental and consummated, one diminishes the number of marriages that are, because sacramental and consummated, absolutely indissoluble. However, this result cannot be called desirable without qualification. The number of marriages to be taken for null and void increases correspondingly. In order to avoid this result some theologians advocate a revision of the traditional doctrine that marriage between Christians, if valid, is also sacramental. But once we assume that a marriage between Christians can be valid without simultaneously being sacramental, a further conclusion emerges: a marriage, if sacramental and consummated, involves the institutional impossibility of a second *sacramental* marriage, but not of a second *nonsacramental* one. Consequently one can easily conceive of circumstances under which divorced and remarried people are to be admitted to the sacrament of the eucharist.

These two examples make clear, I hope, what I understand by a restrictive interpretation of deontological norms. An action considered as wrong regardless of its consequences is subjected to a restrictive definition with regard to its consequences. This procedure, usually being applied spontaneously, may justify the presumption that Catholic moral theology holds deontological norms only *contr'coeur*. It would be interesting to describe and analyze other devices which also serve the purpose of tackling the specific problems of norms considered valid irrespective of their results. For instance, H. Thielicke's doctrine of compromise has the characteristic features of such a device. But for the moment the question at issue is how to account for the principle of double effect. And as I have already pointed out, in my view the principle when applied to deontological norms amounts to a restrictive interpretation of them.

As far as I know, there are only two cases where traditional theology makes use of the principle in a context of purely teleological considerations. These cases are: (1) actions apt to induce other people to a morally wrong behavior *(scandalum activum)*, (2) actions of cooperating with other people in morally wrong behavior *(cooperatio cum peccato alterius)*. Strikingly enough, in the recent past scarcely anyone has made an attempt at clarifying the principle of double effect through a thorough analysis of its application to these cases. Admittedly these two sorts of action are a very peculiar structure and, therefore, difficult to analyze. I assume, however, that theologians would not shrink from this difficulty if they found the traditional doctrine on *"scandalum activum"* and *"cooperatio"* implausible or somehow problematic in its practical consequences.

It is the principle of double effect as applied to deontological norms that in Knauer's, van der Marck's, and also McCormick's eyes stands in need of reconsideration. That strikes me as at least a hint that the problem of the principle is somehow connected with or due to the problem of deontological norms. In fact, if I am not mistaken, the principle as a measure of restrictive interpretation furthers remarkably the cause of teleological considerations. However, usually a deontological remainder is left. And what is more, the line at which teleological considerations are required to stop often seems to be somewhat arbitrary. After these preliminary remarks I shall try to make my view plausible by reconstructing the problems that arise from a deontological prohibition of killing.

The prohibition runs as follows: "You shall not kill either yourself or another innocent person." The practical range of the precept depends upon what is meant by *killing*. I suggest a definition that covers the whole field within the boundaries of which we commonly believe ourselves somehow answerable for our own and other people's lives. I define *to kill* as "to make a decision the result of which one foresees to be one's own or someone else's death." At first glance, at least, it seems conceivable to pass a deontological verdict on killing, in the sense defined, by denying that persons as creatures have the right to make a decision like that. Whoever decides whether human life is preserved or perishes appears to act as lord of life and death. Perhaps one could think of such a decision as an infringement on the Creator's prerogative. If we accept the suggested definition for the moment, the prohibition runs as follows, "You shall not make a decision the result of which you foresee to be your own or someone else's death." However, a prohibition of killing, thus interpreted, leads to consequences which strike most of us as unacceptable or even contradictory.

A few examples of why one may kill oneself or someone else will suffice to prove that. Weary of life, someone takes an overdose of sleeping pills. A second person leaves the last seat in the lifeboat to a fellow traveler. A third takes upon himself the nursing of plague-stricken people, even though fully aware that soon he himself will become infected and die. If we accept the suggested definition of killing, all examples alike are cases of suicide, that is, cases where someone makes a decision, the effect of which he knows to be his own death. A physician performs a craniotomy in order to save the mother's life. A second omits a craniotomy although he knows that his omission will result in the mother's death. A third physician carries out a medically indicated hysterectomy with a pregnant woman. According to the suggested definition, these three examples are also cases of killing an innocent person. All actions just described would have to be morally condemned if we applied to them the deontological prohibition of killing. That stikes us as odd, to put it mildly.

How could we manage to preclude unacceptable consequences like these and still stick to the deontological norm? In any event, the concept of killing has to be narrowed. It must not denote every free decision whose foreseen result is someone's death. A first and extremely important step in this direction offers itself as a matter of course. From the concept of killing we have to exclude any decision of *omitting* an action that could save human life. Thus the classic distinction between killing and letting die is drawn. Only killing has to be regarded as unlawful whatever the consequences, not letting die. Assuredly, when we decide to let somebody die, we have to answer for it. But we can conceive of reasons grave enough to justify our decision. Therefore we have the widely held conviction that a physician is not morally bound to prolong an incurably ill person's life by all means and at all costs.

The distinction between acting and omitting to act is familiar; its soundness seems to be taken for granted. Yet as soon as one looks at it from a teleological standpoint, it strikes one as a trifle less plausible. A free action and a free omission, even though their result is exactly the same (that is, the death of a human being) are assessed in an essentially different manner. Undoubtedly, there is a difference between acting and omitting to act; but on the face of it the difference is rather in the technical device of bringing about a certain result. The only thing that counts morally might seem to be the result, that is, whether a person keeps or loses his life, whereas the technique of producing the effect, as a mere means to an end, seems to be in itself devoid of any moral significance. I know that, on closer inspection, we find ourselves resolutely clinging to the moral significance of the difference between action and omission, at least in some very important cases. I would not dare to deny that we are right in doing so even though I am not in a position to give a satisfactory account of why we are right to do so.

At any rate, in the view of Catholic tradition it is *only killing* an innocent person that is wrongful irrespective of its consequences. By contrast, letting a person die is to be appraised not deontologically, but with regard to its consequences. Death as a nonmoral evil, when compared with other conflicting nonmoral evils, may sometimes turn out to be the lesser one. In such a case it would be permissible or even obligatory to omit everything apt to delay or prevent a person's death. A further question is whether the decision to let die necessarily implies that death is intended. Perhaps the concept of letting die is somewhat woolly. Therefore it is preferable to be cautious. Suppose we decide to let someone die because we think death a benefit to him. At least in a case like that letting die seems to imply intending death, that is, death *qua* benefit.

After introducing the distinction between acting and omitting to act we are in a position to make at least an attempt to understand the principle of double effect. Catholic moral theology excludes from the deontological prohibition of killing not only the omission of an act apt to preserve an innocent person's life. It also draws an extremely subtle distinction between *actions* resulting in somebody's death. Hysterectomy, when the woman is expecting, can be said to have simultaneously a twofold effect: (1) the mother's life is saved; (2) the child's life is destroyed. Insofar as an action receives its specific character from its results, hysterectomy performed under the assumed circumstances is an action of a double character. It is at the same time saving human life from death and putting human life to death. On account of its first character it has to be considered as morally right (with regard to its consequences), on account of its second character it must be regarded as morally wrongful (regardless of its consequences). Taking into consideration the fairly common view that, whereas it is never permissible to kill an innocent person, under certain circumstances an innocent person may be allowed to die, one is inclined to conclude that the hysterectomy ought not to be performed under the given conditions. This conclusion seems to be in accordance with the rule, *"lex positiva valet semper, sed non pro semper; lex negativa valet semper et pro semper."* (A positive law is always valid, but it is not valid for every instance; a negative law is always valid and is so for all instances.)

Kant, if confronted with this problem, would have drawn exactly this conclusion, I presume. By doing so, he would have confirmed his reputation of being a rigorist, but at the same time avoided all suspicion of being a legalistic casuist. In contrast to him, Catholic moral theologians, because, as I assume, they are deeply concerned with the deplorable result of a rigoristic conclusion like that, have resorted to a kind of compromise between the deontological prohibition of killing and teleological considerations. Under the given circumstances hysterectomy is, as a matter of fact, a lifesaving measure as well as an act of killing. Now it seems thinkable that a surgeon decides to perform this action *only because* and *insofar as* it is a therapeutic measure. He is fully aware, of course, that this same action will also cause the child's death. But since he chooses the action merely because it is the only available procedure of saving the mother's life, one seems to be entitled to say: the surgeon *intends* to perform a therapeutic measure, whereas he only *permits* (tolerates) the same action insofar as it is the killing of a child. The action, insofar as it is deliberately intended, is called *"voluntarium directum,"* insofar as merely permitted, *"voluntarium indirectum."* Hence the distinction between direct and indirect killing. The deontological prohibition is restricted to direct killing, while indirect killing is thought to be determined by its consequences, that is, it is to be considered right if justified by a proportionately serious reason.

Usually moral theologians put the matter in a slightly different way. They speak of one action having a double effect, a good and a bad one. Then they stipulate that an action like that is morally right provided the bad effect is only tolerated (not intended) and the good effect is of such an importance as to outweigh the bad effect. I am afraid that this way of wording the principle may be misleading. At any rate, it is not precisely the evil constituting the bad effect that ought not to be intended; rather it is the *action insofar as causing* the evil (or the evil as the result of my action). According to tradition I may be morally justified in wishing a person's death because I think it a great benefit to him. The same ground may entitle me to let him die. In the latter case, it seems to me, I do intend his death. From the traditional deontological point of view it is solely the intention of performing an action precisely as conducive to an innocent person's death that must be rejected absolutely. The reason for this is obvious. The act of killing is considered morally wrong not because of its result, but because of its being performed by someone who is not authorized to do so *(ex defectu iuris in agente).*

Therefore, I think it more appropriate to speak of an action having a double moral character than of an action having a double effect. Presumably we cannot conceive of any human action that has not in some respects good as well as bad results. The principle of double effect, if taken literally, would as a result be applicable to any human action. That appears to explain why Knauer could conceive the idea that the moral quality of any human action is determined by the rules laid down in the so-called principle of double effect. Really, however, this principle refers to actions of a very peculiar sort. They are actions subjected both to a deontological and to a teleological appraisal, actions thought to be wrong independently of their consequences and right on account of their consequences. The problem they raise is primarily not how to weigh their good and bad results, but how to produce the good results without performing an action morally wrong whatever the consequences. That explains why moral theologians take great pains to show that the principle of double effect is compatible with the other principle denying the justification of morally bad means by a good end. The principle of double effect, they assert, cannot be applied if the action, insofar as subject to a deontological appraisal, is related to its good effects as means to its end.

Obviously the principle of double effect narrows the domain of the deontological norm and correspondingly enlarges the field where teleological considerations are recognized as legitimate. One further move in the same direction and the deontological norm resolves itself into a teleological one. Now suppose this further move is made and the act of killing is morally judged with regard to its consequences. Then the principle of double effect appears to lose its function. It can be put aside with impunity. The case of the hysterectomy analyzed above presents itself in a basically different light. The results of the action, if each is taken into account separately, justify only a refutable presumption of the action's moral quality. As an action of killing it is presumably wrong; as an action of saving human life it is presumably right. The actual moral character of the hysterectomy, performed under the assumed circumstances, depends on the question whether or not from an impartial point of view its good effect is preferable. Then it immediately follows that hysterectomy in this case is morally unobjectionable. There appears no need first to determine the agent's intention or the precise causal relation between the good and bad effect. The causal relation seems in itself devoid of any moral significance. Since the conflicting values on both sides are nonmoral in quality, there is no application of the principle that a good end cannot justify a morally bad means. And the agent's intention seems to be already implied in the teleological judgment on hysterectomy. Whoever in the assumed situation carries out the operation knowingly, does in fact do the morally right thing.

Thus far my first attempt to grasp the so-called principle of double effect. Apart from the previously mentioned cases of scandal and cooperation, the principle becomes redundant as soon as one espouses a teleological theory of normative ethics.

McCormick's Criticism

McCormick denies that within the framework of consequentialism the principle of double effect becomes pointless. He attempts to prove that the difference between direct and indirect killing at least sometimes turns out to be morally significant precisely on teleological grounds. Among other arguments he adduces an example well-known to all students of Anglo-American moral philosophy. It is "the case of the rioting mob and the judge." In McCormick's view I "would be forced to conclude that the judge should execute the one innocent man" in order to prevent the death of five other innocent people. An appalling conclusion, as McCormick adds. In doing so the judge would encourage a type of injustice which in the long run would render many more lives vulnerable. The matter would be different if the one innocent man's death were "incidental." In a case like that the long-term effects of direct killing differ from the effects of indirect killing. Consequently, the distinction between direct and indirect killing may turn out to be morally momentous on teleological grounds.

First some remarks about the example. I am afraid McCormick has not chosen a particularly good example to bring his specific point home. I cannot imagine how the judge could save the lives of the five innocent men by anything like the indirect killing of a sixth innocent person. In my view the example could rather serve the purpose of drawing attention to the fact that the difference between killing and letting die seems to be morally relevant in its own right. Philippa Foot employs it to make just this point. But I am far from sure that she is well advised in doing so. She fails to take into account that in a case like that not only the lives of six innocent people are at stake, but the whole institution of criminal law. The form of a teleological argument Juan de Lugo uses to make plausible the absolute inviolability of the seal of confession seems also to account for why the judge must not execute the one innocent man in order to save the lives of the other five innocent people.[5] Incidentally, I take for granted that our being appalled at a certain conclusion at best justifies a refutable presumption that the conclusion is faulty. Not so long ago many bishops and theologians were appalled at the idea of a universal right to religious freedom.

I admit it is not the example that counts but the conclusion, regardless of whether it really follows from the example or not. It is a matter of course among teleologists that long-term effects are also to be taken into consideration. Likewise no teleologist doubts that actions are to be judged differently in case their long-term results differ relevantly. Thus I do not hesitate to agree with McCormick that direct and indirect killing are to be appraised differently provided their long-term consequences differ significantly.

However, it seems to me that McCormick alters the question at issue substantially. Traditional theology is concerned with the comparatively rare cases where killing an innocent person at least prima facie appears to be morally justified on account of its results. But the results do not count if killing an innocent person is wrongful because unauthorized by God. Consequently, tradition asks only whether the contemplated action is to be regarded as unauthorized or not. And it comes to the conclusion that the action is not unauthorized if it can be characterized as indirect killing. In this context, tradition apparently makes the following point: Suppose two actions of killing have exactly the same results. This notwithstanding they are to be judged contrarily if the first action is direct killing, the second indirect killing.

The issue becomes still clearer when we turn to a much discussed case of sterilization. After a certain number of deliveries through cesarean section a woman will be exposed to serious danger in another pregnancy. The danger can be avoided safely either through tubal ligation or through hysterectomy. With regard to their results the tubal ligation seems to be preferable because it is by far less damaging. Yet traditional theology unhesitatingly rejected this procedure. The ground for that is obvious. Under the given circumstances tubal ligation is undoubtedly direct sterilization and therefore wrongful regardless of its consequences. In contrast to that, hysterectomy probably can be regarded as indirect sterilization. For the uterus is already a seriously pathological organ. And because it is an action of indirect sterilization, hysterectomy is right even though it causes comparatively more harm than tubal ligation.

The example, it seems to me, proves clearly that traditional theology holds the following view. Taking into account only their results, an action (a) may be preferable to another action (b). In spite of it, action (a) is wrongful if unauthorized or contrary to the natural purpose of a faculty, whereas action (b) is right if neither unauthorized nor contrary to nature.

From both of the examples it seems clear to me that according to tradition the borderline that separates direct killing and direct sterilization from indirect killing and indirect sterilization marks off an area where deontological considerations resolutely resist all teleological considerations. Now, once the deontological considerations surrender to their teleological opponents unconditionally, the former borderline becomes meaningless. That is the point I have made. And what is McCormick's point? He already takes for granted the overall validity of consequentialism, but believes that nonetheless some sections of the former borderline remain morally relevant.

I am prepared to ascribe to McCormick's view a prima facie plausibility. In most cases deontologists and teleologists agree on what courses of action are right or wrong, even though they disagree on how to account for the rightness or wrongness of an action. As to Catholic moral theology, its deontological arguments, when looked at closely, turn out to be basically teleological in character, though not quite flawless. Killing in self-defense, the death-penalty, and killing in warfare are subject to patently teleological standards. If only the killing of an *innocent* person is said to be invariably wrongful, then it is clear that this restriction is already the outcome of teleological reasoning. To give up the deontological elements of Catholic tradition by no means amounts to a revaluation of all values. Thus it seems not improbable that McCormick's view will prove to be correct.

This view may be divided into two statements: First, not in all, but still in some cases, though all other relevant factors are equal, direct and indirect killing lead to long-term consequences which differ significantly. Second, this difference in long-term consequences is somehow due to the directness and indirectness of killing respectively. If the first statement is true, then perhaps by implication the second is also true. Nonetheless, it would be important to know what precisely accounts for the fact that direct killing as direct and indirect killing as indirect have long-term results which differ relevantly. I am afraid that in this respect McCormick's theory is very difficult to prove. Since he admits that not always, but only sometimes, indirect killing differs from direct killing as regards their results, he is forced to claim that it is not indirectness of killing alone, but indirectness contingently combined with one or other factor that accounts for a morally significant difference in consequences.

To prove the first statement McCormick adduces the doctrine of just warfare. According to this doctrine noncombatants are under no circumstances to be killed directly, whereas their being killed indirectly may be morally permissible. McCormick believes that the invariable wrongness of directly killing noncombatants is based on teleological grounds. He argues:

> direct attacks on noncombatant civilians in wartime, however effective and important they may seem will in the long run release more violence and be more destructive to human life than the lives we might save by directly attacking noncombatants.

I see no reason for disagreeing with McCormick as regards the doctrine of just warfare and its basically teleological foundation. The question is only whether this doctrine is apt to prove the first statement. I doubt it. In its rough outlines the doctrine of just warfare is patterned after the legal institution of self-defense. Just warfare may be regarded as collective self-defense. Now it would seem odd to ask why in the course of defending myself or another I am justified only in fighting, wounding, or even killing the aggressor, and not also a nonaggressor. The reason is all too obvious. I am not defending myself by wounding or killing people who do not attack me. Killing an aggressor and killing a nonaggressor have essentially different results by definition. The same holds good for the distinction between combatants and noncombatants. The combatants are supposed to constitute the actual aggression, while the noncombatants are to be thought of as nonaggressors. Once again, killing combatants and killing noncombatants by definition differ essentially as regards their consequences.

Concerning noncombatants, the question arises as to how in the course of a morally right defense killing people who actually do not participate in the aggression could be justified. It may happen that only in wounding or killing noncombatants is one in a position successfully to defend oneself against the combatants. If so, to spare the lives of some noncombatants involves the factual impossibility of an effective defense against the aggressors. In such a case as this the killing of noncombatants may be morally permissible. Is it reasonable to speak of *indirect* killing under such circumstances?

McCormick describes the course of indirectly killing noncombatants in the following manner: "to attack the enemy's war machine even though some noncombatants (innocents) will be tragically and regretfully killed in the process." This description is fairly vague. Suppose that it is solely by killing some noncombatants that a regiment can gain a tactical position where it can hope to repel the enemy's imminent attack. In my opinion, the killing of noncombatants in a situation like that is direct according to traditional standards. Is it consequently wrongful? Is it wrongful on teleological grounds? Unfortunately, McCormick fails to give any detailed analysis of cases where the killing of noncombatants is to be regarded as indirect. I am fairly sure, if we were to analyze various concrete cases and apply to them the principle of double effect, we would come to results no less implausible than those found in cases of certain surgical operations. And let me hazard a presumption. Suppose we apply the traditional standards to distinguish direct from indirect killing. Then soldiers could often transform direct killing into indirect killing by using weapons of a vaster destructive power. If they employ only handguns and machine guns they may be forced *first* to kill some noncombatants in order to be able to repel the enemy's imminent attack. Had they artillery at their disposal, they could probably say that their action is—just as immediately—repelling the attacking enemy and killing some noncombatants.

To kill noncombatants *directly* means, as McCormick puts it, "to kill them as a means to bringing the enemy to his knees and weakening his will to fight." Provided I understand this description correctly, I admit unhesitatingly that such a procedure strikes me as morally condemnable. But I am far from sure that it strikes me as wrong because it involves the *direct* killing of noncombatants. At least at first and even second glance, it looks like one of the many varieties of extortion. It has a family resemblance with taking hostages, political kidnapping, or the liability of clan and kin, as reintroduced in Nazi Germany. Presumably there is a prima facie wrongfulness in repelling unjust aggressors by inflicting harm on their parents, wives, children, and friends even though the latter actually do not participate in the aggression. The same holds good for criminal law. Therefore no liability of clan and kin.

The rules of just warfare concerning the treatment of noncombatants are, it seems to me, best explained by the principle of *moderamen inculpatae tutelae* (the moderation of a justified defense). That means that in any course of defending others or yourself against an unjust aggression, you are not permitted to do more harm than necessary to repel the aggression effectively. If we accept this principle, we come to the conclusion that in perhaps 99 out of 100 cases killing noncombatants is not only unnecessary, but as a matter of fact, it is also at the same time indirect killing according to traditional standards. Indeed, it is simply a matter of empirical fact that in the course of resisting unjust aggressors one is very seldom confronted with a situation where the direct killing of noncombatants could be considered necessary to repel the aggressors.

As has already been pointed out, to kill civilians as a means to demoralizing the enemy seems to be a different issue. Like other devices of extortion it is presumably somehow wrong in itself. Here, I think, McCormick's very important remark holds good, "A love ethic is, indeed, concerned with effects, but it must also be concerned with how they occur." McCormick adduces the different moral judgment on direct and indirect killing of noncombatants as a proof of his first statement: Other things being equal, direct and indirect killing may have relevantly different long-term results. No doubt, in warfare direct and indirect killing of civilians have relevantly different results; however, there are some other things that are *unequal*. Direct killing is either scarcely ever necessary or it is a means of extortion; indirect killing is sometimes necessary and no means of extortion. Moreover, the principle of *moderamen inculpatae tutelae* seems best suited to explain why, given these inequalities, direct and indirect killing are to be judged differently.

Because McCormick, to my mind at least, does not succeed in proving his first statement (namely, that in some cases even though all other relevant factors are equal, direct and indirect killing lead to different long-term consequences), I feel tempted to leave his second statement undiscussed. For this second statement makes sense only if the first statement is supposed to be true. On the other hand, McCormick takes particularly great pains to establish the second statement. By definition, he argues, direct killing implies an intending will, indirect killing solely a permitting will. This difference, if a real one, must at least sometimes have a bearing on the results of an action, and consequently, on its moral quality. There cannot be any reasonable doubt that "the difference between an intending and permitting will is utterly essential . . . , where moral evil (sin) of another is concerned." Therefore, McCormick argues, this difference must show also where nonmoral evil is concerned. Since I for my part reject the legitimacy of this inference, McCormick fears that I do not take "seriously enough the real contribution of intentionality to the significance of human action."

I feel not particularly inclined to embark on a detailed scrutiny of McCormick's claims, being fully aware of the intricacies one will be faced with in so doing. McCormick himself tries to explain the difference between an intending and a permitting will when nonmoral evils are concerned. He states:

> The intending will is more closely associated with the existence of evil than the merely permitting will. . . . An intending will is more willing that the evil be than is a permitting will.

However, some pages later McCormick himself discloses that this account is open to an objection that is to my mind not only serious, but downright fatal. "The person who is prepared to realize the good even by intending the evil is more willing that the evil exists, but only because he is more willing that the good exists." Moreover, it is true, "the difference between an intending and permitting will is utterly essential

... when moral evil (sin) is concerned." But moral evil (sin) and nonmoral evils differ immensely. So it may be adventuresome to conclude that a crucial difference in our attitude towards sin must reappear also in our attitude towards nonmoral evils.

I am afraid, however, I cannot confine myself to these general remarks. I agree with McCormick that the meaning of the principle of double effect cannot be cleared up except through an elucidation of the distinction between intending and permitting. Thus, though without much hope of more success, I will make a second attempt at clarifying this intriguing principle.

It is important to introduce a distinction here which most moral theologians in this context fail to draw, the distinction between morally good and morally right on the one hand, and between morally bad and morally wrong on the other hand. Suppose a physician motivated only by purely selfish ambition develops a new therapeutic device which he foresees to be really beneficial to a countless number of suffering people. The physician's achievement, evaluated by its consequences, is certainly in accordance with the requirements of the commandment of love. However, *ex hypothesi* the physician does not act from love for his neighbor. Acting from love (agape) is morally good. Doing what on the whole is impartially beneficial to all persons concerned is morally right. Therefore, an action may be morally bad because performed from pure selfishness, but nonetheless be morally right on account of its beneficial consequences.

In the same way Kant distinguishes between acting from a sense of duty *(aus Pflicht)* and doing what is one's duty *(pflichtgemäss)*. Also, the Pauline concept of work-righteousness presupposes this distinction The *work-righteous* is by definition a sinner, that is, morally bad. In spite of it he may be out to do the works the moral law requires, and actually perform them (in paying his debts, refraining from murder, and so on). Someone who is animated by impartial love cannot but choose the course of action he *considers* morally right. But he may make an erroneous judgment and mistake for right what in fact is wrong. In this even his intention is to do what is right. Yet this intention notwithstanding, his action, though morally good, is at the same time morally wrongful. The physician in our example may very well know that his undertaking is morally right. He decides for it not because it is right but because it is apt to promote his own selfish interests. Nonetheless, the moral rightness of his action remains unimpaired. Thus a first conclusion can be drawn. To all appearances, the agent's intention, in as much as constitutive of the moral goodness or badness of his action, has no bearing on the moral rightness or wrongness of the same action.

This conclusion, it appears, is true only for actions which result in nonmoral values and disvalues. There is another and different kind of action that immediately refers to the realization of *moral* values and disvalues. Of particular interest in this context are actions apt to induce others to right or wrong conduct. When confronted with actions of this kind, one cannot avoid disclosing one's own basic moral attitude. What is more, these actions, it seems, are not capable of any moral assessment unless the agent's moral attitude is taken into regard. Is it right or wrong to choose an action apt to induce others to sin?

If we are prepared to accept the teaching of tradition, we have to answer, "It all depends." It is wrong if one chooses the action in order to provoke others to wrong behavior. But then the action is also morally bad. For it is morally bad to approve of anyone's wrong conduct. It is right to perform an action apt to induce others to sin if two conditions are fulfilled. First, if one solely permits and does not intend the other's being induced to sin. And second, if there is a proportionate reason for permitting the other's sin. But if it is right, then the action is also morally good. To permit someone else to commit sin, if opposed to intend someone else's sin, must be a specific aspect of the agent's basic affirmation of moral goodness. In sum, actions which immediately refer to the realization of *moral* values and disvalues apparently do not admit of any moral appraisal unless the agent's basic moral attitude is taken into account. In contrast to this, the rightness or wrongness of actions which result in *nonmoral* values and disvalues seems to be independent of the agent's fundamental moral character.

The main question to be answered now is how intending and permitting are related to one another when they refer to moral values and disvalues. To act from impartial love and to act from pure selfishness imply the agent's most fundamental and hence most comprehensive intention (compare *optio fundamentalis*). By virtue of this overall intention each particular action or omission is morally good or bad respectively. Just as moral goodness and badness are mutually exclusive in the manner of contrary opposites, so are these two overall intentions. One cannot approve of impartial love without unqualified disapproval of selfishness. It is impossible to accept moral goodness or badness as a mere means to a further end. For they are by definition opposite *ultimate ends*. Either one decides for a life of impartial love as an end in itself or one decides to reject it without qualification. To intend something as a mere means does not make sense if the object is moral goodness or badness.

As has just been pointed out, according to tradition unqualified disapproval of moral badness is reconcilable with permitting (tolerating) moral badness. From the foregoing it is clear that it would make no sense to maintain one could permit oneself to decide for moral badness. Where permitting is concerned, one can permit only that someone else freely embrace a morally bad way of life. What is the exact meaning of *permit* in this connection? It is this: "Not intend in any way and yet not prevent it even though one could do so." I see no reason for doubting that this definition makes sense. Yet how could I prevent someone else from making selfishness the overall maxim of his life? Only by thoroughly suppressing his freedom of decision. And how could I achieve this aim with certainty? Probably solely by killing him. Yet the efficacy even of this rather radical procedure can be questioned. There is the theologumenon of final option. If this were true, by killing a person one would only put him in the situation of final option at an earlier date. To all appearances then, it seems that a human being is unable to prevent a fellow human being from deciding for a life of immorality.

If this is so, then the definition given above of *permitting sin* does not apply to any human person. Only of God almighty the Creator can it be said that he "permits moral badness," that is, does not intend it in any way and yet does not prevent it even though he could have done so. This fact may justify the conclusion that the act of permitting moral badness is somehow beyond human understanding. Any further analysis of this act ought to be taken for guesswork, as it were. To suppress a human being's freedom of decision no doubt prevents him from deciding for a life of selfishness; but at the same time it also prevents him from deciding for a life of impartial love. Thus the approval of moral goodness appears to imply the approval of what constitutes the necessary condition of its possibility, a person's freedom of decision. This latter approval in turn involves something that strikes us as a certain readiness to tolerate that this freedom of decision may be used to bring immorality into being. However, only the *possibility,* not the *reality,* of moral badness is the necessary condition of moral badness. Furthermore, the possibility of moral badness, it seems, is tolerable as necessary condition only of *moral* goodness and not as condition of any amount or quality of nonmoral goods.

To sum up. The approval of moral goodness (by identity unqualified disapproval of moral badness) involves the affirmation of freedom of decision as its necessary condition and by implication the toleration of moral badness as eventuality.

This outcome of my first piece of analysis might appear to be incompatible with the traditional doctrine on actions apt to induce others to sin. However, in this context at least, tradition does not clearly distinguish between morally bad and morally wrong. It speaks simply of sin. If we are justified in relying on the analysis just given, we may legitimately conclude that we have to understand by *sin* morally wrong conduct, when tradition speaks of "actions apt to induce others to sin."

In fact, if in this connection we were to understand by *sin* "the fundamental decision for a life of selfishness," then a lot of further serious difficulties arise. Some of them may be briefly mentioned. First, is it possible to foresee with certainty that in a given situation, brought about through my action, someone will be challenged freely to determine himself for a morally good or bad life? Scarcely. Yet suppose such a foresight were possible. Then the result of this free self-determination, whether it will be a free decision for good or bad, seems to be unpredictable.

Second, *being induced to sin* means "freely consent to one's being induced to sin." One could also resist the inducement and thereby wholeheartedly commit oneself to moral goodness. To all appearances an action apt to induce others to sin is at the same time an action apt to induce others to reject sin and approve of a morally good life.

Third, presumably almost any action whatever, if only of a certain existential weight, may turn out to challenge any other person to commit himself for or against morality.

Fourth, suppose by omitting a contemplated action I were able to prevent others from freely determining themselves for moral badness. What kind of reason would be proportionate to justify my not omitting the contemplated action? No amount or quality of nonmoral values could, to my mind, be regarded as proportionate. On the other hand, neither my own moral goodness nor another's moral goodness can be dependent upon any human being's actual moral badness.

Most, if not all, of these difficulties disappear as soon as we understand by *sin* "action or omission insofar as wrongful." We can conceive of various reasons why a human person performs a wrongful action. (a) After leading a life of moral integrity he may change his mind and freely resolve to give way to selfishness (act of free decision). (b) Since he has already made selfishness the overall maxim of his life, he may choose the morally wrong course of action simply because it serves best his own selfish interests (act of choice, prohairesis). Here the biblical saying applies: "A rotten tree produces bad fruit."[6] (c) He may do the morally wrong thing because he mistakes it for right. (d) He may behave in a morally wrong way without being actually accountable for so doing. This case admits of a good deal of varieties.

Cases b, c, and d (in real life, of course, very often scarcely distinguishable) explain why it is possible to foresee and predict in what circumstances a certain group of people or a certain percentage of them are liable or even certain to do the morally wrong thing. Criminal law, for instance, makes use of this predictability. On the other hand, in none of the cases b, c, and d is moral badness originally brought into being. This is obvious as regards cases c and d. But also the wrong deeds of those who have already adopted an immoral way of life do not give birth to moral badness, but make manifest a moral badness already existent. Solely in case a do we have an instance of the authentic origin of actual moral badness. Still, as has been said, it is precisely this case that is not foreseeable and it can be ascertained, if at all, solely after having taken place.

Apart from this case, to speak of actions one knows to be apt to induce others to sin apparently makes good sense if one understands by *sin* "morally wrong conduct." To put it very roughly, from a teleological point of view, an action is wrong if it causes more harm than inevitable. Thus an action apt to provoke others to wrong behavior is an action that through the mediation of other human agents causes unnecessary harm. This harm consists of disvalues, which are nonmoral in quality, to all those who thereby are affected passively. But as has been pointed out, in doing what is wrong the intermediate agents we are considering here do not worsen their own moral character. Hence an action as apt to induce others to wrong conduct is an action as resulting in nonmoral evils. That makes it easy to understand why, as tradition presupposes, the avoidance of (other) nonmoral evils or the production of nonmoral goods may be a commensurate reason for permitting others to sin.

Yet there still remains the central question about what it means, in this connection, solely to permit and not intend the other's wrong conduct. Suppose someone chooses a course of action only because he believes it to be apt to induce others to wrong behavior. In doing so he apparently approves of the wrong action. Without question, to induce others to wrong conduct because one approves of its wrongness is tantamount to intending the other's wrongdoing. The moral badness of a procedure like that is plain. Only the promotion of selfish interests can be the reason for approving of an action of which it has to be said that it effects unnecessary harm if the well-being of all concerned is taken into regard impartially.

To the approval of moral wrongness solely one alternative appears to be conceivable, namely disapproval. Consequently, *to permit other's wrongdoing means to disapprove of it and yet not prevent it.* Whereas we are unable to prevent others from deciding for an immoral way of life (badness), we are frequently in a position to hinder other people's wrongdoing. This is obvious. It may suffice to recall criminal law and its administration. It is easy to grasp why under certain conditions disapproving of wrong behavior not only allows but even requires us to refrain from preventing wrong behavior. Someone who disapproves of unnecessary harm being produced cannot, without inconsistency, be willing to hinder another's causing unnecessary harm if by hindering it he could not help making the situation still worse.

Usually *not prevent* means, in my opinion, the same as "omit a preventive action." But tradition seems to use the expression in a broader sense. Someone who wittingly performs an action apt to provoke others to sin is also said not to prevent others from wrongdoing. The difference between omitting to act and acting, however important elsewhere, has no bearing on the question whether or not somebody only permits another's wrong conduct.

From the foregoing it seems clear that to approve of moral rightness, to disapprove of moral wrongness, and to permit the wrongdoing of others are basically one and the same moral attitude. Consequently, to permit another's wrong conduct is not solely right, but also good. It is not necessary to add the qualification that permitting the wrong behavior of others is morally justified only if there is a proportionately serious reason for not hindering the wrong behavior. To disapprove of wrong behavior and not impede it are consistent with one another solely if the reason for not impeding it is a proportionate one, namely the avoidance of still more harm. In any case, to intend the wrongdoing of others and to permit their wrongdoing are mutually exclusive in the same way as the basic moral attitudes which express themselves in intending or permitting the wrong behavior of others.

As far as I can see, the principle of double effect, as worded by tradition, applies quite naturally to the moral assessment of the kind of actions just analyzed. These actions lead to two sorts of consequences:

(1) nonmoral evils are avoided or nonmoral goods are produced, (2) other persons are induced to wrong conduct, that is, to a kind of conduct which causes more harm than necessary. Actions occasioning another's wrongdoing are morally unobjectionable if and only if the other's wrongdoing is solely permitted, that is to say, if and only if the actions are exclusively performed because otherwise all persons concerned would be worse off on the whole.

The matter becomes rather puzzling as soon as we apply the same principle to an action of killing which at the same time is an action of saving human life. True, in this case too, one consequence consists in the preservation of a nonmoral value. But the other consequence consists in the death of a person and not in anyone's wrong behavior. Or is my own performance of an action of killing wrongful? Indeed, from tradition's deontological viewpoint it is precisely this that is wrong. But how is it feasible to apply the distinction between intending and permitting a morally wrong deed if only the wrongdoer himself can be the person who intends or permits the wrongdoing? Does it make sense to say that I may only permit my own performance of a wrong deed? Scarcely. As tradition teaches, if I merely permit my own action to lead to another's death, then nothing at all happens that could be called wrongful in any sense, provided the good effect of my action is rightly assumed to outweigh the other person's death.

Moreover, the question why it is wrong and bad to intend the wrongdoing of others is at root a question that answers itself. In other words, the proposition: "It is wrong and bad to intend the wrongdoing of others," is analytically true. In contrast to this, intentional killing of a human being, if considered only as such, allows of no definite moral appraisal. The executioner cannot dispatch a murderer without intending death as the result of his action. This intention does not impair the rightness of his action. Hence, if intentionally killing an innocent person is said to be invariably wrong, *the wrongness of the action cannot be derived from the intention of causing death, a nonmoral evil.* The proposition: "It is wrong intentionally to kill an innocent person," is a synthetic one. Tradition accounts for the wrongness of this action by the attempt to show that it is not authorized by God.

Taking this into consideration, it becomes plain that intending and permitting, if related to a particular nonmoral evil as the result of an action, cannot be identified with the agent's attitude to good and bad or right and wrong. It is advisable, therefore, to find out what exactly tradition means when it distinguishes between intending and permitting the death of a human being. For this purpose let us return to our former paradigm.

Suppose a surgeon is about to perform a hysterectomy on a pregnant woman. He is scrupulous and asks himself how he can discover whether he actually only permits and does not intend this operation to result in the child's death. He may say to himself: "I would not be prepared to carry out the operation if it were possible to save the mother's life without acting in a manner which brings about the child's death." Unfortunately this statement, though sincere, leaves his question open. Also, a surgeon who carries out a craniotomy may say to himself: "I would not be prepared to do so, if it were possible to save the mother without the further consequence of the child's death." And there is agreement at least among traditional theologians that this latter surgeon *intends* to kill the child as a necessary means to saving the mother. In the case of the hysterectomy, the mother's survival and the child's death are, so to speak, *collateral* effects of the operation. Thus our scrupulous surgeon can be reassured that he does not intend to kill the child as a means to an end because in the given circumstances he is factually unable to do so. At the same time he is sure that he does not intend to kill the child as an end, because he would not be ready to carry out the operation if he only knew how to save the mother without putting the child to death. Thus he has established two premises which allow him to draw the conclusion that in fact he does only permit this operation to result in the death of the child. In this context, according to tradition, *to permit* means the same as "intend neither as an end nor as a means and yet not prevent."

At first glance one may be inclined to assume that the meaning of *permitting* is virtually the same whether the attitude called *permitting* refers to a particular nonmoral evil or to wrongful behavior. But on closer examination one can hardly fail to notice that *intend as a means* and *permit,* when referring to a nonmoral evil, apparently denote the same mental attitude: "I would not be prepared . . . if. . . ." It is true the causal sequence of the good and bad effect is different according to tradition which speaks of intending as a means or permitting. But this difference, it seems, does not bear upon the agent's attitude towards the evil result of his action. At any rate, whereas intending and permitting someone's wrong conduct are related to one another in the manner of contrary opposites, intending a nonmoral evil as a mere means and permitting a nonmoral evil, considered as attitudes of will, differ in degree, not in kind. In the latter case of nonmoral evil the crucial demarcation line does not run between intending and permitting, but between intending as an end on the one hand and intending as means or permitting on the other hand.

Once again, if there is any difference at all between intending as a means and permitting, then it can be solely a difference of degree. The assumption of a gradual difference, however, inevitably leads us into the insuperable difficulty which McCormick himself raises against his own account: The person who is prepared to realize the good even by intending the evil is more willing that the evil exists, but only because he is more willing that the good exists. Therefore, I am strongly inclined to believe that in point of fact *"intend as a means" and "permit," when referring to a nonmoral evil, denote exactly the same mental attitude*. Tradition, so at least it seems to me, makes an equivocal use of the expression *permit* when it applies the principle of double effect to an action apt to induce to sin as well as to an action like killing. When all is said and done McCormick discloses this equivocation. He clearly conceives of the difference between intending as a means and permitting, if referring to killing, as only a gradual difference, even though he knows perfectly well that intending sin and permitting sin denote the essential difference of opposite attitudes.

It should be clear that all my remarks about the meaning of the expressions *intend* and *permit* refer solely to the use tradition makes of these expressions when propounding and applying the principle of double effect. I do not exclude the possibility or even probability that in other contexts a distinction between intend and permit designates a morally important difference, even as to a person's attitude toward nonmoral values and disvalues.

Thus far my new attempt to grasp the principle of double effect. I am far from sure that I have achieved my aim. It would not take me by surprise were McCormick to force me to reconsider the matter a third or fourth time.

ENDNOTES FOR CHAPTER FIVE

1   P. Knauer, "Das rechtverstandene Prinzip von der Doppelwirkung als Grundnorm jeder Gewissensentsheidung," *Theologie und Glaube* 57 (1967): 107-33.
2   Bruno Schüller, "Direkte Tötung—indirekte Tötung," *Theologie und Philosophie* 47 (1972): 341-57.
3   Rom 13:9.
4   R. Carpentier, "Vers une morale de la charité," *Gregorianum* 34 (1953): 53-54; See also G. Gilleman, *Le primat de la charité en théologie morale* (Paris: Desclee, 1954); O. Lottin, *Morale Fondamentale* (Tournai: Desclee 1954).
5   Juan de Lugo, *Tractatus de fide,* disp. 4, sectio 4, n. 57.
6   Mt 7:18.

CHAPTER SIX

A Commentary
on
the Commentaries

by

Richard A. McCormick, S.J.

In the recently abrogated Common Rules for members of the Society of Jesus, rule number twenty-six of the English version reads as follows:

> All should speak in a low tone of voice, as is proper to religious men, and no one should dispute with another. If there is a difference of opinion and it seems worth discussing, they should propose their views modestly and with kindness. Their sole purpose should be to declare the truth and not to make their own view prevail.

I am sure that the ancient worthies who devised that rule lived to see some remarkable implementations of it in the Counter-Reformation. Be that as it may, a contemporary rendering of the substance of that rule would be the following: a response should aim at enlightenment of the issues. For that is all that each of us in this volume is or should be interested in. However, there are several ways of enlightening the issues. One is to point up the weaknesses and/or inconsistencies in others' reflections. Another is to acknowledge and incorporate their corrections and positive advances into one's own synthesis. I shall try to do both. Briefly, I shall attempt to respond to my colleagues in a way that I hope will respond to the issues.

To clear the way into the issues a word about the term *ambiguity* (the title of the original monograph) is required. Paul Ramsey believes that this term must be restricted to statements. I am both surprised and amused at this insistence. Surprised because there are few who wallow in neologisms and hyphenated creations as freely and happily as this

193

truly fine Christian ethician. Amused because when Ramsey does turn his attention to verbal orthodoxy he comes up with a rigorous narrowing that the experts I have consulted believe is unwarranted by contemporary usage. Furthermore, *Webster's New Collegiate Dictionary* (1973 version) gives as the second definition of the term *ambiguous* the following: "capable of being understood in two or more possible senses." There is nothing in prose, poetry, or the dictionary establishment that demands that the word *ambiguous* be restricted to declarations or statements. Therefore, I shall continue with peaceful grammatical conscience to use it of our choices. For our actions often leave good undone or bring evil into being as they prosecute the good. They therefore have two sides or dimensions and are quite "capable of being understood in two or more possible senses."

This ambiguity has found many witnesses.

> For I do not do the good I want, but the evil I do not want is what I do. Now if I do what I do not want, it is no longer I that do it, but sin which dwells within me. So I find it to be a law that when I want to do right, evil lies close at hand.[1]

This is but a single, even if a classical, statement of the human dilemma. It has been repeated many thousands of times, in poetry, on stage, in confessionals, on the lips of lovers seeking forgiveness, in the solitary murmurs of the individual heart. The jar of our ancient fall profoundly dislocated our whole being and threw us out of harmony, and even as redeemed we must daily die if we are to live. J. Robert Oppenheimer testified to this dislocation when he reportedly stated that "in some crude sense, which no vulgarity, no humor, no overstatement can quite extinguish, the physicists have known sin, and this is a knowledge which they cannot lose." Augustine wrote simply that "whatever we are, we are not what we ought to be." Goethe regretted that God made only one person when there was material in him for two: a rogue and a gentleman. Disraeli rendered it as follows: "Youth is a blunder; manhood is a struggle; old age is a regret." *Simul justus et peccator* is but a lapidary identification of one aspect of the human condition of ambiguity.

Human creaturehood and finitude is another and the one in which the problem treated in this volume roots. Human beings are not disincarnated spirits with instantaneous understanding and freedom. Their knowledge comes slowly, painfully, processively. Their freedom is a gradual achievement. Their choices and actions are limited by space, time, matter. The good they achieve is often at the expense of the good left undone or the evil caused. Their choices are mixed, or, *pace* Ramsey, ambiguous. This intertwining of good and evil in our choices brings ambiguity into the world. The limitations of human beings become eventually the limitations of the world, and the limitations of the world return to us in the form of tragic conflict situations. Thus the good that we do is rarely untainted by hurt, deprivation, imperfection. Our ethical acts are, at best, faint approximations of the kingdom that is to come. We must kill to preserve life and freedom; we protect one through the pain of another; our education is not infrequently punitive; our health is preserved at times only by pain and disfiguring mutilation; we protect our secrets by misstatement and our marriages and population by contraception and sterilization.

Christian theologians—and I write unabashedly as a Catholic Christian theologian here—have struggled with these conflicts for centuries in an effort to contain and reduce them, but above all to discover whether, when, and on what criteria it remains Christian to pursue the good at the cost of evil, or more technically, to discern the rightfulness and wrongfulness of our conduct. Theological compromise with evil has always been an uneasy, fragile thing; for Christians know deep in their hearts and down their pulses that their Lord and Master did not hesitate to demand of them that they swim upstream, that their world view, profoundly stamped by the proleptic presence of the eschatological kingdom, be countercultural, that they suffer at times in dumb, uncomprehending silence and trust. It is a risky venture, therefore, for a Christian to deliberate about the evil he may rightfully do as he attempts to shape his life in love of Christ and the neighbor God's Christ redeemed. But that is precisely what this discussion is all about. How do we come to terms with unavoidable evil? For centuries theologians, especially those of the Catholic tradition, have attempted to do so in certain areas by distinguishing evil that is merely permitted from that which is intended. Thus the distinction between the direct voluntary and the indirect voluntary settled into a state of peaceful possession as a way of living with the hurts and evils inseparable from human handling. The question is: though the possession was peaceful, was it all that accurate and decisive?

It was the purpose of my original essay to pick away at this distinction to test its validity. My reflections were, as I stated, "no more than gropings and explorations undertaken with the confidence that others more competent will carry them further and bring greater clarity to the question." For the record let me add that my original intention (during the period of a research grant in 1971-72 from the Kennedy Institute for the Study of Human Reproduction and Bioethics) was to complete a volume of five or six chapters on some basic assumptions underlying broadly accepted principles for decision making in the area of bioethics. Some of these principles were: the principle of the twofold effect, the principle of totality (if that is indeed different from the twofold effect), the principle of subsidiarity in medico-moral decisions, the relationship of the individual to the common good, the principles underlying the relationship of morality and public policy, and so on. I never got beyond the first chapter, frankly because the matter proved enormously complex. Indeed, the first chapter of this book, which appeared as the Pere Marquette lecture entitled *Ambiguity in Moral Choice,* was never really finished; it simply ground to a halt, with my full awareness that a halt is not an end. Indeed, it may represent nothing more than a crippling stumble.

Somewhat to my surprise, my confidence that "others more competent will carry them further and bring greater clarity to the question" has been realized. It is now my pleasant task to see whether carrying them further has actually resulted in greater clarity and to what extent. There are probably many ways of going about this. One could, for example, disengage five or six recurrent and key issues and attempt to deal with them in precision from the authors who raised them. However, given the prestige of my commentators, the care with which they have worked, the fact that their remarks often root in diverging ways of doing ethics, and the fact that their critiques and alternative suggestions often cast light on the strength or weakness of the direct/indirect distinction, I have decided that I should proceed in two steps. I shall first engage in dialogue with each author individually; then secondly, I shall attempt very briefly at the end to formulate the state of the question as it seems to emerge from this discussion.

But before doing so a few general remarks are in order.

First, I should like to underline the fact that the prime (not the only) issue is the meaning and moral relevance of the distinction between direct and indirect intention as it has come to us through tradition. Certain actions, when done with direct intent (direct voluntary) were regarded as morally wrongful, regardless of the circumstances, consequences, or limited available alternatives. And they were regarded as morally wrong precisely because they were directly willed. Thus if a killing had to be designated as direct (for example, an abortion), it was *thereby* morally wrong. For this reason certain actions viewed as directly willed were beyond the reach of teleological considerations.

It is this understanding of directness and of its morally decisive character that was my main concern and ought to be the main concern of the reflections in this volume. Clearly, if one denies or modifies this morally decisive character, he immediately faces certain other problems of a broader and more methodological kind. For example, if direct killing of a human being is not morally wrong *just because it is direct,* then why is it wrong, if indeed it is? In other words, this discussion necessarily opens into the discussion of moral norms and how they are to be understood. But this is a secondary concern.

The question needs further clarification. There are two ways of approaching the problem we are discussing. The first involves a dominant concern with the intelligibility of the distinction between direct and indirect as morally meaningful or decisive. If no persuasive account of this distinction can be elaborated, then one will either modify it or abandon it—and then accept the consequences of doing so. In this case, the consequence appears to be *some form* of teleology in the understanding of moral norms. The second approach is a dominant concern with avoiding teleological tendencies or adhering to so-called deontological ones, and then adhering to the distinction between direct and indirect voluntariness because if one does not, one is forced to abandon or modify his cherished theories about norms or the understanding of solutions and positions they are thought to yield.

Some of my commentators have gone about the matter in this second way (for example, Ramsey, and to some extent Frankena). This is, in my judgment, not the way to approach the problem. Not only are the terms *deontological* and *teleological (consequential),* as used argumentatively, such huge umbrellas as to be almost useless (a point Ramsey has made), but approaching the problem in this way leaves the problem of prime concern (the moral meaningfulness of direct and indirect) incompletely or poorly analyzed. I think this has happened, as I hope to show.

Secondly, above I used the phrase "direct and indirect intention *as it has come to us through tradition."* Schüller is quite correct in stating that the so-called principle of double effect, at least as a set of formulated rules, appears to be the exclusive property of Catholic moral theology.[2] Outside of Philippa Foot, Paul Ramsey, and perhaps a few others, Schüller was unable to find any non-Catholic who made any use of this principle. The Catholic tradition has generated this principle. This is interesting and important because it highlights the moral relevance this distinction was thought to have. Within the Catholic tradition, the understanding of moral norms and exception making has been along teleological lines as I understand this term (for example promise keeping, secret keeping, falsehood, taking another's property, and so on) except in two instances: killing of innocents and sexual conduct. In these two instances, there was appeal to a special characteristic that made doing these things evil *in se*. In the case of killing, it was lack of right *(defectus juris)*.[3] Where sexual conduct was concerned (for example, contraception), it was unnaturalness. Therefore these last two kinds of actions could be morally justified only if they occurred indirectly. If it can be shown or at least argued that doing the actions in question is not intrinsically evil, or, what is the same, that the special characteristics appealed to are not valid, the need to redouble the intention disappears—or at least the need to redouble the intention as this need was understood in tradition. With the exception of Schüller, my commentators have not understood the tradition sufficiently in this regard. Thus they have turned to other reasons for redoubling the intention, reasons whose persuasiveness we shall have to examine carefully.

Thirdly, I find it both intriguing and illuminating that the contributors to this discussion disagree so thoroughly with each other at key points. I shall advert to this during my subsequent comments; but suffice it here to note that Brody would disagree with Ramsey about commensurability and incommensurability of goods. This is instructive because it reflects the genuine complexity and manysidedness of the problem under discussion.

The most intriguing disagreement concerns my own original presentation. The contributors are unclear or hesitant about what they should call it. Brody states that "it is clear that McCormick is not a consequentialist." Frankena is uncertain. At one point he notes: "The question is what McCormick does. It looks as if he means to steer a course between the situationists' Scylla and Ramsey's Charybdis. . . ." At other points he uses these phrases: "a utilitarian of some sort," "he may still be a straight teleologist of a utilitarian kind," "McCormick may yet be a utilitarian of some sort." Ramsey suspects that I may be a "multivalue consequentialist." Such uncertainties and disagreements are interesting for many reasons. First, they may reflect on the unclarity of my own original monograph. This is certainly a real possibility, especially at one key point, but I prefer to think that they reflect the difficulty of the subject discussed. Secondly, such statements reflect a preoccupation with what happens if one challenges or modifies the traditional moral relevance of the direct/indirect distinction, not precisely a preoccupation with the intelligibility of that distinction itself. Thirdly, disagreements of this kind point to the malleability of terms such as *teleologist, utilitarian, consequentialist,* and *deontologist.* These terms are used as if they were clean-cut typologies and thereby the user gains a certain apologetic leverage over anyone so stereotyped.

However, the terms are simply not that informative. As Paul Ramsey, who retreats into rhetoric with minimum provocation but rarely into fog banks, remarked above:

> Deontological is only an uninformative class-name meaning nonteleological. What the species mean has yet to be explained; and when explanations are given there is usually about as much diversity among the accounts as between any one of them and a teleological ethics.

Schüller has made a similar protest against the logically elegant division deontological/teleological as defined by C. D. Broad. Broad had defined teleological theories as those that determine the moral character of an action exclusively by its consequences. Deontological theories, by contrast, are those that claim there are actions that are morally wrong whatever the consequences. This apparently neat division simply overlooks the vast differences between those who regard themselves as, for example, deontologists. For instance, Kant and W. D. Ross are regarded as being in this category. But there is a chasm between them. Kant held that the duty not to speak a falsehood is absolute; Ross holds it to be a prima facie duty. What is it, then, that divides Kant, Fichte, and the Catholic tradition from Ross, McCloskey, and other critics of utilitarianism? As Schüller puts it in the essay cited in note 2:

> Only Kant, Fichte, and the Catholic tradition assert that there are actions that are morally wrong without any regard for their consequences. W. D. Ross and the modern critics of utilitarianism, on the contrary, assert that for the moral rightness of an action consequences always play a determining role, but not alone. . . . In this light, only Kant and the Catholic tradition, but not the modern critics of utilitarianism, know deontological norms as defined by C. D. Broad.

Much the same could be said of the term *teleological.* A phrase used by Frankena above gives this away. He refers to a "teleologist of a utilitarian kind." Presumably there are teleologists of a nonutilitarian kind, and perhaps many varieties. The importance of noting this is that usage of these terms to pigeonhole a position associates that position with certain dreary and often refuted methodological assumptions, while the flabbiness of the term will not support such necessary association.

Because I shall use the term *teleological* I feel it imperative to say what I mean by that term, whether or not this is what others mean or want the term to mean. With essentially uninformative terms, that is all that can be done. By a teleological norm (a norm teleogically understood), I understand a norm in which consequences always play a determining but not the sole role. I am convinced, incidentally, that all of the contributors to this volume are teleologists in the sense just explained. Some are open teleologists (*pace* his own words, Frankena). Others are crypto-teleologists (for example, Ramsey) who remain in the closet, possibly because they cannot see therein the writing on the wall—namely, the implications of their own positions. Another reason for remaining in the deontological closet is that the areas in question were judged deontologically before, and therefore we have no experience of what would happen if these areas were normed teleologically. This means that we are saying to ourselves, as we hover in the deontological closet: "What will be the implications or consequences if we do judge teleologically?" But such a fear or hesitation already reveals good teleological instincts.

Finally, if one were to tally up the results on the basic issue of moral relevance of the distinction between direct and indirect voluntariety, he would find three distinguishable groupings. The first would include Frankena and Schüller, both of whom would reject the moral relevance of the distinction as it was accepted traditionally. The second would include Ramsey who wants to retain the traditional distinction pretty much intact, with certain qualifications that can be made from his presentation itself. Thirdly, there is Brody whose position on this basic distinction remains a question mark. Even if this categorization is inaccurate, I shall use it to treat in order (1) the question mark, (2) the defender of the traditional distinction, and (3) the challengers or modifiers.

Before embarking on this journey, I must warn the undoubtedly weary reader that because these commentaries concern my own writing, because they go into great detail at times, and because there are many points that suggest comment or disagreement, I am tempted to go into great detail in my response. I shall resist as manfully as possible this temptation and attempt to keep my response close to the heart of the problem. But this austerity should not be interpreted as agreement with or acquiescence in some of the material and interpretations not lifted out for explicit reflection. It means only that given the length of this volume I do not believe that there is a *proportionate reason* for such indulgence.

Baruch Brody

I have included Brody as a question mark because when he discusses the notion of direct and indirect voluntariety (what he loosely and ultimately inaccurately styles "the intended and the foreseen"), he concludes only that "Ramsey is in trouble." I think, but I am not sure—thus the question mark—that Brody sees this trouble as terminal. At a key point in his own analysis of conflict situations, he asserts: "Nor need we consider what means are to be employed (direct versus indirect) because the legitimacy of the means is determined by the nature of his consent." Be that as it may, Brody's essay suggests three areas of commentary: his rejection of my analysis, his rejection of Ramsey, his own alternative proposals.

1. *Brody's rejection of my position.* Brody defines *consequentialism* as follows: "the rightness and wrongness of an action is ultimately based upon the quality of the consequences produced by it." While he admits that I am not a consequentialist in this sense, still he argues that exception making on the basis of consequences is open to the same objections as a full-fledged consequentialist methodology. He argues this because of his understanding of what I have said. Thus: "According to McCormick, that rule (against killing) should be broken whenever breaking it will lead to better results (for example, a lesser evil) than would obtain if the rule were followed." At another point Brody refers to "socially desirable consequences" associated with a policy of permissive abortion and seems to believe he is describing my position.

Hardly. "Better results" and "socially desirable consequences" are far too general and unspecified. The phrase "proportionate reason" is not convertible with the notion of "better results" or "net good." Rather it means that the value being sought will not be undermined by the contemplated action. *Proportionate* in the usage "proportionate reason" refers to a relationship to the basic good in question. Thus, where there is a question of taking life, such taking is proportionate only if it is, all things considered, the better service of *life itself* in the tragic circumstances.

Louis Janssens has put the matter as follows.

> Thomas taught us that the moral end as formal element only deserves to be labeled as the reason and the cause of the exterior action if this action is a means which, in conformity with reason *(secundum rationem)*, has a *debita proportio* to the end, which only in these conditions puts the stamp of its moral goodness on the totality of the act. I mean that no intrinsic contradiction between the means and the end may be found in the total act when the act is placed in the light of reason. Put into terms of the philosophy of values, this means that the means must be consistent with the value of the end. Or according to a more abstract formulation, the principle which has been affirmed in the end must not be negated by the means.[4]

Janssens then applies this to conjugal morality. The marriage act, so asserts *Gaudium et spes,* must be ordered to conjugal love and to the transmission of life, namely, responsible parenthood. Each conjugal act ought to have a proportion to this end. Janssens continues:

> Consequently, if the marriage partners engage in sexual intercourse during the fertile period and thereby most likely will conceive new life, the marital act may not be morally justifiable when they foresee that they will not have the means to provide the proper education for the child. The rhythm method, too, can be immoral if it is used to prevent the measure of responsible parenthood. But the use of contraceptives can be morally justified if these means do not obstruct the partners in the expression of conjugal love and if they keep birth control within the limits of responsible parenthood. Marital intercourse can be called neither moral nor immoral when it is the object of a judgment which considers it without due regard for its end. A moral evaluation is only possible if it is a study of the totality of the conjugal act, namely, when one considers whether or not the conjugal act (means) negates the requirements of love and responsible parenthood (end).[5]

That is my understanding of proportionate reason. And it is a far cry from better results or socially desirable consequences or net good. Therefore, I do not see how proportionate reason as explained is reducible to a consequentialism which speaks about net good, a point I shall return to below.

Many interpreters fail to grasp this notion of proportionate reason. There could be many reasons for this, but one seems central: an action involving evil is too quickly classified as a *moral* evil. Once that is done, the notion of proportion shifts to net benefits. In the study referred to above, Louis Janssens has put this very clearly:

The question to which we refer here is known as the problem of the relation of the *debita proportio* and ontic evil. If the presence of ontic evil as such would always endanger the *debita proportio* of our action, it would be impossible to act morally, because it is impossible to prevent ontic evil. The danger lies in the fact that *moral* evil is mentioned too soon. This happens every time a moral judgment of an exterior act does not include a judgment of the end and of the agent. This is taking ontic evil for moral evil.

Janssens uses as an example the speaking of falsehood.

It is said that "to say something which is not true" is "to lie," and the generally accepted meaning of "to lie" suggests moral disapprobation. This judgment is not sufficiently discriminating to be true. It passes over the distinction between *falsiloquim* (ontic evil) and *mendacium*. Each *falsiloquim* is undoubtedly an ontic evil. . . . But is each *falsiloquium* (ontic evil) at the same time a *mendacium* (moral evil)?

Janssens answers in the negative and uses professional secrecy as an example. If professional secrets are not kept, the very faith in others that is so indispensable to social living is undermined. Furthermore, there are times when mere silence may be interpreted as revelation of the secret.

When someone has no right to know our secret, we must defend our right of secrecy by the necessary means, even by a *falsiloquium* if it is the only means and although it includes an ontic evil.

Franz Scholz has made this point when dealing with the thought of Thomas Aquinas.[6] He notes that the sentence "a good end can justify a physically evil means" stands in agreement with the thought of Aquinas. When treating dispensations from the decalogue, Thomas argued that a dispensation is possible only when there is a difference between the original sense of the norm and its verbal formulation. Scholz uses the fifth commandment as an example. The formulation of this prohibition forbids the taking of human life. Yet there are the instances of war and capital punishment. How do these make sense if the decalogue is "beyond dispensation"?

For Thomas, so Scholz rightly argues, the divine intention is aimed only at the unjust destruction of life *(occisio hominis . . . secundum quod habet rationem indebiti)*. Thus, the object of the fifth commandment is not simply killing, but unjust killing. When killing is justified, it no longer falls under the matter of this prohibition. Thus for Thomas there is a clear distinction between the factual notion (*Tatsachenbegriff*, killing) and the value notion (*Unwertbegriff*, murder). This means, of course, that whatever taking of human life is justified (we can disagree about the range of instances), is justified precisely by the good end—and that only.

Brody's main difficulty with the position I propose is its alleged failure to deal with human rights. Thus he argues that "unless we are prepared to treat individuals as mere means, there are certain of their rights that cannot be violated even if doing so would lead to very desirable consequences."

Brody must be reminded that before one ascribes rights, one must first discuss what is right and wrong. If we agree that it is wrong to kill a human being in certain circumstances, then such killing may be said to violate the victim's rights. His right does not exist independently of the rights and wrongs of killing. Brody's mistake is to conduct the conversation in terms of rights before the rights and wrongs are established that circumscribe human rights. He then uses such rights to invalidate an analysis that seeks to discover the rights and wrongs. The carriage is pulling the horse.

This becomes very clear in Brody's analysis of capital punishment. He ascribes to me the position which holds that the criminal has a full-fledged right to life, but that this right can be outweighed by social benefits. He objects to this—and so would I. If some urgent good or avoidance of evil *justifies* taking the life of a criminal (and I seriously doubt that it does), then one does not say that the benefits outweigh that right, as if it were legitimate to violate rights at times. Whenever one concludes that life may legitimately be taken, he must simultaneously assert that such taking is not a violation of a right. The moral life, after all, is not a fragmented and patchwork thing. It can never be morally right (an objective act of beneficence) to do an injustice. For a *jus* is precisely a moral claim on another's actions or omissions, a claim that makes it morally wrong, for example, to kill. But before one asserts that *jus,* he must get involved in conversation about the rights and wrongs of killing. For example, why is not indirect killing a violation of a right? The one only indirectly killed might make a strong case of this point.

When Brody expresses his own understanding of the rights in the case of capital punishment, he suggests that the criminal "because of his actions, no longer has a full-fledged right to life." But this simply restates the matter; it does not explain it or prove it. For "no longer has a full-fledged right to life" is equivalent to saying "is one whose life may be taken." But that is to be established. Why, because of his actions, does a criminal not have a full-fledged right to life? Were Brody to get down to answering that type of question, he would find himself dealing with a notion very close to proportionate reason.

2. *Brody's rejection of Ramsey.* Here I can be brief because I shall return to the matter at greater length later. Brody has accurately stated Ramsey's dilemma: if the values are incommensurable, then indirectness is needed. But the *reason* to act demands some kind of commensuration. One cannot have it both ways. If Ramsey had focused on the notion of intrinsic evil in the tradition that generated the principle of double effect, he would not have gotten into this problem. By saying that it is the incommensurability of values or goods that forces indirectness Ramsey (a) supposes that certain actions, described in neutral terms, are intrinsically evil; and (b) ignores an analysis of whether this is so. But this is, I think, the heart of our problem.

3. *Brody's alternative proposals.* Brody approaches the problems of lifetaking (abortion, euthanasia) through a consideration of human rights—the right not to be killed and the right to be saved. His approach finesses and thereby begs the crucial ethical issues. In a key sentence, Brody notes that "in general, people can consent to their being deprived of something to which they have a right. . . ." He then concludes that one who acts on the basis of that consent or request does no wrong. The above sentence is crucial because Brody says "*can* consent." However, the entire euthanasia discussion concerns whether a person *may* consent to having his life taken. Obviously, if one *may* so consent, then another does no injustice in acting on such consent. But is a person morally empowered to waive his right to life in these circumstances? The consensus answer for centuries has been in the negative. Because one may waive some rights, it does not follow that he may waive all rights; for rights differ depending on the good at stake. There are rights we refer to as inalienable.

This matter is so important that it deserves a rewording. Among the ways in which rights go out of existence Brody mentions voluntary waiving. Where human life is concerned this must mean that one *may* rightfully say to another: "Take my life." There may be reasons that make this legitimate and rightful. But then one should discuss the reasons—and when he does he will be involved in a discussion of proportionality. Simply to say that the right can be (namely, *may* be) waived is to assume what is to be proved; that one may rightfully say to another "Take my life."

When he attempts to apply this to the save-one-or-lose-two dilemma of pregnancy, Brody says of the fetus that it "is not being unjustly deprived of that life to which it has a right *because it will inevitably die shortly anyway. . . .*" The weakness of this analysis is seen when it is universalized. That is, anyone who will inevitably die shortly anyway is not *unjustly* deprived of his life. This ties the justice and injustice of killing to the imminence and inevitability of death. Such a relationship is a mere assertion. In order for it to stand one must be able to say that it is morally right to kill someone if his death is imminent and inevitable. If that is the situation, then there is no violation of justice. But the ethical argument is not solved by mere assertion. Once again, we see that Brody is involved in a *petitio principii*. He ascribes certain rights and then speaks of the rightness or wrongness of certain actions or omissions. He must, contrarily, first discuss the rightness or wrongness of actions and only then ascribe carefully and precisely the right.

Actually, when all is said and done, Brody is a closet proportionalist. He states that some rights are stronger than others and then concludes:

> If on the basis of the strength of the rights they protect, one rule takes precedence over another, then that justifies an exception.

Now what does this mean? If the right not to be killed is stronger than the right to be saved, that must inevitably mean that there are fewer reasons justifying one than the other. That is, there can be more occasions when it is right *not to save* than there are when it is right *to kill*. That means simply that there are more proportionate reasons for not saving than for killing. If Brody would get behind his rights language to discuss the ethical rights and wrongs that circumscribe rights, he would see that proportionality is inseparable from the notion of a *stronger* and *weaker* right. Ultimately then, Brody has not proposed a different analysis of conflict situations, but only different words—words that both hide the underlying ethical analysis and, I believe to some extent, distance their author from it.

Paul Ramsey

It was to be expected that only heroic efforts by the prodigious Paul Ramsey could reduce his manuscript to a lean one hundred and twenty manuscript pages. "Increase and multiply" is a biblical mandate Ramsey has taken over and spoken to his typewriter with a real vengeance, or, if I may, with a finality disallowing any exceptions by proportionate reason. Amidst it all, I am never sure I have him down pat. Nevertheless the reader should not be misled. There are four or five key ideas in this discussion on which a verdict will depend. However, in attempting to face these key issues, I must not be insensitive to Ramsey's stature as a moral theologian nor to his commitment to truth and logic. Both stature and commitment, the former the result of the latter, mean that Ramsey would not want me to let him get away with unconvincing and inconsistent analyses. I shall try to oblige him, but this attempt will demand some rather detailed, and therefore lengthy, commentary.

With Ramsey let us begin at the very beginning—his beginning. Ramsey starts with the notion of proportionate reason. He states:

> There is, of course, measurable meaning in some judgments of proportion, that is, in cases in which one takes (indirectly) one life to save the only one that can be saved (rather than lose two) in abortion cases.

He then states that "obviously one should choose the lesser of these commensurate evils" but adds that such body counts "are the only instances I can think of in which there is clear commensurate meaning in the final judgment of proportion under the rule of twofold effect."

Now notice what we have here. (1) Ramsey argues that it is precisely incommensurability of goods that demands indirectness of intent. (2) He admits that there is in the case clear commensurability of the goods and evils involved. (3) Yet he asserts in such abortion decisions the notion of indirectness. I must beg Ramsey to explain all of this. If the evils are commensurable (one life versus two deaths in abortion cases) and one should "obviously . . . choose the lesser of these commensurate evils," then what, pray tell, does indirectness have to do with it all? Ramsey has simply smuggled the notion in. Here is an analysis, I submit, whose time has not come, and is not likely to come. It is a clear *petitio principii,* a point on which Frankena and Schüller would certainly agree.

Ramsey labors mightily to show that the warrant for taking fetal life is "what the fetus is doing to the mother" and that therefore the act is targeted against the lethal harm the fetus is causing, and thus not against the fetal life as such. Hence it is indirect. But his struggles are, on his own terms, futile and inconsistent. For the evils involved in the only available alternatives are commensurable, the lesser evil clear, and *that* is why it is morally right to save the one life that one can. Ramsey admits all of this but then incomprehensibly keeps talking about "indirectness" when the only warrant and need for such usage, on his own terms, is incommensurability. This is far more than mysterious. I believe it is simply incoherent.

Let me stay with the classic abortion case for a moment before delving into the unclarities that led Ramsey to this analytic cul-de-sac. I have argued that in the situation when the choice is save the mother or allow both mother and child to die, it is proportionate reason that is the sole justificatory principle. One chooses to save the one life that can be saved *because in such circumstances that is the lesser evil.* Indeed, I once wrote that "it seems clear that directness and indirectness do not really function critically in Ramsey's analysis."[7]

Ramsey vigorously rejects this and sees it as an example of my "penchant for finding proportionate reason sitting under every vine and fig tree. . . ." Here is the case he offers and his reasoning:

> Let us consider certain sorts of birthroom conflicts of life against life which formerly (like craniotomy) would have been deemed to be direct and therefore unjustified killings and which (unlike craniotomy) have *not* been prevented by advancements in medical practice. . . . I have in mind the repeatable (if rare) case of a pregnant woman who has a misplaced, acute appendicitis and who will die from its rupture unless a physician goes straight through the uterus (that is, kills the baby first, then saves her life). Also, there are cases of aneurysm of the aorta in which the wall of the aorta is so weakened that it balloons out behind the pregnant uterus. Again, the physician must first kill the fetus in order to deal with the aneurysm that threatens the mother's life. In both these sorts of cases the baby is in the way, it "shields" the mother from the necessary cure.[8]

In such instances, Ramsey argues (against Grisez) that the child's life may be taken to save the mother, but argues that

> while the life is taken with observable directness, the intention of the action is directed against the lethal process or function of that life. To stop the fetus's death-dealing action (or to remove the fetus's fatal "shielding" nonaction) describes the rectitude of the action of a physician in any surgery he puts forth.

Thus, for Ramsey, it is removal of the child that is intended, not its death; and so " 'removal' is what *is done* and is justified in all cases where 'necessity' foredooms that only one life can be saved."

So it is *removal* as the description of the action that allows Ramsey to conclude to indirectness. But he then limits this description "to cases of necessity or forced choice between saving one life or allowing both to die." Now, we must ask, how can Ramsey so limit the description of abortional interventions? Why cannot such a description be made also of an abortion in incest or rape cases? After all, the child is doing something to the mother in these cases, but what the child is doing is not lethal to itself or the mother. It is, for example, "only" bringing the mother enormous suffering—having to bear the child of a rapist. By limiting the notion of "removal" (and indirectness) to the one saved versus two lost dilemma, Ramsey shows that it is precisely the saving of the only life that can be saved that permits him to argue that in such cases *alone* may the death of the child be said to be indirectly caused. And if that is the case, it is not indirectness that yields the moral rectitude of an abortion, as he insists, but simply the fact that *in such circumstances* this is the best service of life, namely, it is clearly the lesser evil, and there is a proportionate reason.

Ramsey resists this conclusion. Why? In his own words:

> Precisely because by that reasoning—the choice of the lesser evil—I would be justified in killing the child or threatening to kill the child of a criminal in order to stop him from killing my wife and child. One for two.

That would be a telling argument if there were any connection between its conclusion and the foregoing analysis. There is not. Ramsey's argument has supposed that the abortion dilemmas under discussion are simply a matter of "one for two" and that the determination of the lesser evil is *merely quantitative* in the abortion situation, and that therefore wherever a lifesaving versus life-losing situation presents itself, a quantitative calculus is logically in order.

Hardly. In the abortion situation it is not *simply* a save-one versus lose-two dilemma. Something else must be added—and here I should like to acknowledge the suggestions made by James A. Wiseman, O.S.B. Wiseman gives two examples of choices to save life. The first is the classic abortion decision where the choice is to save the mother rather than lose both mother and child. The other Wiseman cites from *Hello Lovers!:*

> Take the case of burning a child with napalm. Let's say that you can, under extreme circumstances, make an act of this kind morally redeemable. Say that by doing so and *only* by doing so, you can bring about the end of the Vietnam war (by satisfying Ho Chi Minh's sadistic pleasure), and say also, as Fr. Wassmer did previously, that the baby is dying of cancer and so on.

This case is presented by William May and is very similar to that of the southern sheriff and rioting lynch mob discussed in this volume.[9]

Now if in the abortion case, the meaning of proportionate reason were *merely* numerical, then it is hard to see how a similar conclusion is not justifiable in the case given above. The difference suggested by Wiseman—and I believe he is correct—is that in the abortion case the deadly deed is intrinsically and inescapably connected with the saving of the mother's life, whether that deadly deed be a craniotomy or the removal of the fetus to get at a life-threatening aneurysm. That is to say, there is in the very nature of the case, no other way of saving the mother. There is an essential link between the means and the end. By contrast, however, such a link does not exist in the second instance. There is no inherent connection between the killing of a child and the change of mind of a military leader or a rioting lynch mob. The connection is, under analysis, adventitious. In the abortion case, no other possibility of saving the mother is conceivable. In the napalm case, however, several other approaches are available, regardless of how pessimistic one would. be about their success. For those who hold to the notion of free will in the doing of evil (and good), there is never an *inherent connection* between killing a child and changing the murderous mind of a military leader or an angry lynch mob. Wiseman thus concludes:

> Life may be directly taken only when there is not only de facto no other way of saving one or more other lives, but when no other way is even *conceivable* with the means truly at our disposal.

Ramsey would have seen and would now admit this crucial difference in the notion of lesser evil if he had looked more carefully at his own wording in the abortion case. There he refers to "necessity and forced choice" and to cases "where 'necessity' foredooms." There is no such forced choice or foredooming by necessity in the napalm case or that of the rioting mob.

I believe Denis O'Callaghan had something like this in mind when he referred to the scholastic tradition on exceptions to moral norms. O'Callaghan wrote:

> If it was honest with itself it would have admitted that it made exceptions where these depended on chance occurrence of circumstances rather than on free human choice. In other words, an exception was admitted when it would not open the door to more and more exceptions, *precisely because the occurrence of the exception was determined by factors of chance outside of human control.*[10]

He gives intervention into ectopic pregnancy as an example. The casuistic tradition, he believes, accepted what is in principle an abortion because it posed no threat to the general position, though this tradition felt obliged to rationalize this by use of the double effect. Tubal pregnancy, as a relatively rare occurrence and one independent of human choice, does not lay the way open to abuse.

O'Callaghan's "chance occurrence of circumstances" and "factors of chance outside of human control" looks very much like Ramsey's "necessity and forced choice" and "where 'necessity' foredooms." What O'Callaghan is saying is that "saving one rather than losing two" is proportionate not merely because of the quantities involved, but because the narrowing of choice involving such commensurable quantities "was determined by factors of chance *outside of human control.*"

John Noonan is very close to this analysis of the situation. To refer to the killing of the fetus in ectopic operations and surgery for removal of a cancerous uterus as "indirect killings" is, he believes, "a confusing and improper use of the metaphor." He continues:

> A clearer presentation of the cases of the cancerous uterus and the ectopic pregnancy would acknowledge them to be true exceptions to the absolute inviolability of the fetus. Why are they not exceptions which would eat up the rule? It depends on what the rule is considered to be. The principle that can be discerned in them is, whenever the embryo is a danger to the life of the mother, an abortion is permissible. At the level of reason nothing more can be asked of the mother. The exceptions do eat up any rule of preferring the fetus to the mother—any rule of fetus first. They do not destroy the rule that the life of the fetus has precedence over other interests of the mother. The exceptions of the ectopic pregnancy and the cancerous uterus are special cases of the general exception to the rule against killing, which permits one to kill in self-defense. Characterization of this kind of killing as "indirect" does not aid analysis.[11]

Noonan's notion of these interventions as exceptions that would not eat up the rule is all but identical to O'Callaghan's "an exception was admitted when it would not open the door to more and more exceptions." And I believe that Noonan's "whenever the embryo is a danger to the life of the mother" is easily convertible with O'Callaghan's more precise statement of the threat depending "on chance occurrences of circumstances rather than on free human choice." For in stating that "other interests of the mother" do not take precedence over the fetus, Noonan is rejecting precisely those interventions traceable to "free human choice."

In summary, then, in the abortion dilemma there is not merely a quantitative analysis being made, but it is made in circumstances where there is an inherent necessity between the means (taking the child's life) and the end (saving the mother where otherwise both mother and child will perish). That is why I said above "one chooses to save the one life that can be saved *because in such circumstances that is the lesser evil.*" In other circumstances, it would not be the lesser evil, and would not be proprotionate. That is what I tried to convey with the phrase used in *Ambiguity in Moral Choice*: "(b) no other way of salvaging it here and now; (c) its protection here and now will not undermine it in the long run." That is also what I had in mind when I said that the essential ingredients that led to the formulation of the rule of double effect are two: the necessity of a certain good and "the inseparability of this good from harm or evil in the circumstances."

If, then, Ramsey's reason for denying that "proportion alone functions critically in this analysis" (abortion case) is that this would lead to the conclusion that I may take one life to save four (or many) lives *in any circumstances,* it is no reason at all. It is but a false (because merely quantitative) notion of proportionate reason and the lesser evil. All one need do is clarify the true notion of proportionate reason and Ramsey's notions of directness and indirectness are bared for what they are, mere appendages.

But before moving to more detailed comment, I should like to put in concise form what I believe to be a fatal argument against Ramsey's reasoning. It is as follows. First, if, as Ramsey admits, in certain circumstances my options are two (save one life, lose two), and, if, as he admits, the goods are commensurable and one ought to save one rather than lose two, then why is indirectness invoked? Thus, indirectness is, at least here, unnecessary. Secondly, if, as Ramsey argues against Grisez, the inseparability of the bad effect from the intended good is not a condition for indirectness, then clearly the evil is the means to the good. Thus we have one clear instance (the abortion case) when the evil of taking life (a basic good) may be intended as a means. But if this is so, it is in principle so with all nonmoral goods, and the operative consideration becomes proportionality.

But Ramsey is committed to the thesis that "any killing of man by man must be 'indirect'."[12] Why he says this, why it is not necessary, and why he misunderstands and rejects any other possible alternative will be the burden of my subsequent remarks. I will organize these remarks under the following headings: (1) turning against a basic good; (2) life as a unique value or basic good; (3) Ramsey's notion of incommensurability; (4) the notion of proprotionate reason; and (5) the relation of the will to evil.

1. *Turning against a basic good*. This formulation is that of Germain Grisez. One of the modes of responsibility with regard to the basic goods, according to Grisez, is that we must never directly turn against them. Why? In Grisez's words:

> To act directly against any of the basic human goods is to spurn one aspect of the total possibility of human perfection, and it is freely to set the will at odds with its own principle of interest in the goods open to us.[13]

In another place Grisez explains this more precisely:

> To act directly against a good is to subordinate that good to whatever leads us to choose such a course of action. We treat an end as if it were a mere means; we treat an aspect of the person as if it were an object of measurable and calculable worth. Yet each of the principles of practical reason is as basic as the other.[14]

This is the analysis upon which Ramsey is obviously heavily reliant. But I am afraid he gives us only warmed-up leftovers from an original menu whose ingredients he has not thoroughly digested. In general, I am very sympathetic to Grisez's (philosophical) analysis of the origin of moral obligation, and that is why I am concerned that it not be undermined by being overstated. Here I will list only a few of the major difficulties I have with Ramsey's analysis.

First, there is the question of the meaning of "turning directly against a basic good." I think I could accept the notion that because life is a basic good, we ought never turn against it in the interest of another basic good. But I have deliberately used the phrase "never turn against it" (rather than "never *directly* turn against it") because the heart of our discussion is whether one who directly intends death in a death-dealing action necessarily turns against a basic good. To affirm identity of the two is to beg the question. That is, it is to say that directly intending death in a choice is equivalent to "turning against" the basic good of life. One can identify those two only by assuming that directness of intent is *morally* distinct from indirectness of intent with regard to the same nonmoral evil.

It seems to me that if the taking of human life is the only choice that is truly lifesaving and life-serving in the circumstances, then one cannot be said to turn against the basic good of life in electing such an alternative.

By inserting *directly* into the wording "turn against a basic good" Ramsey and Grisez have added nothing. Indeed, they have suggested thereby the rather fuzzy possibility that one could only "indirectly turn against the basic good."

This seems clear from Ramsey's own wording. He notes:

> If then incommensurate rights to life come into conflict, one confronts decisional ambiguity whose grammar can only be parsed by the justifiability of never doing any more than indirectly intending to take a human life *if unavoidably the deadly deed must be done.*

Clearly the basic warrant for taking life in such circumstances is that, all things considered, such taking is a life-serving action. That is the only possible meaning of "if unavoidably the deadly deed must be done." Why *must* it be done? There is always the option of allowing both mother and child to die. Several authoritative Catholic documents drew exactly this harsh conclusion.[15] Ramsey rightly argues, however, that "unavoidably the deadly deed *must be* done." Now, if that is right, and I think it is, it is so because in the circumstances taking one life rather than losing two is the lesser evil. This is the sole root warrant for the intervention. Ramsey's subsequent appeal to indirectness is precisely that, subsequent—tacked on, in the interests of getting the killing within the reach of a distinction whose moral relevance he has accepted, but never explained.

My second problem is Ramsey's understanding of "basic good." Not only is he unclear about the notion of "turning against," but nowhere does he unveil to us what these goods are. At one place he says one ought not turn against *"any* human good." At another we read "turning directly against other human goods." In still another the reference is to basic goods. Ramsey even refers to turning "directly against the value of Russian nationhood," whatever that might mean. When interpreting Ross, he suggests the wrongfulness of "turning directly against the claims of reason," "of happiness," and so on.

Yet amidst all these possible but reprehensible moral swervings and veerings, Ramsey wants life (like moral integrity) to be set apart. For him it is more basic than all other goods—though he does suggest that liberty may be on the same plane.

These statements raise all sorts of unanswered questions. What are these goods (Ramsey repeatedly uses the plural) against which we may "never directly turn"? Does the list include instrumental as well as noninstrumental goods? If life is to be set apart as more basic, then may we not turn against less basic goods to preserve a more basic one? If life is, indeed, to be set apart, then how are other goods *equally* basic so that we ought not turn against *"any* human good"? Furthermore, if these goods are all incommensurable (the very basis for Ramsey's use of indirectness), then how is one (life) *more* basic than the others?

More concretely, if it is precisely incommensurability that forces indirectness, then whenever incommensurability exists, one must have indirectness while causing a disvalue. On this reading one could never intend to deceive another, to take his property at times, to cause him any pain whatsoever. For there are certainly many nonmoral values that are incommensurate, for example, money and physical health. But this is certainly not the way tradition has viewed this matter. In other words, Ramsey has no coherent theory to give intelligibility to the notion of turning against human goods, to say nothing of turning directly against them. That is why I have referred to his assertions as warmed-over Grisez.

The matter must be illustrated by a reference to the procreative good. Ramsey notes that Daniel Maguire and I disagree on whether there is ever proportionate reason for direct killing (euthanasia) in terminal cases. He notes that we reach "opposite conclusions on the gravest moral matter" and uses this to reach a twofold conclusion: (1) there is little moral guidance in proportionate reason alone; (2) the difference between Maguire and me is in "temperament or some other factor and not of moral reason in exercise." I shall return below to the kind of guidance proportionate reason is thought to give. Suffice it for the present to say that proportionate reason, *as such,* gives no guidance. It represents a structure of moral reasoning—that is all. But because Ramsey sees Maguire and me disagreeing on the application of this structure, he concludes that moral reason was not in exercise in building the structure. *Non sequitur.*

But let us turn the tables a bit and examine the matter of the procreative good. Grisez sees any contraceptive act as a direct turning against the basic good of procreation. Ramsey, contrarily, does not. Here we have two sensitive and moral men drawing "opposite conclusions on the gravest moral matter." If the notion of incommensurable goods is truly fundamental and clear, then how is it that Ramsey and Grisez can disagree so radically on contraception? Furthermore, Ramsey differs from Grisez on the importance of separability by the agent of the good result from the concomitant evil. Once again, this is a matter of the gravest moral concern (for in Grisez's view it would mean Ramsey is doing moral evil that good may follow). There may be differences in temperament between Ramsey and Grisez, but it could scarcely account for this disagreement. What does account for it is, I believe, Ramsey's quite inscrutable notion of basic good and his equally inscrutable analysis of what must count as turning against such a good. What seems very clearly lacking, then, is any sustained analysis of the meaning of turning against a basic good—or, if I may use Ramsey's phrase, what is missing in the elaboration of these notions is "moral reason in exercise."

2. *Life as a unique value.* After ultimately agreeing with Schüller and me that sin or moral evil must be "set apart" and may never be directly intended, Ramsey argues that there are "other human goods besides moral integrity" that fit this category. Even though he uses the plural, human life is the good he comes down on. He writes:

> Killing a human being must surely be classified with moral evil as something that Christians ought never to encompass with "direct voluntariety."

Life, like moral integrity, must be "set apart."

Ramsey offers two reasons or warrants for saying this. The first is the basic character of human life: "Because a human life is so basic, it is therefore set apart." When one destroys human life, he destroys "in and for him the whole scale of goods and values, the whole world of worth he knows." On this reasoning, Ramsey concludes that "the latter (all other goods and values) are commensurate; he is not."

His second appeal is religious in character. Human beings are the image of God, holy ground.

> For this reason, it seems evident, our tradition of ethics "distanced" from killing to the same degree as from tempting someone to sin. The morality of doing either was not submitted to judgments of proportion alone. . . .

I have a good deal of sympathy for the notion that human life, as the indispensable condition of all other values and worth, enjoys a special place in our evaluations. In this Ramsey would disagree with Grisez, for whom the basic goods are *equally* basic. However, Ramsey sees this special place as one of equality with moral integrity; for he says of human life that it is "utterly incomparable . . . no less than in the case of intending the 'sin' of another." And he further states that "it ought not to be implied that *killing* is any less of a moral evil (even if *death* is a nonmoral evil) than intending the sin of another. . . ."

Here several important rejoinders are called for, because I believe Ramsey is in real trouble with his identification of killing with moral evil. First of all, it is erroneous to say that our tradition "distanced from killing to the same degree as from tempting to sin." It distanced from only certain types of killing; what under examination must be called unjustified killing. Otherwise we should have no theory of capital punishment, self-defense, or just war. In this sense it is true to say that human life is indeed proportionable, but only in a very few carefully specified places. One can use all sorts of feature-dependent explanations of these exceptions, but beneath them all is the proportionability of human life in those cases. However, we have no theory of "justified sinning."

Furthermore, the killing "distanced from" in the tradition (direct, of innocents) was seen as intrinsically evil but *precisely because of a lack of right* given to human beings by God to take life in this way. It was seen as arrogation of God's rights of dominion. However, God *could* command one directly to kill another. Similarly, all theologians in the tradition have admitted that a person may commit suicide if positively empowered to do so by God. Put in slightly different and admittedly anthropomorphic terms, the acid test of the difference between intending death and intending sin is whether it is conceivable that God could intend the death of another. In a centuries-old tradition, there is no doubt on this matter. Of course he could. For what he may empower others to do, he may himself do. God can intend the death of a person as he intervenes to kill him. There is no contradiction involved here.

But it is inconceivable (analytically self-contradictory) that he could intend sin or one's moral ruin in this way. True, he has created free creatures capable of sin. But it is inconceivable that he would *intend* the moral ruin of a person in the same way he could be said to intend that person's death.[16] Therefore, while life is certainly a basic good and killing a basic evil, they assuredly are not to be classified along with *moral* good and *moral* evil. For if God can choose to do an evil for his purposes, we know thereby that the evil is not in the same category as *moral* evil.

My second problem with Ramsey's account is that, when all is said and done, he seems to waver on just why life ought to be set apart and force indirectness on us when we take it. He urges throughout that it is incommensurability that is the reason for this. One can no more measure up or compare human life with other values than one can compare apples with oranges. Fair enough. But in other places it is the fact that life is *utterly* incomparable, imponderable, and so on. Thus he informs us that *"because human life is so basic,* it is therefore set apart" (italics added). This, together with his statement about moral integrity ("a *commanding* moral value incommensurate . . .") leads to the suspicion that it is not precisely the incommensurability of life with other values that leads Ramsey into indirectness, but the fact that it is *so* basic, *so* commanding a value that it is unlike any others in this respect. But does this not lead us to some curious results? One, for instance, would be the implication that some values are "incomparable, imponderable, incommensurable" while others are *utterly* incomparable, *incorrigibly* incommensurable. But is not incommensurability like pregnancy, or is there a condition unknown to us that must be called *utterly* pregnant?

Actually, Ramsey's exhortations about human life not being proportionable seem to stem from and assume that once it is said that killing is not in the same category as moral evil, then it will immediately be the case that a glacial unconcern for human life will be on us and many lives will be taken that would not otherwise. I sympathize with Ramsey's good teleological instincts here, but his assumption is simply not true, not if one is careful in his parsing of proportionality—a matter I shall return to below. Admittedly, if one refuses to identify intending a person's death with intending his moral ruin, and says of the former that it is a nonmoral evil capable of rare justification, one does open himself to face some uncomfortable problems. For instance, the Anglican Study Group, in its *On Dying Well,* has argued that it is not wrongful to kill a soldier being incinerated in a tank's gun turret when the only option is his certain death by excruciating burning.[17] Schüller has raised similar questions without taking a firm position.[18] These problems are, I think, legitimate ones and very uncomfortable indeed. Those who rely on the deceptive decisiveness of the direct/indirect distinction experience no such discomfort. But all this says is that Ramsey is uneasy with uncomfortable problems, not that the direct/indirect distinction can carry the load we give it. He would like things neat and clear from the hand of God. He would, I suspect, rejoice in a Mosaic formulation that runs as follows: "Thou shalt never directly kill an innocent person" complete with divine footnotes about what is direct and who is innocent in our time. That is why he can use a phrase such as "no limit to the revision of the deontological terms of ordinary moral discourse" as if it were a fatal salvo at the notion of proportionate reason. The world would be far less complicated, Ramsey seems to say, if there were far more intrinsic evils meeting us at every turn.

A third point. Ramsey speaks of human persons as images of God, holy ground, redeemed by the blood of Christ. These are the religious warrants to shore up his assertion that we ought not *directly* turn against the good of human life. As he concludes: "To destroy another embodied human life is at once to destroy in and for him the whole scale of goods and values, the whole world of worth he knows." Thus we again encounter the curious conclusion: "That seems to me to be good enough reason for the conclusion that one should never with 'direct voluntariety' take any human life. . . ." To me it would seem good enough reason for never taking any human life—stop. For one who is killed only indirectly has lost his "whole scale of goods and values, the whole world of worth he knows" quite as decisively and definitively as one who is killed directly. Once again we encounter, but in more religious terms, what we saw in Ramsey's treatment of the classic abortion dilemma: the begged question. That is, a morally significant difference is ascribed to direct and indirect taking of the life that is holy ground—when the whole question is precisely whether the difference is morally significant and why. The one who is killed only indirectly is also holy ground. What do fish think of the morality of fishing, so to speak?

Finally, one who puts killing another in the same category as intending his sin is bound to have not only some rarified ideas about the meaning of life, but possibly also flawed notions of moral evil. That is the case with Ramsey. These flawed notions surface any number of times.

For instance, he misunderstands Fuchs's use of the term *premoral* evil. It is true that both killing and intending another's moral ruin are premoral in the sense of "pre" to the agent's act. He may still be contemplating doing either one. They are alike in that. But this does not mean that killing and intending the sin of another are the same *kinds* of action *as evils*. One is intending the *death* of another; the other is intending his *moral ruin*.

Actually Ramsey agrees with Schüller and me that moral integrity is "set apart," that "*no* cause can be sufficiently worthy to warrant that evil." And he explains very well why: "That would be to make oneself good-for-nothing . . . to cut oneself off from life, from the appeal and claims of the good, from God." (Incidentally, once moral evil is described in this way, I have no idea why Ramsey objects to Schüller's statement that "moral evil is by definition unconditional disvalue" and "the exceptionless validity of norms stating it are analytical.")

Yet after this there follows a series of suggestions and objections that seem to question whether Ramsey really means (or understands) what he says. First he suggests that it would not be outrageously unreasonable to believe that directly tempting a person to sin "could be justified because in some cases that had to be done for the sake of an overriding greater nonmoral good." If moral evil is, by definition, precisely "cutting oneself off from good, from God," what possible nonmoral good could override this, be greater than adherence to and union with the source of all good? If Ramsey thinks the possibility is "not outrageously unreasonable," he clearly is willing to tinker with his statement that "sin against conscience is something no one should willfully and directly try to induce in another." But to tinker with that is to misunderstand the very meaning of moral evil. The stuff of moral heroes and martyrs is cut from the Pauline exclamation: "Can anything separate us from the love of Christ?"

Then again there is Ramsey's insistence that nonmoral evils and goods are participatively linked to all of the actions of life. Of course they are. One does not sin or violate his conscience in an abstract world. He sins *in human actions*. Moral evil (sin) is precisely the doing of harmful or destructive things or omitting actions supportive of goods in the self or others when this is perceived by the individual to be wrongful. Because he perceives it to be wrongful, he acts against his conscience in performing this or that action. By this the theologian means that there is *in the action* a perceived aversion from God (*aversio a Deo*) the source of all good. Therefore, when we speak of "intending the sin of another" we mean intending that another act against his conscience *in performing a particular act* (whether that action involve killing, falsehood, taking property, sexual intimacy, and so on).[19] We mean intending the vertical rupture in the horizontal concern. (Schüller has offered a different interpretation of this in this volume.) It is a *moral* evil because one's ultimate destiny, his whole meaning as a person, his relationship to God is at stake. Or, as Ramsey says, "that would be to cut oneself off . . . from God."

Ramsey admits all of this, his sole caveat being that this "'absolutizes' a number of other moral values as well. . . ." What this means is not clear to me. Killing is the one clear case he gives. For he says: "What argument can there be for classifying the slaying of man by man as a nonmoral evil?" One simple answer to that is: ask Abraham. Obviously God could not have commanded Abraham to perform a *moral* evil, and Abraham could not have readied himself out of virtuous obedience to God to kill Isaac if killing were a *moral* evil. (Or is it that the "slaying of man by man" is a *moral* evil only if God does not permit it? But then the whole question is how we know whether he permits it or not. If God can empower killing by a divine revelatory intervention, then how would a similar divine empowering to the same action be an inner contradiction, a violation of life, merely because it is mediated through the natural law, or a person's moral reasoning?)

The other values Ramsey wants to absolutize are injustice, untruthfulness, and infidelity. For he says:

> If then one should never willfully intend the moral evil of another, he should never directly intend another's injustice, untruthfulness, or infidelity under any circumstances; nor himself do injustice, tell an untruth, or prove unfaithful to another.

Ramsey then adds: "But these things can justifiably be in some sense done, provided no species of moral evil is ever directly encompassed within the agent's intention." On this basis he concludes that the direct/indirect distinction has significance "along a whole range of moral dilemmas," not just where sin is involved.

Ramsey's meaning here remains obscure. Clearly, there are many species of moral evil (injustice, infidelity, and so on). But they all are precisely alike in that they are *moral* evils. Whether, however, the direct/indirect distinction has significance "along a whole range of moral dilemmas," depends on what one understands to be a moral dilemma. Ramsey seems to suggest that it occurs where the demands of justice conflict with the demands, for example, of truthfulness or fidelity (moral values). I do not believe that is the case. Rather, nonmoral goods can be conflicted at times. We must determine which deserves the preference *before* we call a certain course of action just or unjust.

The source of Ramsey's obscurity here is suggested by his use of "tell an untruth," specifically his lumping it with injustice and infidelity. These latter two bespeak moral evaluations already made of the available alternative actions *(Wertbegriff)*, whereas "tell an untruth" is merely descriptive *(fasiloquium, Tatsachenbegriff)*. If one identifies the two notions, clearly the direct/indirect distinction applies down a whole range of dilemmas. But they should not be identified.

Similarly, Ramsey has identified too hastily injustice with the "slaying of man by man." Injustice is clearly a *moral* disvalue. Actions that must be called *unjust* are those where a competent moral agent is presumed in their performance to be acting in violation of the moral order. Clearly, then, I may not directly intend another's injustice because that is intending such a violation. But Ramsey wants every "slaying of man by man" to be a *moral* evil, that is, an injustice. That is a totally different matter and his insistence on this point reveals, in spite of his own fine descriptions of violating one's conscience, that he does not really grasp the meaning of moral evil.

By saying that "these things can justifiably be in some sense done," Ramsey meant to say or should have meant to say that what can justifiably be done at times is not injustice, but killing; not a lie, but a falsehood which in the circumstances is an appropriate use of our expressive powers because it protects the very values veracity is intended to protect; not an infidelity, but an action which, though it involves nonmoral evil, ought not to be classified as unfaithful. This same confusion is seen in Ramsey's response to Schüller (his footnote 5) where he imagines that righteousness, fidelity, justice, truthfulness can come into conflict—as if *moral* values could be in conflict. What is in conflict are certain nonmoral goods. Only after we have discerned what values deserve the preference ought we speak of the claims of justice, righteousness, fidelity, and so on. If it is truly moral values that are conflicted, our worldy situation is hopeless. We have no choice at times but to be unjust, unfaithful—to sin even amidst our best efforts. That is, of course, a strong Protestant tradition—but unabashedly Catholic as I am, I shall protest it here. And I think on good grounds. Ramsey complains that I cannot "conceive of conflicts of nonmoral goods or evils that are not resolvable by commensurate reason." That is correct. But why? Because I believe in a providential God in whose world the conflicts we experience do have a resolution. The difficulty in resolving these conflicts should not be identified with "no resolution" and the terribly black conclusion that our only choice is to choose *between* being either just or faithful. Proportionate reason will settle these claims between conflicted nonmoral goods and suggest to us what is, indeed, just, faithful, and so on. Our struggle is to know what is truly proportionate. It is a struggle because our knowing is infected with imperfection, self-interest, sin, and accumulated bad habits.

What finally leads me to believe that Ramsey may not fully appreciate the meaning of the term *moral evil* is his statement: "In any case, reference to God as *summum bonum* of the human will tells us little about value conflicts." I believe it tells us a great deal. If God is truly the *summum bonum*–source and sum of all good—then sin (*aversio a Deo,* rejection of him) is the *summum malum,* the very denial of creaturely meaningfulness. Now clearly the *summum bonum* takes precedence over any other human goods, simply because it includes them all, and is greater than all. Therefore, when any action is said to involve a rejection (sin) of the *summum bonum,* it is by definition an action which turns against and rejects the *summum bonum* for something less. One ought never to do that—a matter that is analytically clear notwithstanding Ramsey's uneven struggle with the matter. That means to me that one may never *sin* to bring about some human good or prevent an evil.[20] Or, what is the same, there is never a proportionate reason for sinning or intending another's sin. If Ramsey means to deny this when he says that "subjective moral integrity is not an 'absolute good'," I must simply disagree with him and urge that he reconsider the matter, though I admit that *unconditioned* is a better term than *absolute.*

In summary, then, Ramsey has made human life *more* fundamental than all other nonmoral values—but in doing so he has put it in the same category as moral integrity insofar as commensurability is concerned. I believe I could agree with the emphasis in the first move, but must reject the excess in the second. Indeed, at some point we must ask Ramsey whether being more fundamental does not imply some kind of commensurability. But that brings us to his notion of incommensurability.

3. *Ramsey's notion of incommensurability.* This is the key notion in Ramsey's analysis. It is what leads him to see moral relevance in the direct/indirect distinction, though I have already pointed out that there are times when he seems to say that it is the greatness of the value (basic, commanding) rather than its incommensurable character that influences him.

Ramsey says that one of his chief questions to me is whether " 'proportionate reason' means the same as 'commensurate reason' in the sense that it leads to measurable choices, to determinate moral judgments." My answer to that is yes, I understand proportionate to mean the same as commensurate. But whether I would agree to the expletive "in the sense that it leads to measurable choices" depends upon how one understands measurable choices. And that depends on what is measuring what.

In my understanding (and that of Knauer, Janssens, and others) it is the end that measures. That is, is the good end being sought by means involving nonmoral evil promoted and not undermined in this action or is it undermined? Or as Janssens puts it:

I mean that no intrinsic contradiction between the means and the end may be found in the total act when the act is placed in the light of reason. Put into terms of the philosophy of values, this means that the means must be consistent with the value of the end. Or, according to a more abstract formulation, the principle which has been affirmed in the end must not be negated by the means.

That is the meaning of *debita proportio* or what I call proportionate reason. It involves Ramsey's "measurable choices" if what is being measured is not incommensurable values or goods, but the relation of means involving nonmoral evil to the end, or what is the same, the status of the end after performing the act involving nonmoral evil or omitting it. I shall return to this under title of proportionate reason. But an example or two may help. The obvious instance is the classic abortion dilemma (save the mother or lose both mother and child). What is being weighed, commensurated, proportioned here is not one life against the other, the value of the mother's life versus the value of the child's.[21] What is being weighed is the relationship of a killing intervention (abortion) to the end (saving life). The means is judged proportionate because *in these circumstances* it is consistent with the end. It is the only response available, even though it involves nonmoral or ontic evil, that affirms the value of the end. Ramsey would admit this, but he states that this is the single instance where the values are commensurate. In other instances (though I know not how many because he has no developed theory of incommensurable goods) there is no such single scale of measurement.

I do not believe that is the case and this brings us to Ramsey's notion of incommensurability. He argues that certain goods are incommensurable one with another and therefore we have no possibility of proportioning or commensurating. We have only indeterminacy. The example he uses is the defense of Russian nationhood. Defending nationhood cost 20,000,000 Russian lives. Not going to war would mean in the circumstances forfeiting nationhood. "Either verdict," he writes, "rests upon a comparison of lives lost with the value of nationhood having a continuing history." But these are incommensurable values; they cannot be weighed against each other and one preferred to the other. Thus indeterminacy. Thus, too, his conclusion that it is "reasonable to say Russia *should have* defended herself at that toll" and "reasonable to say the cost was too great."

Now what is to be said of this? The first thing is that if both conclusions are equally reasonable, we have not simply indeterminacy, but decisional paralysis if the decision taken is to be judged morally right. If one cannot *somehow* overcome this indeterminacy, on what basis could a nation ever go to war with moral uprightness? Secondly, it seems to me that either statement is reasonable to the extent that *some* comparison between the conflicted goods is possible. But Ramsey is asserting incommensurability, straight and simple. That is, no measure is possible. The proper conclusion, then, is that neither statement is reasonable—namely, able to be reasoned when compared to its opposite. And if neither can be reasoned, I fail to see how either could be said to be right or wrong.

Thirdly, granted the theoretical problem of comparing incomparables, what Ramsey calls the "quantity of the qualities" problem, still in daily life we manage satisfactorily enough to reach decisions that involve weighing, balancing, and comparing many a rather incomparable quality in the experience of good hoped for. We manage to arrive at greater good and lesser evil verdicts in many a decision we could not quantify or demonstrate numerically. In most decisions we are comparing what seem to be overlapping species of good or alternative ways of satisfying a single need or passion, but still not goods that fit exactly at points in a single scale so that an Ideal Mathematician could infallibly tell us what is right.

So we choose to smoke or drink or eat creamy butter for enjoyment's sake at the risk of shorter life. We elect a heart bypass operation to relieve oppressive and continuous chest pains although we know the operation is still investigational and itself may kill us. We choose a contemplative or more active career for ourselves.

In all these instances it is not inaccurate to say that we somehow manage to weigh incommensurables, to overcome indeterminancy. As Donald Evans puts it: "Such compromises are a part of everyday morality but they raise serious problems for ethical theory, for their logic and rationale is obscure."[22] In making such compromises we are within the notion of commensurate reason.

Ramsey would admit all this. Indeed, the last three paragraphs are lifted straight from an earlier draft of his essay. On the principle that abandoned property becomes a *res nullius,* I claim these paragraphs for my own. Could it be that Ramsey dropped them because they would weaken his case about not comparing the incomparable when we get to killing? Whatever the reason, it is clear that life is not just incommensurable for Ramsey, but *quite* or *utterly* incommensurable (that qualifier again!). And for this reason, Ramsey is stuck with the kind of indeterminancy that leads to paralysis, with a type of analysis that says of either of two contradictory positions that they are both reasonable, with a position that effectively empties the notion of *justa causa (jus ad bellum)* or its lack in the just-war theory of any decisive power.

A test case will reveal that Ramsey does not, or better, cannot mean what he says (namely that continuing nationhood and loss of life are *simply* incommensurable). Let World War II be the example. Ramsey believes (rightly in my opinion) that the entry of the United States into the war against the Axis aggressor was a morally *right* decision, even though this was accompanied with the foreknowledge that thousands of American troops would perish in the effort. Furthermore, he believes that the pacifist posture toward our entry into World War II was *wrong*. He does not regard either position as equally reasonable, but he sees one as wrong. In other words, the judgment that the defense of our country or nationhood was worth the loss of that foreseen (and perhaps enormous) number of lives was correct. The contrary judgment was not. I do not see how he can make such judgments unless he somehow manages to overcome the utter incommensurability of continuing nationhood with human lives sacrificed. If it is reasonable to argue that we should have entered the war, and reasonable to argue that we should not have, then clearly Ramsey cannot say of the actual decision that it was *right,* and of the pacifist position that it was *wrong*. But that is what he holds—which means that he has managed somehow to commensurate what he holds in theory to be incommensurable.

There are two possible ways out of this impasse. The first is Ramsey's. Proportionate reason is an insufficient guide, he says, "because he who judged the cost disproportionate ought not to have turned directly against the value of Russian nationhood . . ." and he who judged the cost proportionate ought not to have turned directly against human life. I am not sure I know what it means to "turn directly against Russian nationhood" but at any rate this gets us nowhere, and for two reasons.

First, it merely asserts what is to be proved. I would argue that if the cost is proportionate one does not turn against human life in exacting it or against Russian nationhood if the cost is judged disproportionate. To demand beyond proportion indirectness is, then, to beg the question, because it is the very contention of the proportionalist that when the proportion is there, there is no turning against the good of life.

Secondly, Ramsey admits that even if we accept the need for indirectness (*dato non concesso* for the moment), "it would still remain to determine how much death and injury obliquely caused is enough to offset . . . the value of continuing national traditions." He then curiously states that such a determination is "ordinarily the obscure task of proportionate reason." Obscure indeed! For if proportionate reason was inadequate because twenty-million human lives are incommensurable with Russian nationhood, how is the incommensurability any less when the lives are only indirectly taken? Is it not reasonable to argue that twenty-million lives even indirectly taken is too much to pay—and, in Ramsey's words, reasonable to argue that twenty-million lives is not too much to pay? Merely asserting indirectness does not remove the incommensurability problem one whit. If it is incommensurability that forces indirectness, it is still there even after one asserts indirectness. And that clearly questions the moral relevance of indirectness.

That is why Brody is right in saying Ramsey cannot have it both ways. The task of proportionate reason is indeed obscure, in fact impossible, if it is now asked to do what before was said by Ramsey to be impossible. The Gordion knot is still there.

But Ramsey, is right. It is, after all, the task of proportionate reason to make sense of such indeterminate decisions. With W. D. Ross we can admit that "we are faced with great difficulties when we try to commeasure good things of very different types." Great difficulties? Yes. Insuperable ones? No.

That brings us to the second approach when dealing with "good things of very different types." What do we do? *Somehow or other,* in fear and trembling, we commensurate. In a sense we *adopt* a hierarchy. We go to war to protect our freedom. That means we are willing to sacrifice life to protect this good. If "give me liberty or give me death" does not involve *some kind* of commensurating, then I do not know what commensurating means. Our tradition allows violent, even, if necessary, lethal, resistance to rape attempts. If this does not mean measuring *somehow or other* sexual integrity against human life, I fail to see what it means. Our tradition allows (perhaps incorrectly) capital punishment as a protection and deterrent. That involves weighing one individual's life against the common safety which he threatens. There are human goods that we will die for and kill for rather than forfeit—and if that does not involve commensurating, then what is it? Even the traditional doctrine on ordinary/extraordinary means that concluded that a person need not abandon home and friends to save his life in a more salubrious climate, involved a weighing of the basic good of life with loss of intimate contact with friends. The Lord Jesus once said: "What does it profit a man if he gains the whole world and suffers the loss of his soul?" Here he was asserting a chasm or gap, as Ramsey would say, between moral good and other nonmoral goods but not one that makes it impossible to measure. The Son of Man was rather urging us to get our measurements and priorities right.

So we do weigh the apparently incommensurable, at least in *some way or other*. The qualification "some way or other" is important. For commensuration is obviously not a simple, uncomplicated thing. Perhaps this is what Ramsey means by indeterminancy. By saying "some way or other" I mean to suggest that we do all possible to reduce the incommensurability. In ordinary daily living this reduction occurs via personal aims, vocations, life commitments, possibilities. Such personal considerations, while they do not render the incomparable comparable, do provide a perspective, a kind of single scale, within which choice becomes possible and even right.

I believe something similar happens in the moral problems we are discussing. It will be noted that all the examples cited above have to do with life and its loss. The forfeit was considered justified for the sake of national self-determination, sexual freedom (or privacy), public security (common good), the deep need of friendship and the ties of love, and so on. These are all rather basic human concerns and, most crucially, while they are incommensurable as against each other, they are related to each other, or, as Ramsey says, they are "associated goods." That means that harm to one will probably or necessarily harm another—and protection or promotion of one will enhance all. They are of a piece.

This means that the goods that define our flourishing are interrelated in the sense that one who *unjustifiably* takes human life also undermines other human goods, and these human goods once weakened or undermined, will affect the very good of life itself.

To illustrate this let us take Ramsey's justification of contraception. He argues that "in these matters . . . there are no moral judgments for which proportionate reason is not the guiding preference principle." (Incidentally, I find it interesting that Ramsey experiences no discomfort in allowing proportionate reason the role of "guiding preference principle" here, when his overall attitude to the notion of proportionate reason is that it provides no guidance!) He immediately explains this as follows: "Will not the manner of protecting the good (procreative) undermine it in the long run by serious injury to an associated good (the communicative good)?" The "manner of protecting it" means here periodic continence or the so-called rhythm method. Practically this means that the possible ineffectiveness of this method, and forced and perhaps prolonged periods of abstention, can easily harm the communicative good and *thereby* the procreative good itself.[23] The Second Vatican Council said something very similar when it stated that "where the intimacy of married life is broken off, it is not rare for its faithfulness to be imperiled and its quality of fruitfulness ruined." That seems to me to be a reasonable account of things. It is precisely concern for the procreative, but as related to and supported by the communicative good that leads Ramsey to conclude to the moral rectitude of contraception and, if necessary, sterilization.

Clearly *some kind of measuring* is going on there. The incommensurability of goods (procreative, communicative) is reduced by seeing them in interrelationship. And it is this interrelationship that provides the context—a kind of single scale—in which decisions are possible and reasonable, and that makes possible adoption of personal and community policies.

But if Ramsey's analysis of contraception is a reasonable account of things, why could I not reword the matter in the lynch mob case as follows: "Will not the manner of protecting the good (life) undermine it in the long run by serious injury to an associated good (the good and integrity of human liberty)?" If we were to pronounce morally right the taking of one innocent life to appease a lynch mob bent on killing five innocent people, we would approve and universalize extortion to save life. But since that is a serious injury to human freedom and since human freedom is an associated good to human life, it is an undermining of the very good we seek to preserve here and now. It is disproportionate. Why cannot such a case be brought "within the reign of proportionate reason" and on Ramsey's own terms? The only reason is that in Ramsey's view human life is in a category not only different from all other nonmoral goods, but the same as moral integrity. Until and unless he establishes that killing, in contrast to all other disvalues, is a *moral* evil, his reasoning will not stand up.

Ramsey's basic objection to proportionate reason is that in some moral choices "there is no clear single scale." What I have suggested is that the interrelatedness of human goods, their associatedness, means that in a sense there is a single scale, but the means of assessing the greater and lesser evil are more difficult, uncertain, and obscure because the assessment must be done at times through associated goods. One could, for example, argue with Ramsey that his assertion that the procreative good will suffer through impairment of the communicative good in marriage is a false estimate, the result of his own one-sided views on continence, the product of a distorted pansexualistic culture, and so on. One could argue that tinkering with the procreative good (contraception) is precisely the type of interference that undermines fidelity, leads to promiscuity—in a word, undermines the communicative good and thereby also the procreative good. And any such opponent just might be right. I do not think so on this particular point. But that is neither here nor there. What is important is that such assessments are difficult, subject to risk, revisable because they are done through effects on associated values. In other words, the criteria are not as straightforward as they are in the classic abortion case. That is why what is truly proportionate is a risky assessment. It rests upon and calls forth personal and communal adopted priorities that can be distorted and biased. And that is where I find ambiguity in some moral choices.

To reword the matter, I would suggest that the scale is indeed single *in a sense* (through the association of basic goods) but the means of assessing the lesser evil more difficult and hazardous, a prudent bet if you will. When life is at stake (or liberty, or what have we) in certain tragic conflict situations, I am not exactly weighing life *against* other values, but attempting to discover what is the best service of life itself in terms of its relationship to other values. This is how we ought to understand Franz Böckle's statement that any killing is justified by a "rigorous weighing of values" and Schüller's notion that what is ethically wrong involves a distorted weighing of values *(verkehrte Güterabwägung)*.

When all is said and done in regard to incommensurability, I find Ramsey very unclear and uncertain. In one place he accuses Schüller of "*unduly* reducing the incommensurability that is actually constitutive of some sorts of choices among nonmoral goods and evils." What does that mean? How does one reduce this incommensurability *duly*? In another place, when dealing with sterilization and conception control, he says that "commensurate values are at stake; or if not altogether commensurate values, still value conflicts permitting indeterminate choices to be made. . . ." Now what does it mean to be "not altogether commensurate"? And what is it that permits "indeterminate choices to be made" when the values at stake are "not altogether commensurate"? Actually in these realms Ramsey sees proportionate reason as the "guiding preference principle." Now if that is so whether the values are commensurate or not ("not altogether commensurate"), where are we? Especially since it was precisely incommensurability that dethroned proportionate reason and enthroned directness/indirectness? I can only conclude that for Ramsey proportionate reason is usable or not (and directness/indirectness important or not) depending on the answers he wants to arrive at, or has arrived at.

4. *Proportionate reason.* This is a key notion in the writings of Schüller, Knauer, Janssens, Fuchs, Scholtz, Böckle and, indeed, the entire tradition of Catholic moral theology. From Ramsey's essay I must conclude that he does not understand the notion, nor my use of it. Because of the importance of this indictment, it must be carefully spelled out in stages.

a. *Proportionate reason and feature-dependent exceptions.* Ramsey writes that "exceptions, too, would be feature dependent, and not direct appeals to proportionate reason, if that [proportionate reason] means simply quantity of benefits. . . ." No one ever said that proportionate reason means "simply quantity of benefits." But passing over that for the moment, it must be noted that Ramsey contrasts feature-dependent exceptions with proportionate reason. He keeps arguing as if proportionate reason were *distinct from* (as a structure) feature-dependent exceptions. Actually the entire Catholic moral tradition, the authors above, and *Ambiguity in Moral Choice* do not neglect feature dependency in establishing exceptional instances to *replace* them with proportionate reason. Quite the contrary. All we say is that any feature-dependent exception is an example of, a specification of the more general term *proportionate reason.* All such feature-dependent exceptions are as valid and reasonable as the nonmoral evil contained within the action is proportionate.

Take promise keeping as an example. Moral manuals have for centuries listed any number of ways in which a promise ceases to bind as a fidelity contract.[24] Our contention is simply that any feature-dependent exception is an example of proportionate reason. If the feature-dependent exception is not proportionate in the circumstances to the inherent value of promise keeping and what is promised, it is an illegitimate exception, disproportionate, morally wrong. In this light, our existing moral norms must be understood as exceptionless precisely insofar as they resist modification by further feature-dependent exceptions, that is, by proportionate reason.

b. *Proportionate reason as vacuous.* Repeatedly Ramsey refers to the notion as "vague" and even "vacuous," though he slips once in referring to it as "multifaceted." Yet, as I have pointed out, he accepts it as the "guiding preference principle" when contraception is concerned. I will not belabor this inconsistency here but only point out that there is a difference between a general statement and a vacuous one. The notion of proportionate reason never intended to list concretely those instances where a value-violating action is judged to be morally right. Nor did it intend to replace those concrete-value balances, but only to say that whenever one concludes that it is not right to kill, to tell a falsehood, and so on, it is because such disvalues are not proportionately grounded in the circumstances: that when one concludes it is right, it is because of proportionate reason. Of course we must spell out what evils are greater, what values override others at least in our judgment and perspectives. That is the task of concrete or applied moral theology. But even when they are spelled out they will be examples of proportionate reason. Proportionate reason does not decide these concrete issues. It is quite as general as the term *feature dependency.* In fact, I would argue that feature-dependent exception is identical to proportionate reason in meaning.

Thus proportionate reason represents above all a structure of moral reasoning and moral norming, teleological in character, whose thrust is that those concrete norms understood as exceptionless because they propose certain interventions dealing with nonmoral goods as *intrinsic evils* cannot be sustained. Anyone who provides for feature-dependent exceptions to killing, for example, is using the same structure, but different words. That is why I referred to Ramsey as a crypto-teleologist. He can get his "charitable modifications" of the notions of stealing, lying, and murder only by examining what would happen if he did not so modify. The same is true of the move from prima facie duties to actual duties.

A behavioral norm is exceptionless only if it prescribes a value that cannot conflict with other values, or if it does, one that always deserves the preference. *Always deserves the preference* is but a way of saying that (at least in our perspectives) it overrides the other value, is more urgent than the other value, or disallows feature-dependent exceptions. It is a way of saying that choice of the other value would be disproportionate, or, that there is no proportionate reason either thinkable or realistically imaginable for overriding the value. Thus, in summary, proportionate reason is a general term for those characteristics of an action that allow us to conclude that, even though the action involves nonmoral evil, it is morally justifiable when compared to the only alternative (its omission).

Ramsey writes:

> When defenders of proportionate reason say clearly what feature-dependent actions . . . override what others, it will turn out that they are not "consequentialists" in the ordinary sense of that theory of ethics.

That is correct, I believe. But one wonders why Ramsey ever thought they were consequentialists. It must be insisted that when these defenders say clearly *why* one feature-dependent action overrides another, they will be but giving an example of proportionate reason. And when Ramsey tells us *why* he is warranted in building in certain feature-dependent exceptions, he will be giving an example of the more general lesser evil, or proportionate reason.

c. *Proportionate reason and consequentialism.* Throughout his discussion, Ramsey interprets proportionate reason in *Ambiguity in Moral Choice* as if it meant "greatest net good," and "net measurable good" as if it meant weighing all the values against each other and then trying to produce the greatest net good. Thus he suggests that proportionate reason means "quantity of benefits." This is a form of consequentialism, as I understand it, and that is certainly not what I mean by proportionate reason. For I agree that that type of consequentialism is incoherent.

I think I may have led Ramsey to this misunderstanding, and for two reasons. First, I referred to Charles Curran's statement that all the values "must be considered and a final decision made after all the moral values have been *compared.*" This could easily lead one to think that the teleological understanding of behavioral norms I proposed is consequentialist in a quantitative sense (net good). Actually what I meant to suggest was that, there being an interrelationship of all the values, a consideration of these values would or could illumine the matter of proportionality within the act with regard to the value at stake. Thus, to use Ramsey's example, a consideration of what happens to the communicative good when contraception is used or not can illumine whether the use or nonuse of contraception (a nonmoral disvalue) is the best service of the procreative good. For the communicative good is an associated good whose treatment either supports or undermines the procreative good. It is in this sense that I suggested that it is not the end that justifies the means but the ends.

It is not as if we were carving off a little bit of procreative good, a little bit of communicative good, and a little bit of other goods, toting them all up and using the net or sum to tell us which action "produces the best consequences," or "the greatest good for the greatest number." It is not as if we were holding up two basic and incommensurable values, seeing them conflicted, then choosing one as greater or subordinating one to the other on the grounds that this produces the best overall results. That is, I agree, a difficult notion when we are dealing with truly basic goods.

What we are saying is that in a case of conflict of values (let the classic abortion case be the example) where two alternatives are available (abort or not abort), that alternative should be chosen which is *in the circumstances* the best service of life. The "in the circumstances" allows us to isolate those characteristics of the situation (feature-dependent aspects) which alone make the action the best service of the basic value of life, make it proportionate, make it the lesser evil. I described them above—the inherent connection of means to end, the only way possible of saving life.

In other circumstances such characteristics would not exist and the action involving harm (killing) would either be for less urgent (instrumental) values or the manner of protecting life would involve and undermine other associated goods in a way that is detrimental to life itself. In either case the choice is disproportionate.

Secondly, my more serious responsibility for misunderstanding in this matter is my usage in the Hillenbrand Lecture.[25] There I was attempting to establish a *morally* significant difference between omission (withholding or withdrawing certain life-sustaining measures) and commission (positively or directly killing the patient) in treatment of the dying. I wrote that omission and commission "are not morally identical, at least insofar as the moral significance is traceable to, or *revealed by,* effects." I referred to effects and long-range implications "that would spell, *or at least reveal,* the moral difference between omission and commission where the dying are concerned."

The words *traceable to* and *spell* were at that time deliberately qualified by *or at least reveal* because I was uncertain and groping. And that clearly can create the impression that it is the long-range consequences, the net results, that make the direct dispatching of patients morally wrong. That would mean that these consequences would constitute the disproportion. That is misleading. And for this and other verbal (and perhaps even substantive) omissions or commissions, I ask the pardon and absolution of my commentators. In my opinion, consequences,

long-term repercussions, are rather indicators that there was a disproportion within the action. What is disproportionate is the evil to the
intended good within the action. However, consequences can reveal
this disproportionality, especially in difficult and controversial matters.
For disproportionate choices do not spring from nowhere and exist in a
vacuum. They are rooted in subtle and sometimes unrecognized attitudinal and priority shifts, carry with them associated dangers, and can be
expected to have deleterious effects.

The difference between straightforward consequentialism and proportionate reason can be seen from the example of the promise. Ramsey
repeatedly interprets proportionate reason as if it were future consequences (net good) that give meaning to one's present act. Thus he refers
to "immediate behavioral meanings and norms that are not exclusively
judgments of proportion or conclusions from future consequences."
Applying this to a promise would have proportionalists saying that a
promise gets its meaning from consequences, that it is to be kept or not
depending on whether keeping it would produce better net results than
not keeping it.

This is undoubtedly what some consequentialists would say; for it is a
standard objection in the literature dealing with utilitarianism. However, it has very little to do with proportionate reason. A promise has an
inherent meaning and binding force; breaking a promise is always a
disvalue.[26] There are times, however, when it is reasonable and right to
visit the disvalue of a broken promise on the promisee, times when he
would be unreasonable to expect and insist on the keeping of the promise. Those are times when some urgent value overrides the covenant
established in a promise—and both promisor and promisee accept that
possibility and the limits involved when the promise is made. Thus I
have promised a dear friend to be present at his wedding but on the way
encounter an injured person whose life depends on my help and
Samaritanism. I could keep the promise and allow the injured person to
die. I could break it, thus visiting a genuine disvalue on the promisee.
Clearly, I ought to aid the injured party. The reason for that is that
"some values override others" when they are conflicted. But those who
use that formulation sometimes seem not to realize that it is only a
teleological understanding of *pacta sunt servanda* that can get that
override done. By saying some values take precedence over others they
are saying nothing more or less than one who says lesser evil or proportionate reason.

Let us put the example into Ramsey's formulation. "Will not the manner of protecting the good (promise keeping) undermine it in the long run by serious injury to an associated good (human life)?'' Exactly so. If *all* promises had to be kept, no matter what, then people would not make promises and that means undermining the good of promise keeping by removing from our midst the goods we secure through covenants among one another. In other words, in the example above, breaking the promise, while involving nonmoral evil, is not disproportionate.

If Ramsey's analysis of proportionate reason is correct in the case of contraception and sterilization (and I believe it is) then it might apply wherever we are dealing with conflicted *nonmoral* goods or evils. (We have seen that Ramsey does not go this route because for all practical purposes he makes human life an unconditioned good, the taking of which is a *moral* evil.) I believe it does so apply.

Let obliteration bombing be a test case. Those who would defend such counter-people (versus counter-combatant) attacks argue that they will save more lives. This was Truman's argument. The choice is seen as between taking 100,000 Nagasakian lives or losing double or triple that number from both sides in a prolonged conventional war.

If I am right (that proportionate reason reigns even where the taking of human life is concerned), then there must be a way of showing that Truman's understanding of proportion was wrong—if we hold it to be such, as I do. I believe there is.

Let us again use Ramsey's formulation. ''Will not the manner of protecting the good (human life—by ending the war) undermine it in the long run by serious injury to an associated good (human liberty)?'' Making innocent (noncombatant) persons the object of our targeting is a form of extortion in international affairs that contains an implicit denial of human freedom. Human freedom is undermined when extortionary actions are accepted and elevated and universalized. Because such freedom is an associated good upon which the very good of life heavily depends, undermining it in the manner of my defense of life is undermining life itself—is disproportionate.

Let us put this in another way and in explicitly Christian terms. It is the Christian's faith that another's ceasing from his wrongdoing is *never* dependent on my doing nonmoral evil. For the Christian believes that we are truly what we are, redeemed in Christ. We are still threatened by the *reliquiae peccati,* but are free and powerful in Christ's grace. We rejoice in our infirmities that the grace of Christ may abound in us. And we know the powers of that grace—in Magdalen (and many Magdalens), in the martyrs, in the likes of Thomas More, Matthew Talbot, and a host of others. Others can cease their evildoing without our connivance in it, without our doing harm to persuade and entice them. We are free. That is our Christian bet as persons who know our freedom in Christ.

That is why the *essential connection* between aborting and saving the one who can be saved is so important in the classical abortion case. No such connection exists in the instance of the rioting lynch mob. They can cease their evildoing without our doing harm to make them cease. To yield to their demands would be a denial to them of their own freedom. And that freedom is an associated good which must be asserted and protected if the good of life is itself to survive. We may lose some lives in sticking to this conviction, but that is where our trust in God's providence is on the line. Because people can, with God's gracious help, cease evildoing, our doing harm to persuade them to cease is unjustifiable, disproportionate. The Christian reads his proportions not just by looking at numbers, but by looking at many other features of the situation within which the numerical must be interpreted.

Something very similar can, I believe, be said about the conduct of warfare. But before saying it, we must recall the teaching of Pius XII, the most extensive and detailed papal elaboration of the just-war theory in all of hisotry. Pius XII, contrary to some earlier theological formulations, restricted the *jus ad bellum (justa causa* for going to war) to national self-defense. War, he taught, can be justified as a response *ad repellendas injurias* (to repell injury or aggression), not for settlement of other disputes, even the most serious (*ad vindicandas offensiones, ad recuperandas res*). Now the implication of this limitation of just cause to self-defense means that the other nation is the aggressor, in short, is engaged in wrongful conduct. It may (at times) be difficult to say who was the original aggressor but that does not eliminate the need of *an* aggressor as the sole justification for going to war.

If a nation is wrongfully aggressing, once again it is the Christian's faith—and a well-founded one—that that nation can and must cease and desist from wrongful aggression without our harming innocents to make that nation do so. There is no *necessary connection* between our doing harm to noncombatants (for example, killing innocent civilians to stop that nation) and that nation's ceasing unjust aggression. To say that there is would be to insult the humanity of the aggressor by denying his liberty. For unjust aggressors are free to cease unjust aggression. Christ did not invent that idea, of course, but by his graceful redemption he powerfully restated it to a world that too often came to terms with its inhumanities as "necessary," or "culturally imposed."

That is why, I believe, the Christian judges attacks upon noncombatants as disproportionate. In such an attack—even though more lives might be saved than trying to grind the war to a halt by conventional methods—liberty is at stake and to undermine it is to turn against the basic good of life itself. For these goods are, as Ramsey notes about the goods of marriage, associated.

When our actions deny by implication the freedom and responsibility of the aggressor, they deny that same freedom and responsibility in ourselves. And by doing that they remove the conditions for rationality in the conduct of war—which is already at the very margin of the defensible, occurring as it does only after (*ultima ratio*) rational discourse has collapsed. Is anyone willing to assert confidently that there is no connection between Nagasaki-Hiroshima and the senseless slaughters that occurred in South Vietnam? Once the manner of our protection of a basic good reduces or removes by implication the basis for rational limitation of violence (liberty), then irrational (disproportionate) things are going to happen. These irrational things point back to and reveal the disproportion in our original responses.

This matter is so important that it demands restatement. I have said that "that alternative should be chosen which is *in the circumstances* the best service of life." What does that mean? The italicized words are meant to point up in a general way the causal relationship between achieving an urgent good (or preventing an urgent evil) and the causing of evil as the means. *In the circumstances* the relationship between the evil done (abortion) and the good achieved (saving the mother, the only one who can be saved) is a *necessary* one. That is, the abortion of the child is the only way thinkable, given our medical tools, of saving the one who can be saved. Otherwise both mother and baby die.

However, it is possible that the relationship between means and end might be a factually efficacious one without being a necessary one. Take the case of Mrs. Bergmeier who can achieve her liberty from prison and return to her family only by granting sexual relations to the jailer. There is no genuine or necessary connection between sexual relations and the freedom of the woman. The relation is established by the malice of the jailer. Yet it would be factually efficacious. But far from being necessary, the relationship between sexual intimacy and freedom is from the jailer's viewpoint hedonistic, from Mrs. Bergmeier's viewpoint utilitarian. This lack of a necessary connection or causal relationship was what St. Thomas had in mind when he excluded fornication and adultery as means of legitimate self-defense ("non ordinatur ad conservationem propriae vitae *ex necessitate*").

The next question to be asked is this: what is the difference between a means with a necessary causal connection to the urgent good to be preserved (maternal life) and one without such a necessary causal relationship? I suggest using Ramsey's structure, that when there is no essential and necessary causal relationship, then other basic values are brought into play or affected, and in a way that can be undermining of the good of life itself, or whatever urgent good is being preserved through ontic evil. Thus in the Bergmeier case, by yielding to the jailer's sexual demands as a condition of her freedom, Mrs. Bergmeier would be by her very action asserting that the jailer would desist from his unjust detention of her only if she yielded to him. As a matter of fact, he can and ought to desist from such unjust detention; for he is a free and responsible person. To yield to his demands would be to support a denial of his freedom. That is why I said above, while discussing war, that to say there is a necessary connection between another nation's ceasing unjust aggression and our doing harm "would be to insult the humanity of the aggressor by denying his liberty." Exactly the same is true here. To yield to extortion is to deny the extortioner's liberty. And since liberty is a basic value associated with other basic values, to assault it is to assault these others too. Harm to freedom can and does harm other values—in the Bergmeier case, marital fidelity. Therefore, the means in question is disproportionate to the very good being sought. It denies the very value being sought in the end. There may be other ways of attempting an explanation of the implications of *necessary causal relationship*. But this strikes me as at least a plausible beginning.

When one states that in conflict situations where either alternative involves nonmoral evil the lesser evil should be chosen, he supposes that a proper assessment of what is truly the lesser evil has been made. He supposes that one has attended to the association of goods, as Ramsey does when he justifies contraception and sterilization. Once this has been done and the lesser evil established, it is true to say that it is patently absurd to choose the greater evil. Of this Ramsey writes: "So it is; and so, too, is the argument." The reason he gives is that between choosing the lesser evil and choosing the greater evil there is a third alternative: choosing the lesser evil *with indirect voluntariety*. Here, I believe, Ramsey resembles nothing so much as a horseless jockey claiming victory. For what is the lesser evil and what is the greater evil is only determinable after the relevance of the permitting and intending will has been established and weighed into the description of the alternatives. To say otherwise is to assume that indirectness has an independent *moral* significance—which is, of course, to beg the question. And that brings us to the significance of intending and permitting in Ramsey's commentary.

5. *The relation of the will to evil.* Ramsey's very last statement is that Catholic moralists have generalized beyond the cases of contraception and sterilization in saying we may intend nonmoral evils *in se sed non propter se* and that the condition establishing the *non propter se* is proportionate reason. He writes:

> When that analysis is moved to conflicts of incommensurate disvalues and the sin of another or killing a human being is intended *in ordine ad finem proportionatum,* the life and destiny of the human person are wrongly turned into a pure means.

That is a fitting summary of his study for, as I have repeatedly noted, he begs the question under discussion—the moral relevance of directness and indirectness where nonmoral values are involved. Ramsey must say: any killing that turns another person into a means is wrong. But direct killing does this; indirect does not necessarily do it. Therefore direct killing is morally wrong. Now why does not indirect killing, quite as much as direct killing, turn "the life and destiny of our fellow man . . . into a pure means"? That is the whole question.

What is Ramsey's account of the moral significance of directness and indirectness? Only if that is persuasively elaborated will his pure means talk be more than an assertion. He nowhere analyzes the matter himself but is content to state: "I submit, however, that at first McCormick correctly expressed the moral significance of the describable difference between the directly and the indirectly voluntary." I take it that this refers to my statements that

> the intending will (hence the person) is more closely associated with the existence of evil than the merely permitting will [and that] an intending will is more willing that the evil be than is a permitting will.

In such a statement, we must conclude, Ramsey finds the *moral* significance of the direct/indirect distinction.

But he is saddened that I take it all back and establish the "constitutional monarchy" of proportionate reason. For I faced that analysis with the following objection:

> If someone is ready to bring the good into existence only by permitting the evil, it has been suggested that he is less willing that the evil exist. Yet it must be said that he is also less willing that the good exist. Furthermore, the person who is prepared to realize the good even by intending the evil is more willing that the evil exist, but only because he is more willing that the good exist.

Ultimately, therefore, I saw my own explanation undermined.

Here a personal note is required. Before publishing *Ambiguity*, I submitted the text to several colleagues for criticism. One was Bruno Schüller, S. J. The objection stated above was his and I simply incorporated it verbatim into my text. Schüller regards it as an objection fatal to my explanation of the direct/indirect distinction. I believe I would agree with him and would now modify *Ambiguity* appropriately. That means, therefore, that I would say that Ramsey, to the extent that he accepts this as establishing a *morally* significant difference between direct and indirect where nonmoral evils are concerned, is in trouble. Indeed, the trouble is so bad that if Ramsey does not remedy the situation and come up with a convincing analysis (he has not in the essay in this volume) his continued use of direct and indirect as *morally* decisive will remain an assertion only, an assertion that leaves the matter unanalyzed and therefore the question begged.

As will become clear in my final synthesis, I believe that where nonmoral evils are concerned (and killing is among them) the distinction between direct and indirect is merely descriptive. The relationship of the will to the evil caused (whether as means or unavoidable concomitant) serves only to tell us what *end* is aimed at in the action and with what means. In doing this, direct and indirect intent (descriptively different) reveal to us the *significance* of our action. Thus sterility caused by removal of a cancerous uterus is a *life*saving procedure. Sterility caused in order to control conception is a *marriage*-stabilizing and *family*-stabilizing procedure. Whether either intervention was justified depends not on the directness or indirectness of intentionality, but on the goodness of the end and the proportion between the means chosen and the end.

William Frankena

I find Frankena's commentary somewhat frustrating. He seems primarily concerned with whether my method resembles that of others. That is, he works through typologies. Thus at one point I "resemble

Singer's general utilitarianism." At another I am said to have in mind rules "favored by rule-utilitarians like Berkeley and Brandt." At still another I am "seeking a *via media* between Fletcher and Robinson and Berkeley and Ramsey." This is frustrating because by comparing one position to another and allowing implicit critiques to filter through the comparison one must presuppose to some extent the clarity and validity or lack thereof of the positions used as the vehicles of comparison. But nowhere in this study does Frankena sort out the validities and invalidities of these vehicles, their strengths and weaknesses. With a kind of Olympian detachment he uses merely descriptive phrases to refer to them. Thus: "the logical possibility of doing this"; "one can take a deontological line in analyzing and dealing with conflict situations"; "if Donagan's kind of argument is cogent . . ."; "rules of the kind favored by Berkeley and Brandt"; "in moral philosophy a long and honorable tradition rather different from the teleological one McCormick belongs to, one which is also opposed to the Position." And so on.

Throughout Frankena is interested in cleansing my language so that the meaning will be clearer. For this I am grateful. However, this preoccupation points up the different backgrounds from which we have come at the problem. I come at it out of the Catholic tradition, a tradition that has not restricted itself to toying with ethical typologies, but above all has been concerned with the concrete problems of people and their moral justifications. Thus the reasoning and language of the double effect exists not only in theological tomes, but also in papal and episcopal documents that are intended to enlighten the consciences of individuals in an authoritative way. I have taken my start from such documents and such a tradition. And this partially explains some of the obscurities Frankena claims to find in *Ambiguity*.

For instance, while discussing which kinds of effects should be said to be intended (whether those taken as ends, or means, or both), Frankena states that "this is a more disputed matter than McCormick here recognizes." Clearly. It has been known, for instance, for many decades that some theologians would restrict the term *intentio* to the end, and use *electio* for the means. One can find this type of discussion and precision in nearly any one of the standard moral manuals used in the past several hundred years. However, papel documents have repeatedly spoken of the wrongfulness of abortion, whether it be *intended* as a means or as an end. And contemporary Catholic theologians have by and large accepted this usage. That is where I start—with what has been used in authoritative teaching sources and everyday communication of this within the Catholic community. And it explains some of the omissions Frankena correctly attends to.

Where does Frankena stand on the moral weight of direct and indirect as these were used traditionally? It is very hard to say. There are two indications. The first is his statement that his sympathies "are with him (McCormick) and the Reactors rather than with the Position." Secondly, there is his laconic statement "I agree about the Case." Taken together these suggest that Frankena finds no real need for direct and indirect voluntariety in resolving the conflict situations to which this distinction was applied. But from this essay we shall never know; for Frankena leaves the key question at the level of "sympathies" without any subsequent analysis of the problem or its implications.

In this respect I think it is true that Catholic moral theologians have thought more about cases and less about moral theory than moral philosophers. And that moral philosophers have thought less about cases and more about theory. But Frankena is hardly a good example in this essay. He agrees on the classical abortion case without really saying how or why. Secondly, he approves or tolerates "the appalling" as the lesser of two evils without carrying such toleration back to examine what it possibly means for the structure of rightness or wrongness in any conflict instances. So ultimately it is not clear what he thinks about the doctrine of double effect. He largely restricts himself to maneuvering another's statements in and out of typologies. This has two results. First, it saves Frankena the trouble (and us the enlightenment) that would come from a clear analysis of the abortion case and other similar cases. Indeed, it empties the essay of any serious grappling with the direct/indirect distinction. Secondly, it accepts by implication (if typologies are used as references for *critical* comparison) the neatness and accuracy of the typologies used. This is a huge assumption.

A further word on typology is necessary here. By approaching the direct/indirect discussion through the context of ethical typologies, Frankena makes it appear that one who abandons the distinction is vulnerable to the arguments used by contemporary critics of utilitarianism. The argument in substance is something like this: legitimizing the direct doing of certain harms = teleological grounding of norms = reductively utilitarian theory = untenable.

I have already cited Schüller's objection to the apparent elegance of the typologies used in such an equation. Let me now turn to Charles

Curran's discussion of the matter, since it relates recent Catholic writings to these typologies.

Charles E. Curran has written a very useful study in which he compares recent Catholic moral theological studies with the contemporary debates about utilitarianism by moral philosophers.[27] Curran first points out that the objections of philosophers like Rawls, Frankena, and Williams to "utilitarianism, teleology or consequentialism" are threefold: (1) aspects other than consequences must be taken into account; (2) the good cannot be determined independently of the morally right; and (3) not only the consequences of the action but also the way in which the actor brings about the consequences has moral significance. Thus to oppose utilitarianism, teleology, consequentialism (Curran uses the terms as synonyms), these philosophers need not maintain that certain actions are right whatever the consequences.

Secondly, Curran points out that the antiutilitarian argues that, in addition to consequences, other aspects of the action must be considered, for example, the obligation of fidelity in promise keeping. Something other than consequences counts as important in assessing right and wrong, even if these other considerations do not yield an absolute behavioral norm. It is these other considerations that separate Frankena, Rawls, and others from the utilitarian.

Thirdly, there is a third current in philosophical literature represented by G.E.M. Anscombe. Anscombe indicts all of contemporary philosophy because it is even willing to consider the possibility of exceptions based on consequences. Concretely, Anscombe condemns modern moral philosophy "for proposing a philosophy according to which the consequences of such an action could be morally taken into account to determine if one should do such an action." In other words, there are actions which are right or wrong whatever the consequences. Any other position she views as consequentialism. Thus, in her terminology, W.D. Ross is a consequentialist.

In summarizing, Curran puts it as follows:

> An overview of the philosophical literature indicates that there are three different positions, but terminology differs in describing these different opinions. The following descriptions will not agree with the terminology employed by many of the authors themselves, but it seems to be necessary to bring about needed clarifications. The first position is properly described as utilitarianism, strict teleology or strict consequentialism. The third position, Anscombe and others, may be described as nonconsequentialism or

even deontology—some actions are wrong no matter what the consequences. I will call the middle position a mixed consequentialism or mixed teleology. This middle position differs from strict teleology or strict consequentialism because it maintains the following three points. (1) Moral obligation arises from elements other than consequences. (2) The good is not separate from the right. (3) The way in which the good or evil is achieved by the agent is a moral consideration. Since such an opinion does not necessarily hold that certain actions are always wrong no matter what the consequences, it has been called consequentialist by Anscombe.

When I first encountered Curran's threefold division of positions within modern philosophy, I was pleasantly surprised. I had arrived independently at a similar division. Specifically, I had concluded to the usefulness of the following divisions: (1) absolute deontologists (Kant, Catholic tradition on certin points [for example, contraception], Grisez, Anscombe); (2) absolute consequentialists (J. Fletcher, some utilitarians); and (3) moderate teleologists (Ross, McCloskey, Frankena, Fuchs, Schüller, Knauer, and McCormick, among others).

Curran next asks where reforming Catholic moral theologians fit into this division. Exactly as I had, he concludes that

> as the debate progressed it became quite evident that the reforming Catholic theologians, generally speaking, do not embrace utilitarianism or what Rawls, Frankena, Williams and others have called teleology or consequentialism.

They are Curran's mixed consequentialists or my moderate teleologists. Why? Because these theologians, in their explanations of *materia apta* (Janssens), commensurate reason (Knauer), proportionate reason (Schüller), insist that other elements than consequences function in moral rightness and wrongness. I would include myself among those who so insist.

This point is crucial in this discussion, I believe. For if a careful reading of both contemporary philosophy and recent Catholic theological analyses reveals that there are not two positions only (deontological, teleological) but rather three, then objections leveled against the reforming tendencies and *Ambiguity* on the grounds that they are consequentialist lose their effectiveness. Frankena's use of typologies fails, I believe, to make these clarifications. Indeed, in Anscombe's terms—if not in Frankena's—Frankena is a consequentialist; for he is willing to contemplate doing what he calls "the appalling."

All this means that my response to Frankena must take the form of some questions.

The very first question I want to return to Frankena is about his agreement with the classical abortion case. It is the situation of save the mother or lose both mother and nonviable fetus. And let us make it very specific. The instance we have in mind is that where the baby must be killed in order to get at the mortal threat to the mother (for example, the aneurysm). Frankena agrees that we ought to abort. That means that he believes it is the morally right thing to do. Why does he agree? Not clear. Is such an abortion a direct but justifiable one? Or is it an indirect abortion? And what difference would it make anyway whether we call it direct or indirect? In Frankena, not clear.

Is it morally right because it is one of those appalling things we have to do as the lesser of two evils? Not clear. Frankena believes that intending/permitting have moral relevance but adds that "facts about what I take as an end, what I take as a means, and what I permit are more relevant to judgments about the moral quality of my character or will." I confess that I do not understand "more relevant." Does that mean that intending/permitting are still relevant, but less so, where rightness and wrongness of action are concerned? And if there is genuine relevance, what is it—especially if Frankena's sympathies are, as he says, with the revisionists where direct/indirect are involved? The fact that Frankena agrees with the solution, yet does not provide any intelligible account of why he does so, confirms his statement that at least some moral philosophers have thought more about theory than cases. Indeed, I would turn that a bit and say that they have thought too little about the theoretical implications of cases, and to that extent have thought less about theory than they sometimes think. Or is it, finally, that the theory they have thought about has little to do with reality?

This matter is of the utmost importance. Frankena approves the abortion but does not come clean and clear on why. This means that not only are we left in the dark on his views on the major issue of this volume, but it means that he comfortably avoids the hard questions associated with conflict resolution in general. Concretely: (1) if Frankena believes the abortion is somehow indirect and justifiable as such, then he owes us an explanation of the moral relevance of directness/indirectness; (2) if he believes it is direct but justifiable, then we eagerly await an analysis of directness and of his principle of justification; (3) if he believes these terms are in this instance irrelevant to the moral rightness of the abortion, then I know of no other rationale for the conclusion he draws than that doing the abortion is the lesser of two evils. If this is his ultimate justification, then is it not also the truly relevant consideration whenever we are dealing with unavoidable evils and the lesser can be determined? And if that is the case, is not Frankena committed to a teleological understanding of ethical norms? Frankena concedes that "what is appalling may sometimes . . . be morally tolerable as the lesser of two evils." That *sometimes* is an engaging little word. It cries out for clarification. But once he has said that, he is foursquare behind the major thesis of *Ambiguity* and may eventually turn out to be what we insiders call a moderate teleologist in his understanding of normative statements. The only remaining task is to get clear on the ways we discover what is objectively the lesser evil. And once we do that, I would cease describing the evil we justifiably cause or permit as "appalling"—for that term suggests moral disapprobation. It suggests something we *ought not have done*—and therefore "are appalled" at its being done. I would use nonmoral or premoral evil or tragic necessity.

My second question to Frankena concerns his resistance to what seems to me the obvious teleology in his statements about the lesser evil. He says: "Like many others, I have myself contended that a principle of justice is needed for an adequate morality *in addition* to any principle of beneficence or utility. . . ." Thus Frankena resists a teleological understanding of moral norms—even though I believe he is logically committed to such an understanding—because such an understanding commits us to the sufficiency of the principle of beneficence. He believes that we need justice in addition to beneficence (or utility).

This "principle of justice" adduced by Frankena is likened by him to Donagan's absolute principle of never treating an individual merely as a means. Here two things might be said. One concerns the meaning of that principle, the second touches Frankena's usage of justice in addition to beneficence.

As to the principle of "never treating an individual merely as a means," I would suggest that this is a highly indeterminate notion, and when pushed begs the very question we are concerned with. Under analysis, it really means *abused*. And when put that way, no one can qualify it or disagree with it. However, the principle tells us little about when one must be said to be treated as a means. Concretely, why is someone "only indirectly killed" not also treated as a means? (What do fish think of the morality of fishing, as I have asked?) His or her death is foreseen, it is the result of my action, I could have foregone that action and so on. To reply that it is not treating the individual as a means because the killing is indirect, or that it is treating the individual as a mere means because the killing is direct, clearly begs the question. So when Frankena adduces this maxim as something a teleological understanding of norms cannot handle, his objection seems to me to have lost its teeth. For instance, is the fetus used as a mere means when it is killed to save the mother in the aneurysm case? If it is a direct killing, most who hold "The Position" would answer yes. Yet Frankena would approve the abortion—as I would. Is he, therefore, saying that it is permissible to use an individual as a mere means *in this case only?* Or is he saying (as I would) that when killing represents the lesser evil, it does not involve one in treating an individual as a mere means, whether the killing be direct or not? We just do not know, because Frankena has avoided a careful analysis of the relevance of direct and indirect voluntariety.

As for myself, I would only suggest that a person must be said to be used as a means only when he can be said to be reasonably unwilling (even by construction) that the action visiting harm on him be done. That does not tell us much concretely, but it does dissociate "as a means only" from its necessary connection with directness as traditionally understood.

The second point concerns Frankena's use of justice in addition to beneficence, and for that matter, of David Lyons's appeal to justice and fairness in addition to beneficence. The Christian theologian is perplexed by the notion of love implied in such fragmentation. As Schüller puts it:

> The Christian theologian who, under the influence of Romans 3:8-10, declares that love as benevolence and beneficence must be seen as the final criterion for the moral rightness of an action, does not understand under "love" something next to justice and fairness. Rather he understands by this term the general root of all other particular principles.[28]

It is a strange concept of love that has nothing to do with justice and fairness, as if these were separate and independent sources of moral rightness.

Let me adduce an example of fairness that has been used in the philosophical literature. A person wants a certain political candidate elected. He knows that a vast majority of citizens feel the same way and will vote for this candidate; so he himself stays home. Viewed in terms of consequences, his vote would be useless. Therefore, as useless, it is not morally right if it is viewed within a teleological framework. Yet it is unfair, for the stay-at-home enjoys the good of getting his candidate elected even though he spares himself the trouble of a trip to the polls. Therefore, it is asserted, beyond love (as usefulness, *beneficentia*) there is required a principle of fairness.

I do not wish to deny that fairness demands the person's vote. Rather I am amazed that one thinks that such fairness has nothing to do with what we Christians call love of neighbor. I am further surprised at how narrowly the critics of utilitarianism interpret the term *useless*. Of course, the vote is in one sense useless (it will not change results). But precisely because the vote is useless, it has the peculiar aptitude to be an expression of solidarity, much as the gesture of the woman who poured perfume over the head of Jesus was seen as useless by some but was actually an act of love.[29] We should not confuse the principle of utility (*beneficentia*) with mere efficiency.

It may take a little more coaxing than I have done here; but if such coaxing is successful in persuading Frankena that an adequate concept of *beneficentia* includes justice and fairness (even though there remain unfinished tasks in elaborating this inclusion), then nothing prevents us from calling Frankena a teleologist. Schüller has summarized this very well as follows:

> Traditional moral theology factually represents a deontological theory. Frankena does the same thing. But they do this from reasons that have nothing in common. Frankena believes he must hold a deontological theory because the necessary principle of justice is logically independent of the principle of love. Traditional moral theology states, on the contrary—so it seems to me—that the principle of justice is contained already in the principle of love. Therefore traditional moral theology must deny that Frankena has a legitimate ground for counting himself a deontologist. This theology itself represents a deontological theory, because it believes that there is, first, a class of actions that are morally wrong because of their unnaturalness (contraception). Second, there is a class of actions that must be seen as wrong because of a lack of divine permission (such as killing of the innocent). As far as I can see, Frankena, on the basis of the rest of his ethics, must contest that these two classes are justified. Therefore he could not admit that Catholic tradition has a legitimate ground for holding to a deontological theory. If one admits that Frankena is correct, yet if he holds with Catholic tradition that the principle of justice (and fairness) is contained in the principle of love, *then the result is a teleological theory of moral norms.*[30]

A couple of final points. Frankena states that I contend that judicial murder "can always be shown to be wrong in this world by a consideration of its long-run effects." From what I have written above on

Ramsey's commentary, it should be clear how this statement must be interpreted. Specifically, I would argue that because of the association of basic goods, an assault on one (liberty) will bring harm to another (life) and that therefore judicial murder is *in itself* a disproportionate means. It is not *materia apta* to the goal (preservation of life) because it denies in the means the very value sought in the end. In doing so, it will certainly have long-range consequences, but it is not these that constitute the disproportion; they help to reveal it. Thus the term consequences, as I would read it, refers to the present support of or undermining of the value being sought, a support or undermining that occurs through association with other goods.

I would further add—in explanation of Frankena's phrase "can be shown"—that the harm to life through harm to an associated good (liberty) is often grasped spontaneously, nondiscursively, and therefore obscurely to a large extent. Thus if judicial murder appalls us, assaults our *Gemüt,* our sense of profanation, we grasp something about its moral quality prior to discursive ethical deliberation. I believe and do not apologize for the fact that our emotions and religious commitments do function in our value judgments in a way that is sometimes beyond reduction to reasoning processes or analytic arguments.

At this point I would like to say a word about two aspects of moral knowing that are important to the problem discussed in this volume. The first concerns what I call the connatural and prediscursive element in moral knowledge. The second, which is closely associated with this, touches on personal and communal hierarchy of values, what I want to refer to as adoption of a hierarchy.

I cannot treat extensively here the connatural and prediscursive elements in moral knowledge. But two statements can be adduced to point to what I have in mind. The first is secular-scientific, the second religious. But they are driving at pretty much the same point.

Nobel laureate Peter Medawar, while discussing the line between a humanizing and dehumanizing use of technology, states that the answer we give in practice

> is founded not upon abstract moralizing but upon a certain natural sense of the fitness of things, a feeling that is shared by most kind and reasonable people even if we cannot define it in philosophically defensible or legally accountable terms.[31]

In his discussion of genetic manipulation (and specifically, donor insemination) Karl Rahner insists that there is what he calls a "moral instinct of faith." This instinct can be called by any number of different names; but the point is that there is a component to moral judgment that cannot be adequately subject to analytic reflection. But it is this component that is chiefly responsible for one's ultimate judgments on concrete moral questions. In this sense these ultimate judgments are not simply the sum of the rational considerations and analyses one is capable of objectifying and no adequate understanding of proportionate reason implies this. For this reason Rahner states explicitly that

> all the "reasons" which are intended to form the basis for rejecting genetic manipulation (namely, A.I.D.) are to be understood, at the very outset, as only so many references to the moral faith-instinct. . . . For in my view the moral faith-instinct is aware of its right and obligation to reject genetic manipulation, even without going through (or being able to go through) an adequate process of reflection.[32]

What is to be concluded from this? I would say that, even though our spontaneous and instinctive moral judgments can be affected by cultural distortions and can be confused with rather obvious but deeply ingrained conventional fears and biases, still they remain a more reliable test of the humanizing and dehumanizing, of the morally right and wrong, of proportion, than our discursive arguments. Thus if our moral sensitivities are outraged by the sheriff who would frame and execute one innocent man to pacify a riot-prone mob bent on indiscriminate killing, I am initially prepared to trust this instinctive reaction.

Even more specifically, I have suggested that when the causal relationship between the means (involving nonmoral or premoral evil) and the end is not a necessary one, then other basic and associated goods are brought into play and in a way that can be detrimental to the very good one is seeking to realize. I would suggest here that this detrimental relationship is something we understand in an intuitive, prediscursive way, without the full ability to state it adequately in rational analysis. Thus when we conclude that counter-people (versus counter-force) bombing, even though it may end a war more quickly, contradicts the very values (life) we are trying to preserve, we conclude this on the basis of an association and interdependence between the basic values of life and liberty that is understood in a connatural, prediscursive way.

Now we turn to the matter of adoption of a hierarchy of values. One of the basic objections to a teleological understanding of moral norms is that it involves commensurating the incommensurable, at least at times. I would grant that the basic goods are incommensurable. One cannot measure one *against* the other if they are indeed basic. But perhaps we can *adopt* a hierarchy of values, either personally or societally. It seems to me that this is what is really happening in the resolution of many conflict cases involving basic human goods.

Let warfare be an example. Do we not go to war (involving killing, the suppression of a basic human good) to protect our political freedom? Is there not *some kind* of commensuration there even though the values involved are "objectively incommensurable"? Have we not corporately concluded ("adopted a hierarchy") that political freedom is so basic a value that it is worth sacrificing lives to preserve it? It seems so. It seems that we might argue that the conclusions of traditional Christian ethics here (the just-war theory) are the community's adoption of a hierarchy of values which relates the violence and death involved in war to other basic values.

The theory of war of some ethicians (for example, Schüller) analogizes off of personal self-defense. That is, it finds justification of defense on the assumption that the enemy is intent on killing us, as is the case with defense against an unjust aggressor against one's individual life. But this overlooks the fact that all the aggressor need want and ordinarily wants is political control of our society. If we would simply hand over such control, the enemy would not employ guns and bombs, and therefore would not kill. It is our unwillingness to forfeit political self-determination that leads us to marshall armies and weapons, namely, to prepare violent resistance. In other words, the justification for war is not in the first the fact that the enemy is aggressing against our *lives;* it is rather first that he aggresses against (covets) our political freedom. *Our resistance* to that aggression makes it a matter of aggression against our lives. But the justification for our resistance is a judgment that political freedom is a treasured good, even worth sacrificing life for if we have to. Does not such a judgment involve, if not commensuration of loss of some *lives* versus loss of political *freedom,* at least the corporate adoption of a hierarchy wherein we say our freedom is worth this sacrifice? It seems so.

One might face the problem I have raised by arguing as John Locke does. Locke argued, as Ramsey notes, to an inalienable right of liberty on the grounds that a real threat to that is tantamount to a threat against an individual's life. Locke wrote:

> He who attempts to get another man into his absolute power [should be understood to have] a design upon his life. For I have reason to conclude that he who would get me into his power without my consent, would use me as he pleased when he got me there. . . ."[33]

Thus, on Locke's reasoning, life-taking defense against an intent on denying my freedom is in a real sense life-taking in defense of life itself.

Locke's "reason to conclude" is quite valid, I think. But it will be noticed that Locke's argument is really very similar to my *association of basic goods*. While human life and human liberty are objectively incommensurable values, they are associated values. Otherwise Locke could not conclude, as he does, that "I have reason to conclude." And because they are associated values, the community may make this association, namely, adopt a hierarchy (or better, a policy with regard to interrelatedness) of values. Thus, I see "association of basic values," "proportionate reason," and "adoption of a hierarchy of values" as attempting to say the same thing, or at least as very closely related.

A further strong support of the notion of association of basic values is found in the cluster theory of the virtues—those dispositions that control our responses to basic human values. According to this theory, the virtuous disposition is a kind of seamless fabric, as strong or weak as its individual threads. In other words, weaken one virtue and all are thereby weakened.

In summary, then, proportionate reason as I understand it can be explained in several different ways, no one of which need reduce to "greatest net good." Namely, one can speak of association of basic goods (rather than commensuration); one can speak of corporate *adoption* of a hierarchy; or one can speak of a certain equivalence (aggression against liberty is tantamount to aggression against life). That is why I repeatedly referred above to a "weighing *of some kind*." Proportionate reason could be used to state any one of these positions, no one of which need involve a toting up of "net good."

My final question to Frankena concerns his use of Ross's position. He grants that Ross's distinction between prima facie rightness and wrongness and actual rightness and wrongness demands some kind of weighing of alternatives. But this weighing, he says, is between rightness and wrongness, not between goods and evils. In this vein Ross speaks of "one duty more pressing than the other."[34] Or again, he speaks of "prima facie rightness in the respects in which its prima facie right most outweighs is prima facie wrongness." It is the terms *outweighs* and *more pressing* that I wish to attend to, especially their implications.

Ross is notoriously unhelpful in providing guidance for the difference between prima facie and actual rightness and wrongness ("for the rest the decision rests with perception").[35] But can the difference be explained without some reference to goods and evils? I think not. Ross admits that prima facie rightness (promise keeping) may not be actual rightness. Actual rightness could be not keeping the promise. This can mean only one thing to me: that a more urgent *good* is at stake in some way. That is what a "duty more pressing" means to me. In other words, after having made a promise an agent has two choices: (1) keep it, regardless of the harm done to the promisee and others; or (2) not keep it, while attending to something much more urgent that has intervened unforeseen and made claims upon us. The only reason I can see for not keeping the promise is that another good is at stake (for example, a dying person to attend to, encountered on my way to a friend's wedding, a wedding I have promised to attend). I call this proportionate reason.

In summary, then, I should like to invite Frankena, as a self-proclaimed outsider in these matters, but one from whom we have all learned so much, to consult the long scholastic tradition and even the moral manuals on applied moral theology. He will find there much more precision, on, for example, promise keeping, than one finds in Ross, a much more disciplined and rigorous analysis of what constitutes proportionate reason.

Bruno Schüller

Schüller's commentary is, in my judgment, the most illuminating one in this volume. Because our agreement on these matters is so extensive, I must admit that my evaluation is likely to be biased. However, the reason for this evaluation is his careful exploration of the notions of intending and permitting (as in the double effect) in two different instances: actions involving the wrongdoing of others and actions causing nonmoral evils such as death. I agree with Schüller that if we are to achieve any deepened knowledge of the relevance of the direct/indirect distinction it must be through an analysis of the intending/permitting distinction. I shall return to this shortly.

In his remarks, Schüller asserts that he is unclear as to where our disagreement begins. At the time of writing *Ambiguity* I thought that Schüller had not sufficiently grappled with the significance of intentionality in his dismissal of the notions of direct/indirect where nonmoral evils are concerned. That is, Schüller had concluded, as I read him, that the direct/indirect distinction was without *any* moral significance. It was merely descriptive. I could not accept this. My dissatisfaction centered on and peaked with what I believed to be Schüller's inability to deal consistently with the accepted, and I think still viable, notions of direct and indirect killing in warfare, if he dismissed the distinction as being without decisive moral relevance. It was into this lacuna that I moved in an attempt to maintain and show a difference between the two. This difference I located in long-term effects, equivalently arguing that one (direct) killing is always wrong in warfare *because* of disastrous long-term effects, whereas the other, as indirect, would not produce such effects and was therefore at times justifiable. This clearly puts the emphasis on consequences in a way which led several of my readers to see a radically consequentialist methodology lurking below, and even above, the surface.

I made this move because I was, and still am, convinced that the very processes that produced the direct/indirect distinction (restrictive interpretation, as Schüller notes) committed one in consistency to a teleological understanding of behavioral or concrete moral norms. My original dissatisfaction with Schüller's analysis, therefore, rested on a certain incompleteness of explanation in his study, things left unsaid.

Specifically, while denying any decisive moral relevance to directness and indirectness as such, Schüller, it seemed to me, had not sufficiently analyzed the difference between actions involving the incidental (indirect) death of noncombatants and those that deliberately and directly destroyed noncombatants (the same number as would die by indirectness) to bring pressure on the aggressor. I tried to trace this difference to directness and indirectness *as such*—through the effects of either. Schüller contends, and I believe rightly, that the actions are different and our task is to identify those features that make the acts different. Doing so we shall see that it is not precisely directness and indirectness that lead to different long-term results, but those characteristics of the actions that make them different actions. To what extent his explanation is successful I shall suggest below.

What has Schüller done? I believe it may be useful to attempt to summarize his very compact and closely reasoned study.

Since the moral relevance of the direct/indirect distinction is tied to the notions of an intending and permitting will, Schüller attempts to unpack the moral significance of these will-postures. As I understand him, he does this by focusing on "basic moral attitudes," "the agent's attitude to good and bad, right and wrong," "the agent's attitude towards the evil results of his actions," "attitudes of will," and "mental attitudes." These are his phrases and they seem to me to be his key referents for unlocking the meaning of permit/intend. What is objectionable is an *attitude of approval* toward either another's wrongful conduct (namely sin, but in the nuanced sense of actions causing more harm than necessary) or the nonmoral evils associated inseparably with one's own actions. Approval and disapproval are contrary opposites. As long as the attitude revealed in my action inducing another to wrongful conduct or causing a nonmoral evil entails approval, the action in question is morally wrong.

Now the *attitude of approval* is revealed when one intends another's wrongdoing (moral evil); it is not present when one merely permits it (not intend it and yet not prevent it even though one could). For one may disapprove and still not prevent another's wrongdoing, whereas if one intends it, he must be said to approve it. As Schüller puts it,

> to intend the wrongdoing of others and to permit their wrongdoing are mutually exclusive in the same way as the basic moral attitudes which express themselves in intending or permitting the wrong behavior of others.

Or even more generally, he states that "to approve of moral rightness, to disapprove of moral wrongness, and to permit the wrongdoing of others *are basically one and the same moral attitude."* Since this is so, the principle of double effect (involving a distinction between intending and permitting) has a legitimate place where actions inducing others to wrongdoing are concerned.

This same analysis does not hold when we are dealing with nonmoral evils such as sterilization and death-causing actions. That is, intending and permitting are not contrary opposites revealing contrary attitudes (approval versus disapproval). Thus the intention of causing death is not the reason for the wrongfulness. For merely "permitting" and "intending *as a means"* may reveal the same basic attitude: "I would not carry it out if it were possible to achieve the good effect without causing the bad one." This same basic attitude associated with permitting and intending as a means is *disapproval.* Thus Schüller's conclusion:

> Whereas intending and permitting someone else's wrong conduct are related to one another in the manner of contrary opposites, intending a nonmoral evil as a mere means and permitting a nonmoral evil, *considered as attitudes of will,* differ, if at all, at most gradually.

On this basis Schüller concludes that the direct/indirect distinction where nonmoral evils are concerned is not morally decisive, at least as recent Catholic tradition has viewed this decisiveness (wrong *because* directly intended).

In summary, then, Schüller argues that where nonmoral evils are concerned, intending and permitting are as morally significant as they entail approval or disapproval of the nonmoral evil. But intending as a means and permitting both may reveal disapproval ("I would not carry out . . ."). Therefore, it is not intentional (*direct,* as a means) killing that is wrong, but only that killing that entails *approval*—namely, killing intended as an end and unnecessary killing. And I suspect that Schüller would say that these two categories (as an end and unnecessary) are practically the same.

I think Schüller is correct in his basic assertion (versus Grisez and Ramsey) that a killing of a human being is not morally wrongful precisely because it is direct. (Grisez and Ramsey maintain, it will be recalled, that any killing of a human being, to be morally right, must be indirect.) Furthermore, I believe the general lines of his analysis of intending/ permitting are very illuminating. In this vein, his challenge to my analysis is successful. I had attempted to show a difference in direct and indirect killing through appeal to deleterious consequences and to assert that these consequences are due precisely to the *directness* of the killing. I then concluded to the practical absoluteness of norms prohibiting direct killing of noncombatants in warfare on the basis of these teleological considerations. I believe this is unsatisfactory and have attempted to explain above how I would now argue moral wrongfulness of such killing. In short, such killing is disproportionate to the good being sought because it undermines through the association of basic human goods the very good of life. Briefly, all things considered, it cannot be said to be necessary. I believe Schüller is saying much the same thing, though I do not wish to put words in his mouth or thoughts in his analysis that are misleading.

Because I believe the basic lines of his analysis are correct, I wish to put some questions to this analysis and make some comments on it; questions and comments that may help to sharpen the continuing discussion of this most difficult and intriguing matter.

1. *Intending wrongful action as a means.* As I understand him, Schüller argues that where nonmoral evils are concerned, intending and permitting are as significant morally as they entail *approval* or *disapproval*. But, intending as a means and permitting are both compatible with disapproval ("I would not carry it out if . . ."). Therefore, he reasons, it is not intentional (*direct,* as a means) killing that is wrong, but

only that killing that entails approval of wrongdoing. This would be *unnecessary* killing.

This analysis, he argues, does not apply where the wrongdoing of others is concerned. Intending and permitting (disapprove but not prevent when one could) are contrary opposites. They are related to the agent's attitude to good and evil, right and wrong. Briefly, intending wrongdoing always involves *approval*, where permitting does not.

Here the following problem occurs. If intending nonmoral evil *as a means* does not involve approval, why would intending another's wrongdoing *as a means* necessarily involve approval? Could another's wrongdoing not be the necessary means in the circumstances to a lesser evil or greater good? Or again, if one "chooses a course of action *only* because he believes it to be apt to induce others to wrong behavior" (Schüller), he approves wrongful conduct. But what if one chooses a course of action not only because he believes it apt to induce others to wrong behavior, but also because this wrong behavior seems the only way to achieve greater nonmoral goods?

An example will help. Titius is bent on murder out of rage and revenge. Helpless before his unwavering determination, I persuaded him not to murder Bertha, but only to rob her and kill her dearly beloved pets. These latter acts are morally wrong. They are intended by me *as means* to save Bertha's life. I persuade to (intend) the lesser evil to prevent the greater. As I persuade to it, could I not argue that "I would not be prepared to perform this action if the result (saving Bertha's life) could be achieved in any other way"? In other words, intending wrongdoing *as a means* does not seem necessarily to entail approval.

This matter can be pressed from a slightly different perspective, that of scandal. Schüller has reinterpreted the traditional teaching on scandal (actions occasioning the *sin* of another). He points out that *sin* should, in the context of the teaching on scandal *(scandalum activum)*, mean "morally wrongful action." By this he means "producing more harm than necessary." This is the meaning to be given to the term *sin* because the relation of my action to the free morally *bad* self determination of another *(optio fundamentalis)* is uncertain and unknowable. In this I believe Schüller is correct. When sin is understood as *morally wrongful action,* then Schüller concludes: "This makes it easy to understand why . . . for permitting others to sin the avoidance of other nonmoral evils . . . may be a commensurate reason." By contrast, if sin means free morally bad self-determination, it is difficult to see what nonmoral goods would suffice as commensurate reason.

So far so good. But this reinterpretation does not explain why tradition would *never* allow intending the sin of another. For if sin should be understood as wrongful conduct (not *bad* conduct), why can it not be intended as a necessary means at least in cases such as that of Titius above?

Schüller's answer to this might be that a wrongful action is *never* a necessary means for the avoidance of greater nonmoral evils. For wrongful action is, by definition, an action causing more harm *than necessary*. Thus he might deny the moral legitimacy of persuading Titius only to rob and not kill Bertha because robbing is unnecessary. Titius ought not kill Bertha and is free to abstain from doing so. I have argued this way myself above. However, the notion of "more than necessary" remains obscure, or at least not sufficiently developed in Schüller's study. And that brings me to a second and closely related comment.

2. *Schüller's account of warfare and extortion.* One of my major intellectual problems in dealing with the notions of direct and indirect was their usage in the conduct of war. Concretely, it appeared to me that if we abandon the distinction in question as morally decisive, then it would be difficult to condemn the direct killing of noncombatants if by doing so the defender could achieve the same desirable good—victory, repulsion of the aggressors, or what have we—that is achieved by permissible bombing with incidental (indirect) deaths of the same number of noncombatants.

Schüller turns to this problem. He believes that it is not precisely *directness* of killing (noncombatants) that is wrong but rather the action is extortion. The rules of just war concerning noncombatants are best explained, he feels, by the principle of *moderamen inculpatae tutelae* (do no more harm than necessary to repel the aggression effectively). But because noncombatants are not the aggressors, "one is very seldom confronted with a situation where the direct killing of noncombatants could be considered necessary to repel the aggressors." Briefly, directly killing noncombatants is morally wrong because it is unnecessary.

Here several comments are in order. First, Schüller's attitude toward direct killing of noncombatants, which he calls extortion, is a bit vague. At one place he says of it "prima facie wrongfulness." In another it is said to be presumably somehow wrong in itself. In another it is said to be unnecessary in 99 cases out of 100.

Secondly, according to *moderamen inculpatae tutelae*, only that force necessary to repel the aggressor ought to be used. But if, de facto, force brought against a nonaggressor (noncombatant) will discourage the aggressor *with less overall damage,* why is it not an example of *moderamen?* This was Truman's reasoning when he used atomic bombs on Hiroshima and Nagasaki, as I noted. Schüller's answer to this is that such bombing is extortionary. But then, what is wrong with a little extortion if it prevents even greater nonmoral evils? His answer to that, if the case of the rioting mob and the judge be any indication, is that "not only the lives of six innocent people are concerned, but the whole institution of criminal law."

But what does it mean to say "the whole institution of criminal law" is at stake? Elsewhere Schüller expands this a bit.[36] He says that the conclusion that the sheriff should frame the one to save others is justified only if this conclusion, raised to a universally acknowledged and practiced rule, would actually promote the common good. Because that is at least highly doubtful, such an exception must be judged contrary to the common good and unjust. But why would it be contrary to the common good if raised to a universally acknowledged and practiced rule? Schüller does not develop this.

For me the answer to that is that what appears to be a lifesaving action by the judge is really at odds with the very value of life—is disproportionate. I have suggested above why I believe that is the case, namely, extortion by definition accepts the necessity of doing nonmoral evil to get others to cease their wrongdoing. The acceptance of such a necessity is an implied denial of human freedom. But since human freedom is a basic value associated with other basic values (in this case, life), undermining it *also thereby undermines life.* In sum, extortion, as life undermining, is not *materia apta* (Janssens), is disproportionate.

What I am driving at, of course, is that Schüller has defined wrongful behavior as that which does more harm *than necessary.* Yet he has given us no systematic explanation of the factors that make some harms necessary and others unnecessary. Until that is done the account of proportion and disproportion remains incomplete and vulnerable. Concretely, Schüller argues that in 99 cases of 100, direct killing of noncombatants is unnecessary. The situation where I must do such direct killing is, he says, "very seldom." I am concerned about this one out of a hundred, this "extremely seldom" instance where it is necessary. Hiroshima? And more specifically, I am concerned about *what makes it necessary.* It is only when we know this that we will be positioned to say whether extortion is "somehow wrong in itself," or only prima facie wrongful. I believe that it is wrong in itself, and for the reasons given above. That is, I believe it is disproportionate to the very value being sought.

3. *Teleological method and the notion of proportion.* It is clear that both Schüller and I adopt a teleological understanding of moral norms, at least what I have called "moderate teleology." Exception making is traceable to and based on a truly proportionate reason. However, it is not clear to me how he would understand proportionality. And even more appositely, there may be in my own understanding of this some confusion and obscurity, perhaps even error. An attempt to set this forth may be of some help. If nothing else, it may reveal my own difficulties in closer perspective.

Proportionate reason (and in this sense, a teleological approach to norms) can mean at least two different things—at least, I believe they are different. (1) An act is wrong because of the bad consequences it *will have,* because of what is *likely to follow* upon it, both in the short and long run. This is "consequentialism" in the strict sense, if it is these considerations alone that determine rightness and wrongness. (2) An act is wrong because its very description, when carefully made (and not without some intuitive elements) entails an attack on the value it seeks to serve. The acceptance of such an act as right will, of course, have deleterious consequences. But these do not *constitute* its wrongfulness. Bad consequences occur because the act was *in itself disproportionate* in some way. I trace this disproportion, this "attack on the value it seeks to serve," to the fact that the harm done in realizing the good is *unnecessary*—as explained earlier. Harm done stands in a *necessary* relationship to evil to be avoided or good achieved when it is the only way possible, essentially and deterministically, for the evil to be avoided or the good achieved—as in the case of saving at least the mother versus allowing both mother and child to die when these are my only alternatives.

It is in this second sense that proportion should be understood. I believe Schüller might disagree with this. But I am not sure. Nonetheless, I shall leave the matter there, to the greater perspicacity and tender mercies of future commentators.

Before leaving Schüller and trying to draw up an intelligible summary of where the discussion rests, it would be both useful and ecumenical to attempt to combine elements of Ramsey with Schüller and myself.

An action, like killing, is morally wrongful when it must be said to turn against a basic good. It is an action entailing an attitude of will, a mental attitude against a basic good (life); an attitude describable as approval of the evil (Schüller). This cannot be identified with intending the evil as a means (*direct* as traditionally understood, and as Ramsey, Grisez and others hold). It happens when (1) the evil is intended as an end, or must be said to be so intended; or (2) when it is caused without necessity. When, however, it is reluctantly caused because *necessary* (whether permitted as a nonmeans, or intended as a means), it does not entail a bad moral will, or "turning against a basic good."

The sole remaining question (and the key question) is: when and on what grounds must a killing action, for example, be said to be *necessary* (namely, if omitted, more harm to life will be inevitable)? Obviously, life itself or a value quite as urgent (adoption of a hierarchy) must be at stake. Killing for lesser reasons is unnecessary and disproportionate. This is not an object of dispute in this volume. My own suggestion, and hence my explication of a key aspect of proportionate reason, is: when the killing is the *only way imaginable* to prevent greater loss of life. When it is not the only way available, and the evil could be avoided, even improbably, without causing the harm (especially by a cessation from wrongdoing or the threat thereof on the part of others), then causing the harm is *unnecessary.* Because there is not a *necessary* connection between avoiding the evil or achieving the good and intending harm as a means, other basic goods (for example, liberty) are brought into play in using the harmful means. Because of the association of basic goods, undermining one undermines others, and thus the very value at stake, for example, life, will suffer more if the killing is done. That is, the action is disproportionate.

Thus, whether or not the evil (nonmoral) intended as a means is proportionate is determined not quantitatively, but all things considered, by carefully weighing the association of basic goods.

Conclusion

This volume has been concerned with the moral significance of the distinction between direct and indirect as it has been interpreted and taught for many decades, especially within the Catholic community. My own conclusion, after weighing carefully the contributions of the thoughtful and eminent commentators in this volume is that where nonmoral evils are concerned (deceiving in speech, killing, sterilizing) the distinction has no moral decisiveness *as such.*

By the term *as such* I mean to say two things. First, I mean that a killing, for example, is not wrongful simply because it is direct *in the traditional sense*. Concretely, an abortion may be direct and still morally permissible. Nor do I believe Ramsey has succeeded in giving moral weight to the distinction with his modifications of directness—namely, by appeal to what the fetus is doing to the mother—or his insistence on incommensurability. Therefore, it is not clear that one must be said to turn against (or set oneself against) a basic good when one directly intends a nonmoral evil in the traditional sense. In this sense I would agree with W. Brugger that it is morally justifiable to intend (*in se, sed non propter se*) a nonmoral evil as a means for the sake of a prevailing good (*bonum praevalens*).[37]

Secondly, by saying *as such* I mean to continue to argue that direct and indirect do have descriptive significance. That is, what is directly intended as a means tells us what the agent is doing. It describes what one is aiming at, with what means or with what collateral harm. That in turn reveals to us the meaning of the action. The meaning of the action suggests to us which values (goods) are involved in this or that choice and how they are involved. Knowing this we are positioned to develop a judgment of proportion, namely, a judgment as to whether we are causing less harm by performing the action or omitting it. In other words, we are positioned to judge whether the action is describable, all things considered, as an act of beneficence in a conflicting world, or what is the same, whether there is a proportionate reason for performing it even though harm is inevitable.

Finally, I am persuaded by Schüller that the meaning of intending/permitting is found in their relationship to the basic moral attitudes of approval or disapproval. In *Ambiguity in Moral Choice* I had argued that the will relates differently to what it intends and permits. However, the key issue is the *moral* significance of this difference. Schüller argues that the *moral* difference is located in the attitudes of approval or disapproval that are revealed in one or the other. I believe I was not too far from this in *Ambiguity* when I wrote that "an intending will represents a closer relation of the agent to the disvalue and therefore indicates a greater willingness that the disvalue occur." Furthermore, I spoke of "general reluctance that the evil must be brought about . . . is presumably common to both instances" (of intending and permitting). What I did not do is identify this general reluctance as the key element in deciding whether direct (as a means) and indirect intent have *moral* significance as such.

The matter can be restated as follows. I wrote: "the intending will is
. . . more 'willing' that the evil exist." Schüller has in effect denied this.
I believe he is right. Where moral evil is concerned (understanding this
in Schüller's nuanced analysis as *unnecessary* harm), intending it necessarily involves approval of it precisely because it is unnecessary. Such
approval is tied to and reveals fundamentally bad moral attitudes and
dispositions. To use Ramsey's rendering, it involves us in turning
against a basic good. But where nonmoral evils are concerned, this is not
the case. Intending as a means and permitting are vehicles of the same
mental attitudes: "I would not be prepared to perform this act if. . . ."
This is an attitude of fundamental disapproval. Incidentally, I believe
this analysis responds to the aretaic concerns of William Frankena—
namely, that the direct/indirect distinction be related more than it has
been to the dispositions of the agent.

In terms of approval and disapproval, then, permitting and intending
as a means can pertain to the same moral category (disapproval) where
nonmoral evils are concerned, whereas intending as an end necessarily
implies approval. In this analysis the traditional moral decisiveness of
the direct (as a means) and indirect intent disappears. If this is correct,
we would have to conclude that the mistake of the tradition was to
believe that intending as a means necessarily involves approval.

Since the meaning of direct and indirect is tied to intending and
permitting, I am prepared to agree that the direct/indirect distinction is
only as *morally* meaningful as the difference between intending (as a
means) and permitting can be shown to be. I believe that Schüller is
correct in insisting that the distinction between these two is gradual at
most.

If this is accurate, those actions considered wrong when involving
direct intent of the disvalue as a means, and hence giving rise to deontological norms, must be interpreted teleologically. Our only problem,
then, is to discover plausible teleological analyses of why norms considered practically exceptionless are so.

In *Ambiguity in Moral Choice* I had argued, using direct killing of
noncombatants as an example, that it is (1) long-term effects that constitute the decisive immorality of this; and (2) that these effects are traceable to directness itself. I would now revise that argument, thanks to the
various prods administered by my commentators, above all by Schüller.
Certainly disproportionate actions (unnecessary harm) can be expected
to have deleterious long-term effects. But these effects are not the
determinants of wrongfulness in the types of cases under discussion.

Wrongfulness must be attributed to a lack of proportion. By that I mean that the value I am pursuing is being pursued in a way calculated in human judgment (not without prediscursive elements) to undermine it. I would further explain (tentatively) the disproportion in terms of an association of basic goods whereby the manner of protecting or pursuing a good brings other values or goods into play and can be responsible for disproportion as a result. In other words, I would abandon the *long-term effects* explanation of teleology; but I see no reason for abandoning the teleology itself.

This discussion will continue as it should. It is an extremely interesting gathering place for serious moral issues, many of which could not be developed, let alone solved, in this volume. Moral choice in a world of conflict may be either far more mysterious or far simpler than our essays suggest. I suspect that it is the former. Whatever the case, the commentators in this book deserve sincere thanks for their insightful comments and for the kindness that prompted them to respond to my original modest probe. They have provided *vires a tergo* toward achieving, if not clarity, then at least more intelligent confusion about the ambiguities of moral choice and of moral thought about such choice.

ENDNOTES FOR CHAPTER SIX

1   Rom 7: 10-21.
2   Bruno Schüller, "Neuere Beiträge zum Thema 'Begründung sittlicher Normen'," *Theologische Berichte* 4 (Einsiedeln: Benziger, 1974): 109-81, at 126.
3   One could include here also the dissolution of consummated sacramental marriages. This type of dissolution was said to be beyond any human power *(defectus juris)*.
4   Louis Janssens, "Ontic Evil and Moral Evil," *Louvain Studies* 4 (1972): 115-56, at 142.
5   Ibid., pp. 143-44.
6   Franz Scholz, "Durch ethische Grenzsituationen aufgeworfene Normenprobleme," *Theologisch-praktische Quartalschrift* 123 (1975): 341-55.
7   Richard A. McCormick, "Notes on Moral Theology: The Abortion Dossier," *Theological Studies* 35 (1974): 312-59, at 349.
8   Paul Ramsey, "Abortion—A Review Article," *Thomist* 37 (1973): 174-226, at 214.

9   Joseph Fletcher and Thomas Wassmer, *Hello, Lovers!*, ed. William E. May (Washington: Corpus Books, 1970) pp. 47-48.

10 Denis O'Callaghan, "Moral Principle and Exception," *Furrow* 22 (1971): 686-96.

11 John T. Noonan, Jr., "How to Argue About Abortion," in *Life or Death–Who Controls?*, eds. Nancy C. Ostheimer and John M. Ostheimer (New York: Springer Publishing Co., 1976), pp. 119-40, at 125.

12 Ramsey, "Abortion—A Review Article," p. 220.

13 Germain Grisez, *Contraception and the Natural Law* (Milwaukee: Bruce, 1964), p. 83.

14 Germain Grisez, *Abortion: The Myths, the Realities, and the Arguments* (New York: Corpus Books, 1970), p. 319.

15 Thus, for example, Pius XI *(Casti Conubii)* wrote: "As to the 'medical and therapeutic indication' to which, using their own words, we have made reference, Venerable Brethren, however much we may pity the mother whose health and even life is gravely imperiled in the performance of the duty allotted to her by nature, nevertheless what could ever be a sufficient reason for excusing in any way the direct murder of the innocent? This is precisely what we are dealing with here." *(Acta Apostolicae Sedis* 22 [1930]: 539-92.) Theologians not infrequently stated the matter as follows: better two deaths than one murder.

16 The sufficient reason for God's action is always his own goodness. But sin (the primary analogate thereof, mortal sin) is by definition *aversio a Deo,* aversion from God's goodness. To say that God could intend sin would be to predicate simultaneous contradictories of him; that he does and does not have as sufficient reason his own goodness.

17 Anglican Study Group, *On Dying Well* (London: Church Information Office, Church House, 1975).

18 Bruno Schüller, "Zur Problematik allgemein verbindlicher ethischer Grundsätze," *Theologie und Philosophie* 45 (1970): 1-23.

19 I say "we mean" referring to the manner in which traditional Catholic treatises understood the matter. In this volume Schüller has suggested a reinterpretation of this tradition, or at least a modification of it. My language here prescinds for the moment from Schüller's modification.

20 The scholastic tradition proposed the maxim *"omnis finis habet rationem boni."* In this perspective there is no end that justifies sinning (moral evil) simply because any other end or good, as a sharing in or refraction of the *summum,* should not be preferred to the *summum.*

21 This, of course, would be possible where one had to choose between either the life of the mother or that of the infant.

22 Donald Evans, "Paul Ramsey on Exceptionless Moral Rules," *American Journal of Jurisprudence* 16 (1971): 184-214, at 191.

23   I say "possible ineffectiveness" because there are those who maintain that when properly practiced (precise knowledge, high motivation, etc.), periodic continence has a very high rate of success.

24   For instance, see Marcellinus Zalba, S.J., *Theologiae Moralis Summa* (Madrid: La Editorial Catolica, 1957), vol. II, n. 958.

25   Richard A. McCormick, "The New Medicine and Morality," *Theology Digest* 21 (1973): 308-21.

26   Thus the inaccuracy of Ramsey's statement: "McCormick's suggestion is that a concrete prohibition like the one in question—and thus his explanation of why any behavioral rule is *generally valid in the first place*. . ." (my emphasis). Norms prohibiting nonmoral disvalues are *generally valid in the first place* because we are dealing with disvalues.

27   Charles E. Curran, "Utilitarianism and Contemporary Moral Theology: Situating the Debates," *Louvain Studies* 6 (1977): 239-55.

28   Schüller, "Neuere Beiträge," p. 170.

29   MK 14: 3-19.

30   Schüller, "Neuere Beiträge," p. 176.

31   Peter B. Medawar, *The Hope of Progress* (New York: Doubleday and Co., 1973), p. 84.

32   Karl Rahner, "The Problem of Genetic Manipulation," vol. 9, *Theological Investigations* (New York: Herder and Herder, 1972), p. 243.

33   Cited in Ramsey's contribution above.

34   W. D. Ross, *The Right and the Good* (Oxford: Clarendon Press, 1965), p. 31.

35   Ibid., p. 42.

36   Schüller, "Neuere Beiträge," p. 173.

37   W. Brugger, *Theologia naturalis* (Pullach: Berchmanskolleg, 1959), p. 412.